inconsistent presentations of what Jesus was really all about. One Jesus was a pacifist. Another Jesus acted like a warrior. One Jesus just came to die. Another Jesus came to show us how to live. One Jesus showed us the supremacy of deep inner spirituality. Another Jesus just wanted to meet people's physical needs. Sometimes I was told to interpret his actions as a metaphor and other times I was supposed to mimic his exact moves step by step. Which one is it?

I began to wonder if people in positions of authority had really discovered what Jesus was all about. What if pastors were confidently presenting the way of Jesus without doing enough homework? What if authors were selling me on a view of Jesus that had more to do with current trends than historical reality? I was nervous that conference speakers were creating messages to deliver first and then finding a way to make Jesus' life support their ideas. That was unacceptable to me.

In response I started seriously researching Jesus' life. If I was going to follow Jesus, I needed to know how he navigated his world. I needed to know the purpose behind the limited number of concrete actions that have been passed down to us from his earthly life. I didn't want to pick out my favorite Jesus from all the options and fabricate a personalized religion. I didn't want to go with my gut and imagine Jesus was exactly who I wanted him to be. I wanted to know who he really was no matter how appealing that may or may not be to me.

Over the years, I have busted my butt to know him. I have become both a student and teacher of Jesus' way. My hunger to figure out what Jesus was really doing led me to the highest levels of academic learning. I studied Greek and Hebrew and Aramaic as I explored the art and science of interpreting Scripture in undergraduate and post-graduate degrees from Columbia International University. Then, I picked up German and French and travelled to Israel, Egypt, Turkey and Greece as I completed a Ph.D. from Trinity Evangelical Divinity School. My specialty became the historical context of Jesus and the Gospels. I spent years reading ancient texts about Jesus' culture, picking apart the political power struggles of his day, and mapping the history and values at the forefront of people's mind who first encountered Jesus. The findings have been incredible. What I learned has given me a fuller view of the entire world in which Jesus lived and more specifically why he did what he did.

The pinnacle of my research—my dissertation—was published by T&T Clark out of London in 2010. Although I was pleased with the outcome, I knew what I had discovered had to be shared with a broader audience of people on the same path. I didn't want to keep what I had learned all to myself. So I became a Bible professor. As a professor, I taught college and seminary courses on Biblical interpretation, Jesus and the Gospels, and the Bible's historical background. What a blast! I loved it. I loved watching my students experience the thrill of finally understanding the mission of Jesus and the reason behind each mysterious action. Getting the chance to help people who want to follow Jesus finally understand where he was going is an absolute thrill.

But I didn't want this message to get stuck in college courses or academic circles. So I began sharing at Sunday school classes and church retreats, at Bible conference centers and summer programs for men. I'd talk about it over dinner and share tidbits in every context with an interested audience. However, each time I would share about the purpose behind one of Jesus' mysterious actions, people would ask how they could get more. I didn't have a simple answer. That's why I wrote this book.

In the following pages, you are going to see Jesus in action and understand why he did what he did. In chapter 2 he will be announcing an alternative path to peace with distinct policies and ironic messengers. In chapter 3 he is welcoming outsiders and breaking down cultural barriers with each miraculous healing. In chapter 4 he is acting out his message before explaining it. In chapter 5 he is correcting your false imaginations about the powers that be and how you need not fear them. In chapter 6 he is surprising people with reminders of where the true source of life lies when he turns water into wine. In chapter 7 he is demolishing cultural promises about the latest self-help solutions. And in chapter 8 he is ceremonializing habits of recommitment to all his ways so that our relationship doesn't get one-sided. That's just a few actions we cover in this book.

I do hope the following pages have the ability to speak to multiple audiences. If you come to this book with a passion to follow Jesus and a desire to figure out where else he leads people beyond what you know, you should be satisfied. If you're reading these words after years of wondering if you've really been given an accurate picture of Jesus' mission, you can finally relax in the confidence of knowing how to affirm or adjust that picture. Or maybe you've been turned off by simplistic interpretations that made Jesus out to be nothing more than a divine man who stopped by earth to show us how he can forgive your sins. If that's you, get ready for a dynamic introduction to a man on a mission who fully engaged his culture and contemporaries to fight for a world rooted in justice, truth, and love. Seeing the way in which Jesus' entrance and actions in the eastern Roman Empire pushed to reform accepted cultural norms will give you a whole new imagination for what it means to follow him today. Depending on your background and personality, the fresh content may excite you with new paths to follow or sober you up with the difficulty of the way. In either case, you will have the concrete opportunity to follow Jesus with the confidence of knowing what he was actually doing. I think you will enjoy the ride.

To be frank, I cannot say it has been an easy road to search beyond conflicting explanations of Jesus' actions and arrive at evidence-based conclusions about their meanings. I have had to work hard and long as a student of Jesus' way. My wife can tell you that I have worn myself out learning languages, persevering through 16-hour research sessions, traveling the Mediterranean, and spending late nights in libraries and museums.

My hope is that my last ten years can help you with your next ten years. I hope you will experience multiple "Ah ha!" moments as we head back in time to figure out why Jesus did what he did. I certainly loved each light bulb that turned on in my understanding of Jesus' way. It has fired me up. And I consider it a privilege to share it with you.

To prepare you for what's coming, I want you to know that our journey takes us back in time. I will be introducing you to ancient stories, ideas and cultural patterns that are not commonly written about in popular books. These glimpses into the world that gave shape to Jesus' life are the key to revealing the purposes behind the actions he took. I won't be filling up the pages with footnotes of all my sources, but I will provide you with some basic resources and advice on how to continue studying Jesus' life this way in the final chapter.

To be clear, most of the historical background connections I will make in each chapter had already been discovered by some other archaeologist, historian, or scholar. My main work has been to track down, test, expand and then simplify the research to share it with non-technical audiences. Too many insights about Jesus' way of living have been lost in the technical vocabulary of insular academic circles. I know. I've lived there.

A few of the cultural connections that explain Jesus' actions are my original research findings. I cannot summarize what it has taken to chase a million rabbit trails to finally resurrect the original meaning of Jesus' actions. The process of building the case, sharing it in writing and testing the evidence and interpretations among colleagues and at society meetings of biblical scholars has taken years. It has truly been a labor of love. With all that work behind me, I am now offering to you the most accurate picture I know of the way Jesus has called us to follow.

Since I wouldn't want to put anyone through what I have endured (minus the world's best gelato I ate every day while studying in Athens), I have invested good sums of mental energy into presenting what I've learned in an inviting, accessible, and even humorous manner. I can't promise that you'll appreciate my jokes or even get my dry humor, but I've done my best to communicate substantial research in a conversational style. I hope you laugh just as much as you learn. I hope everything is simple to understand even though Jesus' way will always be difficult to follow.

Let me give one final word before you begin. All the talk about research and historical context may distract you from the ultimate goal of my writing. I have not set out to write a biblical encyclopedia for the masses or get you hooked on fun ancient Middle Eastern stories (as if there were any). The goal of each chapter is to unveil the meaning behind Jesus' actions so you know what it looks like to follow him. Once you know why he did it, you will be able to look for opportunities to accomplish the same purpose in new ways today.

Each mysterious episode in Jesus' life that we explore will ultimately lead to a discussion about our response. I want to bridge the gap between the "then" of Scripture and the "now" of our daily decisions. To help you respond and follow, I include a couple consistent elements in every content chapter.

First, I end every chapter with three questions about how to reenact the way of Jesus. The questions normally come after a final section about concrete directions from Jesus' example that we can apply. The three simple questions do not ask you to rehearse what you read but rather to go beyond the book. The goal is to discover culturally appropriate ways to imitate the point behind Jesus' doings in the flow of your everyday life. Each question is designed to fuel a conversation among you and your friends. Those group conversations are meant to become feasible action plans. After all, Jesus has called us to follow him not just to know what that would look like if we did.

Second, I have spread throughout the book a couple dozen real life examples of nonprofit organizations reenacting the purpose of Jesus' mysterious actions (see Appendix A). Why? I want to expose you to game-changing projects and programs that you'd otherwise never know. I want you to see that people are changing the world by embodying Jesus' way today. I want you to have concrete opportunities to join with them or simply be encouraged by them as you feel the momentum of Jesus' followers organizing together to reenact his way.

In case you are wondering, I do not pick the nonprofit stories out of a hat or collect them from friends. In my current job as the Director of Research at Excellence in Giving (www.ExcellenceinGiving.com), I am constantly evaluating the strategy and impact of Christian ministries. I subject them to rigorous tests of leadership quality, strategy execution, financial management and demonstrated impact. I perform these evaluations and other research assignments to advise some of the nation's most generous families on where to give more than $20 million each year. That is where I have identified the litany of inspiring stories in the book. So you can have confidence that I have done my homework before highlighting their impact.

Now you may be surprised to learn that I have switched from life as a Bible professor to life as a philanthropic advisor. My family and friends still ask me when I'm going to return to teaching. I do understand that the switch from Bible teacher to philanthropic advisor may not be intuitive. If you can't follow that twist in my personal story, here is the simple theme connecting both professions. Whereas before I taught Bible students how to discover the way of Jesus as a professor, now my work at Excellence in Giving allows me to direct high-capacity philanthropists toward supporting organizations whose work reenacts the way of Jesus. The purpose of finding and following his way remains the same. Only the means have changed.

If you want to know more about me, just ask. I'd be happy to correspond as I am able or to come teach your group of action-oriented Jesus followers a little more about the meanings behind Jesus' actions that I could not fit in this book. Send me a message at Facebook.com/reenactingtheway or email me at **paul@reenactingtheway.com**. My work and family keep me quite busy, but I'm always open to new ways to promote and explore the way that Jesus lived and called us to follow.

Now get ready to understand and imitate Jesus in ways you never thought possible.

Chapter 1

Doing Things to Make a Point:
Jesus in His Context and Us in Ours

Focal Point: How do we figure out the point Jesus made through his actions and then reenact his purpose faithfully and creatively today?

Actions Speak Louder Than Words (When We Know What They Mean)

Endless books have been written about the teachings of Jesus. The topics have been categorized and the principles applied to one generation after the next. Fewer books have set out to explain his actions. That is what we are going to do. We are going to figure out the meaning of Jesus' most mysterious actions in the Gospels. Then we're going to take action ourselves.

We all know the adage, "Actions speak louder than words." However, not many of us understand what Jesus' more mysterious actions were trying to say. For example, why did Jesus only heal certain types of diseases? Why did Jesus have 12 baskets of food left over after feeding the 5,000 but 7 baskets after feeding 4,000? What statement did Jesus make when he healed a lame man who thought a magical, bubbling pool could do so? We are going to answer each one of these questions and all those from the introduction along the way. We are going to look past his sayings and ask tough questions about his doings. In the end, we are going to find that Jesus' nearly inexplicable actions were making culturally relevant statements to his contemporaries.

We have to remember when we read the Bible that it is retelling stories from a different time and place. If Jesus would have proclaimed, "The kingdom of God is like Facebook—it will begin with a few college-age guys and turn into a global network," nobody in first century Israel would have had a clue what he meant. They had no framework for understanding Facebook, college, or global online networks. That is why Jesus had to compare the kingdom of God to a mustard seed that grew into a huge tree. First century Israelites could actually figure out what that meant.

That is often the way it works with us. We read Jesus' words and hear what he did, but we have no way to figure out what he meant. The reason is the massive time and culture gap between us and him. His words and his actions had all kinds of cultural references and subtle inferences that intrigued his original audience. Unfortunately, they leave us in the dark. We miss the point because we are from a different time and place.

SHAKING YOUR HEAD AMONG ALBANIANS

The difficulty we have interpreting Jesus' actions can be similar to the culture gap I encountered in Kosovo. After NATO intervened to stop the 1999 Serbian-led genocide of Kosovars, I went to Pristina, Kosovo to help organize and promote the first post-conflict citywide celebration of Christmas. I went with some friends from a church in the U.S. and teamed up with some Albanians to organize, promote, and operate the events. Needless to say, we had a few cultural and communication barriers to overcome.

Some of the Albanians had intermediate English skills while others had beginner skills. I had no skills when it came to the Albanian language. I couldn't even pronounce the name of their language, *Shqip*. So we did our best to communicate. I have to believe that we at least sometimes understood one another even though my "Quick Guide to Albanian" didn't seem adequate for the job.

The communication problem came to a head when the confusion of languages also became a confusion of cultural habits. Here's how it went down. The main event at our Christmas Eve outdoor celebration was a live concert featuring a traveling Christian band. The Christian band played a variety of original songs and worship songs that led up to the lead singer's testimony. The lead singer had escaped a life of drunkenness because of an encounter with Jesus. His testimony was timely for an eastern European audience that commonly struggles with alcoholism.

When all was said and done for the week, we went out to buy "thank you" gifts for the participants, including the band. We looked around at a nearby corner store, and my new-found Albanian friends narrowed down the options to two choices: a 12-pack of German beer or a bottle of French wine.

I have to say I was quite confused. How did it make sense to get alcohol for a former alcoholic? Why not buy some Vicodin for former prescription drug addicts or some blue hats and handkerchiefs for former Crypts? I had to do something to intervene. Thankfully the perfect opportunity presented itself to me.

One Albanian friend asked me: should we get them the beer? I wanted to say, "No you idiot. You don't fuel former addictions." But I had aced all my cultural anthropology classes and knew better. I would be a bit more tactful. So instead of directly saying no, I shook my head left and right to give a negative response without being too assertive. They received it well just as I had planned. Then they asked: should we get them the wine? Again, I shook my head. To my surprise, they said "OK" and headed off.

Later that night, I watched the band's lead singer open up his gift and couldn't believe my eyes. Instead of giving him one or the other, they gave him both. What!?! It immediately made no sense. I had kindly told them not to purchase either for this former alcoholic. I was beginning to wonder if the Albanian culture was one where you lie to someone's face in the moment just to maintain the relationship as long as you can.

Then it hit me. I remembered an experience earlier in the week at a trendy coffee house we visited one night. I ordered a "chai," and they asked if I wanted to add a shot of "vodka." I shook my head "no." Only when I began drinking my "chai," it had the powerful and unfamiliar taste of fire. There were no Indian spices like the Oregon Chai I had expected. My request to pass on the liquor had somehow gotten lost in translation.

Trying to save face after gulping raspberry tea spiked with vodka failed. I was 19 years old and had never tasted liquid fire in my throat. Coughing and spitting back into my cup while my face turned red quickly gave away my unpreparedness. Needless to say, everyone had a good laugh at my expense.

I later found out that shaking your head left and right means "yes" in Albanian culture and moving your head up and down means "no." So when I declined the "vodka" shot by shaking my head left and right, I had actually said "yes." When I was asked at the end of the week if we should get the band beer or wine, my intention to kindly say "no" was foiled. My actions had said "yes" to both. It was a complete cultural reversal.

PREPARE TO GO BACK IN TIME

To make sure we don't think Jesus' "yes" means "no," we are going to go back in time. Unfortunately, that process doesn't involve a twenty-first century time machine or bolts of lightning striking the flux capacitors on a DeLorean at 10:04pm. It means we have to do our homework. That is why you will find a bunch of ancient documents from the Eastern Mediterranean world cited throughout this book. It may not sound fun at first, but it is necessary. You have to read about the world in which Jesus and his disciples lived to truly understand what they did. That is the only way to understand the subtle yet profound statements Jesus made with his actions.

I promise to keep the citations short and throw in the best jokes I know. I'll limit the ancient sources to the most important background documents that bring out specific cultural meanings for first century audiences.

However, I will not cheapen your reading experience by dumbing down the depth of the historical background information. My suspicion is that most of you will enjoy reading the primary sources for yourselves in the manageable portions I provide. You are probably just as frustrated as I am that so few broadly distributed Christian books reveal the substance and sources behind their conclusions. I actually had one publisher turn down this book proposal because "it has too much depth for the average Christian reader." That's insulting.

As I have presented this research at retreats, in college courses, to friends over dinner, and in different countries, I have consistently found audiences interested in reading the ancient literary evidence for themselves. The experience alone ushers you into the world that brings Jesus' actions to life. So get ready for excerpts from Rabbis and Roman historians and blurbs from the Dead Sea Scrolls and ancient Greek inscriptions. The way you imagined Jesus doing what he did is going to change. Here is a taste of what's to come.

WEARING YOUR IDENTITY ON THE EDGE OF YOUR PRAYER SHAWL

"If I only touch the edge of his prayer shawl, I will get well." That was the logic of a large number of Israelites who encountered Jesus. Personally I would have taken a different approach. I would have wanted a more memorable experience. Maybe a secret potion or some holy water to pour on my head for seven days would be more impressive. If I was going to be healed, I'd want a little more showmanship than the tassels on the edge of a prayer shawl.

One particular woman thought the edge of Jesus' prayer shawl could stop a 12-year hemorrhage. It was a bold (somewhat difficult to understand) belief. She didn't want him to touch her head, to say a prayer, or to make a magical elixir. She just wanted to grab a corner of his shawl.

At first glance, this lady seems to have an ill-conceived belief in the power of prayer shawls. I personally think they are a fashion nightmare and have never found one with the redeeming value of healing power. But Matthew 9:20-22 records her exceptional story.

> A woman who had been suffering from a hemorrhage for
> twelve years, came up behind Jesus and touched the tassels

of his shawl. In her head she was thinking, "If I only
touch his garment, I will get well." Jesus turned around to
look at her and said, "Daughter, be encouraged; your faith
has made you well." At once the woman was made well.

This story leaves me with one big question: Why did Jesus interpret her grasping for the "tassels of his shawl" as true faith?

From our modern perspective, the story looks like the bold move of a fanatic who sees her favorite Hollywood star. It's like a crowd full of young girls who all want to rip a piece of clothing off of Justin Bieber as he passes by. In the mental scenario I imagine, this woman is like the one teenager who is able to jump across the security line and grab the corner of Justin's hipster coat. She gets an instant adrenaline rush and all her ills are healed. At least that's what I imagine. But the analogy breaks down with the idea that girls believe Justin Bieber's clothes could end their battle with sickle cell anemia or hyperthyroidism.

Jesus does not mistake this woman's desperate grasp for an awestruck female fan. He takes her very seriously. He looks at her passionate pursuit of the tassels on his prayer shawl as a definitive act of faith. How can that be? It doesn't make plain sense. To figure out what is really happening, we need to start with a simpler question. Why was Jesus even wearing tassels on the edge of his prayer shawl in the first place?

INTERPRETING THE TASSELS

Tassels happen to be a central element to a divine command in the Torah. In Numbers 15:38-39a the Lord tells Moses that Jewish men needed to wear tassels as a reminder.

> Speak to the sons of Israel, and tell them that they shall
> make for themselves tassels on the corners of their
> garments throughout their generations, and that they shall
> put on the tassel of each corner a cord of blue. It shall be a
> tassel for you to look at and remember all the
> commandments of the LORD.

By the first century CE, Jewish customs had developed to the point where religious leaders primarily wore prayer shawls with one tassel on all four corners. Each tassel had a blue cord woven into it per the instructions in Numbers 15:38. Since Jesus played the role of a Rabbi in Israel, we would expect him to wear a similar prayer shawl with four tassels (the picture on the right shows the corner of a Jewish prayer shawl with a tassel tied onto it). It would have been a sign of his commitment to obey God's commands. It would have marked him as a teacher who had expertise in interpreting the terse Hebrew laws. It would have also given him the chance to fulfill a mysterious prophecy.

Rabbis in Jesus' day had developed a number of common methods for interpreting the Hebrew Scriptures. Many of the interpretive techniques are denounced in Christian Seminary "Hermeneutics" classes today (the ones I teach included), but they were popular in the first century.

One of the interpretive techniques is called *Gezerah Shawah*. Don't worry if you can't pronounce it. *Gezerah Shawah* is similar to what we call "cross-referencing" today. An interpreter finds a word or phrase in one verse and then traces it to other verses where it occurs. The goal is to find additional insight on a particular topic or to explain the meaning of one verse through the ideas found in another verse with similar language.

When Rabbis applied the *Gezerah Shawah* technique to Numbers 15:38, it led them to Malachi 4:2. The connection came from the common word "corners"—*kanaph* in Hebrew. In Numbers 15:38 *kanaph* refers to the corners of the garments where Israelite men were supposed to attach tassels. In Malachi 4:2 it is difficult at first to find the word in the English translation. Try and pick it out from the following quote: "For you who fear My name, the sun of righteousness will rise with healing in its wings."

At first glance, you cannot find a word in the English translation that seems anything like *kanaph* since *kanaph* is translated "corners" or "edges" in Numbers 15:38. The trick to locating it is understanding the range of meaning for *kanaph*. *Kanaph* generally refers to the edge of something. In the case of a rectangular garment, it represents the "corners" where tassels are attached. In the case of a bird, it represents its "wings."

In Malachi 4:2, rabbinic interpreters believed that the "sun of righteousness" was a reference to the Messiah who would come to save his people from their oppression. The fact that the Messiah would have "wings" did not make much sense. So they used *Gezerah Shawah* to interpret the "wings" (*kanaph*) of the Messiah as the "corners" (*kanaph*) of his outer garment. Since Malachi 4:2 stated that the Messiah would have "healing in his *kanaph*," Rabbis conjectured that the Messiah would have healing power in the tassels of his robe (*Exodus Rabbah* 31:10). We have no way of knowing exactly when Rabbis first popularized this interpretation, but it makes complete sense out of our story.

Why did Jesus interpret the lady's grasping for the "tassels on his prayer shawl" as true faith? The answer is simple to understand now. Jesus knew she grabbed his tassels because she believed he was God's anointed Savior. Her actions made a clear statement about her beliefs. In fact, her grasping was her faith. That is why he said, "Your faith has made you well." The woman was somehow familiar with the messianic interpretation of Malachi 4:2 and found the miraculous power right where she expected it to be.

According to Mark 6:56 and Matthew 14:36, she wasn't the only one. "Wherever Jesus entered villages or cities or countryside, people laid the sick in the market places and implored him that they might just touch the fringe of his cloak. As many as touched it were being cured." It was a nationwide phenomenon.
When you don't know the background information, you don't know why Jesus healed people who grabbed his tassels. You don't know what the action meant. But a quick tour through rabbinic

interpretations of the time clears it all up. That is what we plan to do throughout the rest of this book. We are going to make sense out of the confusing and mysterious moments of Jesus' active life.

WHAT JESUS DID AND WHAT WE DO NOW

Some people have dismissed historical background investigation thinking it does no good when applying the Bible. Cynics will say it simply leads to History channel specials that question the Bible's accuracy. I can understand the frustration. I've seen the online videos that portray Jesus as an Egyptian magician based on astrological "evidence." I've watched random Greek texts turn Jesus into a Greek egalitarian philosopher because an historian at DePaul said so. I've read the books about how the Gospel of Thomas proves Jesus is a confused and esoteric apocalyptic prophet. These wild hypotheses can make any observer leery of new "historical data."

However, the historical background is a non-negotiable for anyone who wants to follow Jesus. I plan to prove this statement by the end of the book. Historical background information does not rewrite what Jesus did or who he was. It simply reveals it. If you happen to be someone who wants to reenact his ways, the fact is: you can't follow him if you don't know what he was doing.

Think about the problems we have when reenacting what Jesus did. If you read that Jesus flipped over tables and whipped unfair businessmen on Temple grounds, does that mean we have the right to throw a temper tantrum and physically harass unjust people? If so, I have always thought the concession prices on nachos and warm pretzels at stadiums were rapacious. Do I have the right to smash their hot dog warmers and flip over some grills?

There are many confusing questions along these same lines. If Jesus walks on water, should we likewise stop using life jackets as a sign of our faith? If Jesus mashed up his spit with some Mediterranean mud and wiped it on a blind man's face, should we start carrying around a Ziploc bag of dirt in case we run into a blind person? Most of us either ignore these strange actions of Jesus in the Bible, or we settle for generic interpretations. We take his actions, mix them with our assumptions, and produce advice for life that reflects more our opinions than his intentions.

MISSING THE POINT WITH FIRE ANTS

I still remember a night in Mexico where my feet paid the price for another man's ignorance of Jesus' intentions. I had been building a home in Juarez for an impoverished member of a local church. We had a team of over 30 young adults working on multiple homes in 107° F weather. Each night we would gather at a campsite in the middle of the desert to debrief and discuss the experience.

One night, the trip leaders read the story of Jesus washing the disciples' feet and organized a modern-day reenactment ceremony around our campfire. I knew that a few denominations considered "foot washing" one of the ecclesiastical sacraments so I didn't protest. However, I questioned the connection between the meaning of "foot washing" for a first century audience and for a twenty-first century audience in a different culture. "Foot washing" was normal in first century Israel but just awkward and impractical today. Of course, I kept those questions to myself.

The trip leaders began the ceremony after dark and slowly washed the feet of each trip participant in a methodical manner. As they approached me, I took off my boots and smart wool socks as instructed. I will say that I found it a bit non-sensical that they applied no soap (since that had been developed during the two intervening Millennia). In my opinion, if Jesus actually intended to clean the disciples' feet, why not use our advanced technology to better serve everyone on the trip? But that's just me. I shrugged off my skepticism thinking it was just the heat stroke talking. I decided to focus on their kind-hearted, symbolic gesture and leave my criticism undisclosed. That lasted for about two minutes.

After they finished wetting and drying my feet, I put my socks back on and began lacing up my boots. The socks created a mysterious tingling on my feet at first, and I wondered if there truly was something magical about the act of "foot washing." Could my feet be having a truly unique spiritual experience? As I put the second boot over my sock, I quickly changed my mind. The tingling turned into stinging and burning. My freshly "washed" feet were now covered by a farm of fire ants that had taken up residence inside my socks. My quiet acceptance of a poorly imitated action of Jesus became a frantic flailing that involved socks, shoes, sand, and some choice phrases being flung around the campfire. I could not believe that a "foot washing" ceremony designed to humbly serve me had sent burning venom into my epidermis. I was not impressed.

If the Mexico trip leaders were trying to do what Jesus did for his disciples, then they had failed miserably. I was experiencing something more akin to the Temple merchants who got whipped than the disciples who were loved in a culturally profound way. Needless to say, I haven't participated in any "foot washings" since.

If the trip leaders would have spent more time understanding the specific historical context of "foot washing," they could have figured out a more contextually appropriate way to imitate Jesus' action. They would have understood the point Jesus made through those actions and faithfully created a way to do the same for us that night. For example, they could have performed a service for us that is both meaningful and regularly practiced by those in modern-day service industries, just like the servant did in Jesus' day. They could have provided us with hot water for a shower (since we were in a waterless desert). They could have handed out steamed towels to refresh our faces. They could have given us some cold Cokes or a cup of ice cream. They could have shined our work boots at the end of the week or cleaned our sweat-stained hats. All of those actions would have both imitated the modern-day service industry and been meaningful in our situation. But instead they performed an impractical and ultimately painful service.

I want you to get the point back then so you can get it right today. I hope to inspire more faithful and creative reenactments of Jesus' actions in every chapter that follows. If we carefully explore the most relevant historical references, we can match his purposes with appropriate actions today. If you get what Jesus was doing first, you can reenact his purposes fittingly in our place and time—without anyone's feet covered in fire ants.

When it comes to Jesus' death, almost every person who looks to Jesus for forgiveness finds symbolic meaning in his crucifixion. No one who calls him 'Savior' also interprets his death as mere proof of his humanity. You won't find people wearing crosses to remember that Jesus died like a Roman criminal. That was not the symbolic message in his act of death. The crucifixion may have proved Jesus had a real human body that spilled blood when whips, nails, and spears pierced his skin. However, it has an entirely different significance for all those who have followed him over the centuries.

Jesus' act of dying has always been revered as an act of sacrifice. It was a demonstration of his willingness to take the punishment that others deserve for their cruel and malicious behavior. Most of his followers throughout the centuries have focused on this meaning to his death. They have not settled for its "face value" meaning that he exhibited the signs of mortality.

However, the same believers who see his act of dying as an act of atonement for sin often fail to pursue the deeper significance of all his other actions. Particularly, his (often mysterious) miraculous actions are reduced in significance to simple demonstrations of divine power rather than specific statements about the way God wants to reorder our world. That is a tendency I want to correct.

We must understand that Jesus falls into a long line of God's prophets who acted out their messages. The prophet Ezekiel built a model of the city of Jerusalem and laid down buck naked next to it for a year. He was trying to catch people's attention (that's also why you don't see "Ezekiel" films alongside films about Joseph, Moses, and David). Elijah called down lightning to burn up a bull. That wasn't a random idea but a specific challenge to a pagan God that claimed to control thunder and lightning. An unnamed prophet in the book of Acts tied himself up with belts to predict a famine. His uncommon activity was intended to make an indelible impression on his audience. Jesus did the same thing.

We must realize that Jesus took action to send specific messages to the world—to reveal a way that we should follow. His actions were not generic. Each decision recorded in the Gospels is rife with the intentionality of a man on a mission. He understood the culture and context in which he lived and set out to reorder it. So we cannot simply observe his actions without asking what it meant to those around him. There are messages we will miss and paths we will walk by if we are not careful. Just imagine what it would be like if his death on the cross was given no more value than proof of his humanity. It would change everything.

FOLLOWING JESUS WHEN YOU KNOW WHAT HE WAS DOING

We can't view Jesus as a talking head if we want to follow him. His words do teach us, but his actions have a message we better not miss. He put too much purpose into his actions for us to overlook the details. So in these pages, we are going to dig into those details and revive the past to figure out his purposes. If we can find the symbolic meaning of his actions, then we will have found a mission for us to remake in our culture. We will have uncovered a trajectory to point us in new directions today. We will learn how to follow him.

This kind of "following" is radically different from our usual assumptions. When we imagine "following," it often looks like horses in a single-file line on a trail ride. The trail guide is out in front, and all the other horses just follow the nearest tail. Improvisation is frowned on. Success is a line of horses that stick their shoes in the same dirt as the horse in front of them. You're allowed to stop and relieve yourself when you must, but you cannot deviate from the trail. No creative adaptation to new settings is required. That type of mindless tail-chasing does not work when you are following Jesus.

The problem is that the trail Jesus walked on has disappeared. The cultural context has completely changed. Healers used to spit on mud and put it on people's faces. That doesn't happen anymore (thank God!). The Romans used to rule the world, but that ended centuries ago. There used to be a Jewish Temple in Jerusalem, but it crumbled in 70 CE. The world that Jesus knew is not the world that we know. That means we have to chart a new path that faithfully reflects the purposes of his actions but creatively connects with new cultures.

In each chapter, we will explore ways to reenact the purpose of Jesus' mysterious actions. I will include stories from a couple dozen non-profit organizations operating around the world. Since I have spent years evaluating the work of hundreds of faith-based non-profits, I will introduce you to some of the most outstanding programs that are embodying Jesus' actions and getting results. These organizations are doing today what Jesus did back then. Their stories often go unnoticed, but the nobility and transformative power of their work deserves our attention. Some stories will make you cry. Some stories will inspire you to give. Some stories will make you act. All of them should give you a tangible picture of what it means to follow Jesus around the globe in the twenty-first century.

REENACTING THE PURPOSE OF JESUS' ACTIONS

Jesus didn't say, "Come follow me," because of how interesting it would be to watch what he does. He wanted generations of people after him to create fresh ways of doing what he did. So I'm going to introduce a way of interpreting the Bible that moves from Scripture to a script—from a book to an action plan. I want you to see the steps that I use and have a plan to re-create them. I want you to confidently find and follow the purposes of other actions that Jesus and key biblical characters took in Scripture. If I succeed, you will look and listen to the activity of Scripture in new ways. You will discover the biblical trajectories that tell us where to blaze new trails today.

As a Bible professor who has studied, taught, and practiced "Biblical interpretation" for almost a decade, I have created a simple model for reenacting biblical activity. It is a two-step process. It can be used to reenact Jesus' way or any other action in the Bible. I could write an entire book about how to perform each step, but let me summarize it concisely for you and give a quick example.

STEP ONE:	*First*, figure out what a biblical author or character is doing.
STEP TWO:	*Second*, devise a way to imitate that action in your own subculture.

I call it the "Reenactment Model." You can see the 5 sub-steps in the outline below.

REENACTMENT MODEL

I. What is the biblical author or character in the story doing?

    A. What cultural norm is being challenged or borrowed by the biblical author?

    B. How does the Bible direct its ancient readers to take on that cultural norm?

II. How can we similarly imitate what the biblical author or character is doing?

    A. What cultural norm could we similarly challenge or borrow?

    B. Which entities (media, people, companies, etc.) in your culture represent those values?

    C. What *specific and feasible action* could we do today to take on a contemporary cultural norm?

I will use the Reenactment Model for analyzing every story of Jesus that we explore. The goal is to figure out the point Jesus made through his actions and then consider how we could faithfully but creatively reenact its purpose. Since this model for interpreting the Bible can work with passages that aren't action-packed stories, let me show you how it works with a teaching section from a New Testament epistle.

The first step will be to figure out what the author is doing to his audience with his words. How is Peter re-directing them? It is a different paradigm from the typical approach that focuses on extracting timeless principles or commands from what an author says. Once we figure out what an author is doing, we will look at ways to reenact the author's purpose.

DOING THINGS WITH WORDS: 1 PETER 4:1-2

Read the passage from 1 Peter and then follow the steps to reenactment.

> Therefore, since Christ has suffered in the flesh, arm yourselves also with the same purpose, because he who has suffered in the flesh has ceased from sin. Now you can live the rest of the time in the flesh no longer for base human desires, but for the will of God.

We are going to walk through the "Reenactment Model" focusing on Peter's command to embrace life's difficulties for the redemptive purpose they offer.

I. What is the biblical author or character in the story doing?

A. What cultural norm is being challenged or borrowed by the author?

Suffering in a Roman world brought shame. There was no value in public humiliation or discrimination. Suffering was a problem not a point of pride. Romans prided themselves on victories not defeats. When Peter instructs his audience to "arm yourselves," his audience would have expected him to follow it up with the phrase "for victory" or "for battle." Instead he commands his audience to prepare themselves for suffering, and he ascribes great value to that suffering. Simply put, Peter's words challenge the Roman aversion to suffering.

B. How does the Bible direct its ancient readers to take on that cultural norm?

Peter subverts the shame Romans attached to suffering. He claims the result of suffering is not humiliation but deep moral development. Those who suffer will "live the rest of the time in the flesh no longer for base human desires but for the will of God." For Peter, suffering is not a matter of shame. It is a formative process for people who want to move their priorities beyond basic human impulses. It has a redemptive purpose. Peter is exposing the superficiality of the Roman aversion to struggles. He is calling his audience to a new kind of culture with a new set of values. Suffering is a good thing.

That is what Peter was doing. Now back to our world.

II. How can we similarly imitate what the biblical author or character is doing?

A. What cultural norm could we similarly challenge or borrow?

My American culture avoids suffering at all costs. Most prayer requests I have ever heard ask God to stop pain and problems. Very few requests ask God to build character through problems. Why is that? I think it has to do with our cultural values. In the United States, we value "getting the most for the least."

We want to get everything and pay nothing. We want a luxury car for economy car prices. We want juicy, organic strawberries for the price of unripe, out-of-season strawberries. We want to lose weight without working hard. We want to be on top of the corporate ladder without ever climbing the lower rungs. We are addicted to shortcuts and discounts.

Our passion for "getting the most for the least" weaves into the way we understand the path of Christ. We want the character and self-control of a holy person without the formative experiences that create them. We want the faith and heart of David without knowing his years of starvation and death threats. We want the deep joy of appreciating what truly matters in life but not the loss that leads us to such realization. So we pray for God to give us everything without suffering for anything. It is a cultural blind spot.

B. Which entities (media, people, companies, etc.) in your culture represent those values?

Any company that promises great products and services for "FREE" plays into this cultural value. Any spiritual message that says peace and joy and hope are yours for "FREE" is selling superficial abstractions to a suffer-free world. Even when kids use "cheat" codes to advance to new levels in video games, they are being trained to find workarounds rather than develop a good "work ethic." We don't consciously recognize this effect, but it is prevalent.

One of my favorite examples is the AB Shocker. According to the infomercial, I can theoretically get well-defined abdominal muscles without doing a single sit-up. I don't have to carve out time, break a sweat, or lift a leg. I just put an electric belt around my abdomen, and it will "shock me into shape." How easy! I get everything I want, and I don't have to suffer along the way. How could I turn that deal down?

In the Christian world, "discipleship cruises" do the same thing. They promise personal development without personal difficulty. I know this critique will offend some people, but it fits squarely inside the cultural preference of "getting the most out of the least."

We somehow believe that character can be refined *not* by the heat of troubles but by ocean breezes, island beaches, and a few meetings along the way. I understand the value of retreats, but they only have value for those who live their life on the offensive. For a "getaway" to create space for reflection, you must be getting away from the difficulties and stress of staying true in trying times.

Christian cruises are a problem if they make us believe we can embrace pleasure as a path to character. If you want to form character and find wisdom, go install latrines and fuel-efficient stoves in the poor communities of Jamaica rather than spending time on its sandy shores. There is no easy path to deep character development.

C. What *specific and feasible action* could we do today to take on a contemporary cultural norm?

Let me give it to you straight. We can stop praying to avoid suffering and start embracing the benefit of suffering. That is how to accomplish today what Peter was commanding back then. We have to cut through escapist theology and embrace problems as the path "to live for the will of God."

I can never forget the reaction I received after telling a group of freshmen in high school to stop praying for an end to suffering in the lives of their favorite aunts and family pets. Between my seminary education and doctoral degree, I taught a few high school Bible classes at a Christian academy. In our homeroom period, we would often take prayer requests before school started. One morning I couldn't handle the barrage of requests for an aunt's broken leg, a lost dog, and the pain of unemployment. I stopped taking requests and started asking questions. I asked: "Is God focused on preventing all suffering in our lives or shaping who we are in the middle of it?"

I gave a mini-lecture about all the places in the Bible where God authorized suffering or described it as a means of character building. I told them how God cared more about freedom from self-interest than freedom from problems. Some of the students thought I was crazy. They had never had a teacher who questioned the validity of praying for Uncle John's prostate cancer treatment. It created a memorable dissonance on the countenance of my students.

Now I am not suggesting that God doesn't heal people. The Bible is full of healings. However, each one of those healings had the purpose of facilitating additional ministry. Typically that ministry witnesses to people cut off from a relationship with God. It is meant to restore the relationship. That is why the most healings happening around the world are in the context of evangelistic ministries. We will continue this discussion and explore the meaning behind Jesus' healing miracles more closely in chapter three.

If we are going to fight against our culture's passion for "getting the most out of the least," we are going to question accepted religious practices. We are going to reinvent the meaning of difficulty. We are going to redefine problems as the necessary path to character formation. When the fabric of our lives is ripped apart, we get a chance to develop strong moral fiber. It isn't as easy as it sounds on paper, but it is one way to reenact the purpose of Peter's words.

Reenacting the point of Peter's words challenges our cultural norms. It offends those that prefer to absorb culture, even Christian culture, rather than follow Jesus. We have to be willing to embrace that unsettling activity. That does not mean we purposefully offend our fellow travelers. We must strive to be as delicate as can be in the process. But we can't cave to cultural pressure.

If we follow Jesus well, the political giants of our time and the religious powers that be will get angry. Jesus' path provoked his death, and our reenactment will lead to exclusion and negative consequences—or at least some nasty blogs and shameful tweets. Debunking values like "getting the most for the least" is not an easy road.

THE DIFFICULTY OF FINDING THE WAY

This model for reading across the pages of the Bible and into our world is no easy task. That's probably why few take this road. It's much more convenient to stack up a list of 26 doctrines to believe, 329 sins to avoid, and 134 righteous acts to repeat. Why cultivate wisdom when you can just create a monolithic mold for everyone?

If you want to follow Jesus, you must use discerning eyes when others' vision goes blurry. You can't opt for passivity. Following Jesus doesn't happen on accident in any culture. You also can't actively avoid everything in your culture. Boycotting everybody doesn't create a meaningful solution to any problem.
Disengagement is not the path Jesus took to influence the people he met. He took the path of discerning engagement. He found ways to act symbolically and reshape the world that others assumed was carved in stone.

To be honest, this approach won't appeal to religious adherents who just use God to feel better about themselves. Active engagement in the world is only a distraction to the spiritual woman or man who mainly seeks an individualized spiritual escape. For those people who are focused on justifying themselves and tending to their inner being, engaging the world diverts them from caring for their soul. But Jesus didn't come just so you can have a meaningful spiritual experience. He came to restore the world to what it was meant to be. Reducing him to a divine pet that sits in your spiritual purse and strokes your ego is an insult to the life he lived.

True imitation of Christ requires us to join his mission of the restoration of all things. It requires both faithfulness and creativity. We must faithfully reenact why he did what he did. And we must creatively carve out paths in our culture that carry the same symbolic meaning. You will need every mental resource you have to chart this course and every ounce of commitment you can muster to walk forward.

GET A GROUP AND GET GOING

In my experience, you will need the support of a community to motivate that faithfulness and to check your creativity. We were meant to live in encouraging communities that inspire us to action and keep our dumb ideas in check. So I'd encourage you to think about reading the rest of this book with a group of friends if you're not doing so already.

At the end of each chapter, I have listed three questions to stimulate conversation in your community—conversations that should help form faithful and creative responses to what you learn. I hope you use those questions in your group to engage in the difficult and desperately important task of following Jesus on a new trail. And I hope you experience the thrill of following Jesus when you actually know what he was doing. Here's the first set of three questions to facilitate your discovery of how to reenact the way (of Jesus).

Reenacting the Way

1. Have you given more attention to the teachings of Jesus than the unique purposes of his actions? If so, what do you think you have missed out on?

2. How similar or different is the Reenactment Model of biblical interpretation from the way you normally read and respond to Scripture?

3. When have you felt like it was hard to follow Jesus because you couldn't figure out what he was doing? Are you willing to put in the work to both figure out what he and others in the Bible were doing and faithfully create a way to take similar action in your subculture? Be honest.

CHAPTER 2

THE BIRTH OF AN EMPEROR:
AN ALTERNATIVE PATH TO PEACE AND JOY

Focal Point: How does Jesus' entrance into the Roman Empire expand our vision of how he saves the world and where we can join him in bringing order and peace to all people?

WHAT A BIRTH MEANS TO A MOM

For many of us the story of our birth provides little more than a nostalgic moment at family gatherings. One parent (if you're so blessed to have a relationship with one) smiles wide and recounts the anecdote for the hundredth time to the chagrin of all those who must endure it. My mother is guilty of it all the time. On a visit to see how tall the grandchildren are, she will often corner a new friend or colleague of mine and open the barrel of tales. Typically they begin on a somber note.

Immediately after I was born, the doctor gave me a five percent chance to survive due to projected kidney problems. So she speaks of hours and days spent holding me with the expectation that I could die at any moment. Certainly it is a serious matter that commands the attention of the listener, willingly or unwillingly. How did she find the strength to hold a dying baby? Of course, there is no real suspense since I'm sitting in the same room healthy as can be.

When my near-death encounter does not move everyone to tears, my mom keeps a second birth story in her pocket. She interjects how I had tied the umbilical cord in a knot while in the womb. "It is a miracle he's alive today," she says, normally adding, "God must have created him for an important purpose." With this statement, my birth story turns into a mandate for meaningful living. It puts serious pressure on me to do things that matter. Every good thing I do now becomes potential material for my mother to link back to my providential preservation at birth.

Sometimes I wonder if other more mundane factors were involved in the umbilical cord knot. Maybe I did not appreciate the menu so I cut off the supply. Or maybe I wanted to give my kidneys a break so they could develop under a reduced water supply. Maybe I just knew how cold it would be in Wisconsin in January and thought the umbilical cord could double as a scarf. In any case, that is my story, and it hardly discloses my adult character or potential contribution to the world—at least to most people other than my mom.

THE MEANING OF ANCIENT BIRTHS

Ancient accounts of great figures such as Alexander the Great or Caesar Augustus demonstrate that a man's coming greatness reveals itself through extraordinary signs at birth. The signs go way beyond a knot and some kidney problems. Birth narratives and their accompanying events were not anecdotes for the royal family to exchange with interested guests. Extraordinary birth stories were told to reveal character and future exploits. It is how biographers in the ancient Mediterranean world (everything from Rome to Greece to Israel) hailed the superiority of one great man among other men.

In Plutarch's description of the birth of Alexander the Great, note how special attention is given to coincidental events and their significance. Don't worry if you've never heard of Plutarch. Just trust me that he was an important Greek historian and biographer. His story of Alexander's birth was typical for the Greco-Roman world into which Jesus was born.

> Alexander was born early in the month of Hecatombaeon (Lous is its Macedonian name), on the sixth—the very day the temple of Ephesian Artemis was burned down. In referring to that event

Hegesias the Magnesian made a witty remark, the coolness of which might have extinguished that blaze. For he said that the temple was probably burned down because Artemis was occupied with Alexander's delivery. All the Magi who were currently residing in Ephesus believed that the destruction of the temple foreshadowed another disaster, and ran through the town striking their faces and shouting that that day had given birth to ruin and dire misery for Asia.

On the same day, three pieces of news reached Philip (Alexander's dad), who had just captured Potidaea: Parmenio's defeat of the Illyrians in a great battle; the victory of Philip's racehorse at the Olympic Games; and the birth of Alexander. Pleased as he surely was with these tidings, Philip was even more elated by the prophets, who declared that his son, as he had been born on the day of a triple victory, would be unconquerable.[1]

The events on the day of Alexander's birth warranted bold conclusions. Because the Temple of Artemis burned down in Ephesus when Alexander was born, the magi proclaimed the coming destruction of the Persians who ruled the area. And Alexander was the man to do it. The activity around his birth prophesied the greatness of a man who would conquer the known world of his day. It was no coincidence. This was no mere anecdote. The signs around his birth proclaimed Alexander's significance. These events were given much more meaning than a nostalgic memory for mom.

If the signs around ancient births deliver symbolic messages, it makes me wonder what missing messages are tucked into the birth narratives of Jesus. What statement is being made by the sequence of events around Jesus' birth? That is what we are going to explore in this chapter.

On a side note, it also makes me wonder why the Soviets invaded Afghanistan on the day I was born. Maybe I was supposed to invade Afghanistan one day. Maybe I was meant to join the war against the Taliban and completely missed my destiny. Maybe I could have

---

[1] Plutarch, *Life of Alexander* 3 as translated in *Alexander the Great: Selections From Arrian, Diodorus, Plutarch, and Quintus Curtius* (eds. James S. Romm and Pamela Mensch; Indianapolis, Ind.: Hackett, 2005), 2-3.

stopped the latest conflict from becoming a double-digit year operation if I had cried less as a baby. In any case, that is not the focus of this chapter. (However, if you do have any insightful observations about what it means for my future, please write. FYI, I am neither Russian nor Communist but my mother has made me multiple Afghan blankets over the years—maybe that's what it foreshadowed.)

Each Gospel Takes a Different Approach to Jesus' Birth

A quick survey of the four canonical Gospels reveals that only Matthew and Luke wrote birth stories. The earliest Gospel Mark provides no such account, and John's Gospel focuses on the divine origin of Jesus of Nazareth rather than his physical birth.

When we turn to Matthew and Luke's accounts of the birth, we find two very different stories. In the nitty gritty details, we find logistical differences in the genealogies. We also find differences in geographical movements. Joseph and Mary start out in two different towns (Matthew puts them in Bethlehem and Luke starts in Nazareth). Luke and Matthew then send off the young family in two different directions following the birth (Luke takes them back to Nazareth and Matthew sends them to Egypt). It's important to ask "why."

In the big picture, Matthew's account presents Jesus in terms most meaningful to Jews, and Luke describes Jesus' birth in uniquely Gentile terms. Their audiences demanded two different depictions of his birth. If each Gospel was to accomplish the ancient goal of foreshadowing greatness before its demonstration in the life of a man, then they could not tell the same story and create the intended impact on two different audiences.

So how do Matthew and Luke contextualize their birth narratives for different audiences? The answer begins to take shape when the particular titles and descriptions of Jesus' significance are compared and contrasted between Matthew and Luke. For our purposes we will focus on Matthew 1:18-2:12 and Luke 2:1-20.

Remember, both texts do have similarities. For example, they name the child *Jesus* and call him the *Messiah*. Those basic similarities are commonly recognized and will not be discussed here. We are interested in the dissimilarities. We seek to unmute the message hidden in those differences. We want to find out what more Jesus' birth story says about him than the words themselves betray at first glance.

JESUS FOR THE JEWS: MATTHEW'S GOSPEL

In Matthew a distinct connection between Jesus and the Jewish mindset appears. First, Jesus' name is explicitly connected to the salvation of the Jews. *Yeshua* in Hebrew means "he who saves." Matthew 1:21 explains that Jesus has arrived to "save his people from their sins." Matthew doesn't say Jesus will save "all people." The "one who saves" is going to save "his people."

It should be no surprise that Matthew explicitly directs Jesus' rescue mission to God's chosen people. Matthew is writing a biography of Jesus for a Jewish audience. He wants them to see how God is making good on his prophetic promises to restore and to forgive his people for their sins.

As Matthew continues the birth story, he specifically presents Jesus as the fulfillment of Isaiah's prophecy. Jesus is identified with the child named Immanuel who would represent God's presence among his people (Matthew 1:23). He is the living embodiment of a divine promise recorded in Isaiah 7:14. He is the long awaited return of God's presence to his people.

The same connection between Jewish Scriptures and Jesus' birth is made when Micah is invoked to elucidate the location of Jesus' birth in Bethlehem. Matthew 2:6 cites Micah 5:2 to explain that the coming king would be born in Bethlehem. However, Matthew doesn't just use the location from Micah. Matthew also quotes Micah to explain that Jesus is the realization of God's promise to send "a ruler who shall shepherd my people Israel." Jesus is not being introduced as the "Lord of the world" but the "ruler of the

Jews." Jesus is coming to fulfill promises to his people and that is exactly what Matthew's Jewish audience needed to hear.

This fact becomes clear in the final way that Matthew distinguishes his presentation of Jesus' birth from Luke. Specifically note the title for the child placed on the lips of the magi who inquire in Matthew 2:2, "Where is he who has been born *king of the Jews*?" There is no emphasis here on the king of the earth or the king of kings. Matthew wants his Jewish audience to recognize first and foremost that Jesus is the king of the Jews, the promised ruler of Israel.

THE DEATH OF DEATH

Presenting Jesus in a way that connects with specific ethnic and religious groups didn't stop with Matthew's Gospel. One modern-day organization called *T4 Global* is continuing the tradition. *T4 Global* is currently helping a group of Samburu Pastors in Kenya bridge village life among the Samburu to a unique presentation of Jesus.

In Samburu religious tradition, God demands sacrifices to appease his wrath. So the Samburu sacrifice lambs without blemish, slaughtering and spreading the blood to cover the errors of their ways. The similarities to ancient Israelite sacrifices are somewhat eerie. The reasons for the sacrifices are almost identical to the Old Covenant as well. The people of the village sacrifice lambs for three reasons: reconciliation, sanctification, and substitution. For as long as they can remember, the Samburu have slaughtered lambs to make up for their sins.

All of these sacrifices give hope to the village that God will see the blood and stop the punishment the Samburu deserve. God's wrath will be delayed. Unfortunately, the elders believe that the sacrifices can never end. For every failure, a lamb must be offered.

In response to this common village practice, Samburu pastors are constructing a series of stories that begin with the early sacrifices of Genesis and move up to Jesus' symbolic death. These stories teach the Samburu that God did command his people long ago to offer sacrifices for sin. However, the history of sacrifices came to an end in Christ.

The major turning point in the biblical stories for the Samburu comes when John the Baptist identifies Jesus as the "Lamb of God who takes away the sin of the world." This identification makes a radical claim in Samburu culture. Jesus is the sacrifice to end all sacrifices. The sacrificial stories transition from the despair of endless sacrifice and ritual to the hope of One who was called "the Lamb." In the story of the life and death of this "Lamb of God," they hear of a slaughter that ends all slaughter. They hear about a death that reconciles, sanctifies, and substitutes—an all in one sacrifice. For the Samburu this solution delivers them from a perpetual system of death and despair to the life-giving, once-for-all act of Christ. Nothing else has to die and no one else has to fear. The story of Jesus is no irrelevant foreign religion to the Samburu. It has become the most relevant story they have ever heard in their lives.

Jesus' story not only frees the Samburu from fear and endless sacrifice. He also puts an end to an unnecessary economic struggle. For a community of herdsman, the constant sacrifice of lambs is a costly expression of appeasement. People get trapped in poverty because they feel trapped in sin. With the work of Samburu pastors and *T4 Global* technology, the religiously motivated economic toll of killing lambs is being stopped. Constant guilt can be removed by Christ, and therefore income for the herdsmen increased. Their lives are being changed because the symbolic actions of Jesus are being connected to the world they know in profoundly practical ways.

Who knew telling the story right could save so many African sheep and the families that depend on them for income! I'll certainly never leave out Jesus' claim to be the "Lamb of God who takes away the sin of the world" if I meet some Samburu in Kenya. That specific presentation of Jesus changes everything for them. And that is why Matthew told the right story of Jesus to the Jews and Luke wrote the perfect script for a Roman audience.

The titles and descriptions for Jesus radically change when you move from Matthew to Luke's birth story. If you miss that divergence, you miss Luke's point. The exclusivity of Jesus for the Jews disappears and a whole host of new titles and descriptions take center stage in the words of Luke's angelic herald. Luke calls Jesus a Savior "for all people." Jesus will bring "peace on earth." He is the Lord of the whole earth not just king of the Jews. The uniqueness of these titles and descriptions has been lost in modern-day retellings of Jesus' birth. They have become stock phrases in nativity pageants and Peanuts holiday specials.

However, there is more going on here than a universal "Jesus for the Gentiles" introduction. Luke is doing something more significant than we typically realize. To figure out what he is doing with these titles and expressions, we must sketch out the way in which Luke has situated his birth narrative in the larger story of the Roman Empire. Remember Luke had a Roman audience that didn't grow up watching *Charlie Brown's Christmas*. They had other traditions come to mind when they heard Luke's story about Jesus' birth.

In Luke's account of Jesus' birth, he immediately connects it to a Roman census issued by Caesar Augustus. Luke 2:1 reads, "In those days a decree went out from Caesar Augustus that all the world should be registered." Of all the coordinating events and figures that he could have mentioned, Luke wants his readers to place Jesus' birth during the reign of Augustus in the Roman Empire. Being the only mention of Augustus (at least by name) in the entire New Testament, it stands out and begs the question: "Why?" What is it that Luke wants us to see? How exactly does the birth of Jesus relate to Augustus's Roman Empire?

For those 3 of you out there who have been asking this question your whole life, get ready for the culmination of all your dreams. For the rest of you, just go with it for a few pages. It's going to get good.

It has been noted by many commentators that Luke's Gospel and his record of the Acts of the Apostles are structured around inverted geographical movements. In Luke's Gospel, the story of Jesus begins with the reference to the Roman Empire we just read. Then Luke's Gospel spends a good deal of time in Galilee and ends in Jerusalem. In the book of Acts the disciples reverse the order. They begin in Jerusalem and move into Judea and Samaria. Then Paul travels throughout the empire, and the story ends in Rome. Do you follow the inverted order of geographic movement?

The location of activity moves from Rome to Jerusalem in Luke's Gospel and then in reverse from Jerusalem to Rome in Acts. In fact Luke believes this geographical movement from Rome to Jerusalem is so important in his gospel that he places all of Jesus' post-resurrection appearances in the holy city (instead of following Matthew and Mark's preference for Galilee appearances). This proclivity in Luke begs the question: Why has Luke been so deliberate in connecting the good news of Jesus first and last to Rome?

The answer to this question will grow out of our subsequent journey through Roman imperial propaganda from the time of Augustus. We are going to read how Romans interpreted the birth of Augustus and see where the legends connect with Luke 2. Don't worry. I will cite English translations and keep the quotes to a minimum. I won't let you drown in a sea of Latin literature about gods and myths and togas. However, I will give you enough material to know what Luke's audience knew about the birth and legends of Caesar Augustus and how it all collides with Luke's version of Jesus' birth.

THE GOSPEL OF AUGUSTUS

In 9 BCE the Proconsul of Asia, Paulus Fabius Maximus, advised the *koinon* of Asia (a.k.a., the governing assembly of the Roman province of Asia) to change their calendars from the local lunar calendar to the solar calendar used in Rome. I know. It's such a big event you are wondering how you hadn't heard about it before.

In the Proconsul's recommendation, he specifically suggested that the first of the year be placed on September 23, the birthday of Caesar Augustus. His reasoning was simple. Since the birth of Augustus ushered in a new age of peace and prosperity, his birthday should become the first day of every year. (By the way, I've tried to do the same thing for my birthday at work, but I still can't get an extra New Year's vacation day. So I don't recommend going through the hassle of printing new calendars).

The governing assembly received the idea readily and awarded a crown to Paulus Fabius Maximus for construing such a brilliant way to honor the emperor. They all knew this idea would please the emperor and possibly attract more imperial tax dollars. So they had to put together a good PR campaign to milk it for all it was worth.

In order to effect this change in the lives of everyday people throughout the province of Asia, they composed a declaration. The declaration honored Augustus for his salvation of the world and ordered everyone to throw out the old calendars. The most complete version of this inscription was recovered at a city called Priene (not too far from Ephesus) and has been translated below. Read it carefully and listen for the same language you've read in Luke's birth story of Jesus.

In her display of concern and generosity on our behalf, Providence, who orders all our lives, has adorned our lives with the highest good, namely Augustus. Providence has filled Augustus with divine power for the benefit of humanity, and in her beneficence has granted us and those who will come after us [a Saviour] who has made war to cease and who shall put everything [in peaceful order] . . . And Caesar, [when he was manifest], transcended the expectations of [all who had anticipated the good news], not only by surpassing the benefits conferred by his predecessors but by leaving no expectation of surpassing him to those who would come after him, with the result that the birthday of our god signaled the **beginning of good news for the world** because of him.[2]

---

[2] Lines 34-41 quoted from Graham Stanton, *Jesus and Gospel* (Cambridge: Cambridge Univ Pr, 2004), 32. Fragments of this inscription have also been located at other cities.

For the Christian reader this inscription sounds full of heretical language. It seems to apply titles and roles to Augustus that are religious in nature and only appropriate for Jesus. Yet, the language is fully political. These are the grandiose titles that Roman politicians employed for propagandistic purposes.

In the time of Augustus, a Savior full of divine power whose birth signaled good news for the world was nothing other than an ideal emperor. In the recommendation that Paulus Fabius Maximus sent to the *koinon* of Asia he even wrote concerning Augustus's birthday, "We could justly consider that day to be equal to the beginning of all things . . . the beginning of life and of existence, and the end of regrets about having been born." It seems ridiculous to us, but it captured the significant shift in political and social stability that Caesar Augustus established.

The birth of Caesar Augustus created a new world of peace and joy out of existing disarray and despair. It was so monumental that we now call this time period in Rome the *Pax Romana*, or Roman peace. Some have even called it the *Pax Augusta* since he established it. We must understand that what we merely consider an important period in the political history of Rome was to them their salvation. The birth of an emperor who brings peace to a world that had been destabilized by armed conflict is good news—it is a gospel worthy to be proclaimed in all the world and remembered by all who have enjoyed his benefits.

THE GOSPEL OF JESUS AND AUGUSTUS

If this type of adulation for Augustus represents the political propaganda of the day, how should we rethink our reading of Luke's birth narrative? How does the good news of Jesus' birth relate to the good news of Augustus's birth? Note the strong similarities of language and ideas between the inscription and excerpts from Luke 2:1-20 on the next page.

Greek Inscription	*Luke 2:1-20*
"Savior"	"Savior"
"made war to cease and who shall put everything [in peaceful order]"	"Peace on earth among men"
"the birthday of our god signaled the beginning of good news"	"I bring you good news of great joy"
"for the world"	"for all the people"

The so-called "Christian" or "religious" language of Luke's birth narrative takes on new significance when heard within the world in which it was composed. Luke's audience believed the Roman emperor was the savior. The birth of the emperor Augustus was good news for all people because he brought peace to a world at war. When the angels use language of savior, peace, and good news for all people, it is a direct challenge to the Roman emperor. Jesus is taking control. He is going to institute policies to benefit the world and lead every nation toward a social revolution that leaves peace and order where conflict once reigned.

In that context, the announcement of Jesus as "savior" would not be heard as the revelation of a *personal* savior who intends to bring peace to one's soul. It is much bigger than that. It is an emperor who would rule the world. However, many of us associate "savior" with someone who just takes care of our sins or personal problems. No doubt other passages of Scripture teach that Jesus does that. But the story of Jesus' birth tells us his vision for saving goes way beyond a personal spiritual experience. It has ramifications for the entire world and all of its social structures.

The announcement of the savior of the world is exactly that—a savior who intends to take a society in disarray and restore it to peaceful order once again. People stuck in cycles of violence and suffering should hear a promise of comfort and coming stability. Their despair should turn to hope.

In a Roman world, the arrival of a Savior would not mean that a few individuals can now be snatched away to heaven from the perils of this planet. It's not that individualistic or isolated in scope. The peace is being brought to the whole earth. The entire game has changed. God has sent someone to set all things right. Although evangelicals tend to focus on a personal spiritual experience that Jesus seeks within people, he was introduced as the emperor who would put an end to earth's conflicts and replace despair with joy for all people. That's no isolated or internal vision for saving the world.

PEACE-BUILDING INITIATIVES IN AFRICA

The African Leadership and Reconciliation Ministry ("ALARM") understands the large-scale purpose of Jesus' plan for peace. ALARM has an entire branch of their operations focused on building peace in Sub-Saharan Africa. The *Peace-Building and Reconciliation Initiative* has had significant success in bringing together community representatives from different tribes, regions and religions in conflict with each other. A recent beneficiary has been the town of Eldoret in western Kenya.

The ethnic violence that broke out in December 2007 after Kenya's disputed presidential election affected Eldoret in horrifying ways. Many people lost their lives, and those who survived the conflict often became Internally Displaced Persons ("IDPs"). In one particularly horrific incident, a mob of youth set fire to a church in Eldoret where over 50 people had gathered for protection. All were burnt alive.

In January 2008, at the height of the crisis, ALARM sent two staff members to Eldoret to develop a plan with Church leaders that would facilitate reconciliation. They began with a meeting of Church leaders from opposing tribes. To no one's surprise, it didn't fix everything in an instant. Genuine dialogue was difficult since it was the first time for these pastors to face each other after the violence erupted. The gathering did, however, represent a critical first step.

Two weeks later, the ALARM team returned to Eldoret for a two-day "Trauma Healing and Peace Building" meeting. This time more Church leaders attended and honest dialogue ensued. Pastors confessed their error in picking political sides and supporting particular ethnic groups during the elections. They confessed to their role in nurturing the violence. The honesty and contrition pointed toward the hope of reconciliation.

When the violence subsided in March 2008, ALARM's Africa Director was chosen to chair a newly formed alliance of churches, known as the Hope for Kenya Forum. The Forum's purpose was to restore peaceful relationships between warring factions in Kenya. ALARM organized several conferences to this end in Eldoret and other towns across Kenya. ALARM's President Celestin Musekura facilitated the meetings with leaders from every major Kenyan church and denomination. He called for the healing, forgiveness, and restoration of the nation.

One particular initiative that came out of the meetings was Operation "Tukule Chakula Kwa Nyumba" (Operation "Let's Break Bread Together at Home"). Some of the pastors who attended the first ALARM meeting decided to practice what they had learned about peace-building and reconciliation. Led by Pastor Martin Shikuku, the pastors initiated peace activities within and beyond the Church through shared meals.

The goal of Operation "Tukule Chakula Kwa Nyumba" was to unite people from different tribes around a delicious, satisfying meal. The meal would be the first time since the post-election violence that disputing tribes would come together. Sharing food provided the space to re-learn how to trust, work and live with each other. In preparing this community event, each disputing ethnic group was asked to assign 10 women and several youth to cook the day's meal in a common kitchen. Just cooking together was a sign of peace returning to a volatile region.

On April 9, 2008, approximately 300 people attended the shared meal. Mrs. Emily Chengo, the ALARM Africa Director, spoke at the event. She presented the need to pursue alternative conflict resolution methods. Since the event fell on the day before Good

Friday, Emily spoke of God's gift of reconciliation to humanity. She said that eating together symbolizes a new beginning of interaction and dialogue. She in essence called them back to the very purpose of Jesus' coming announced at his birth. Jesus had come to bring peace.

Due to the unique nature of this event, government leaders invited members of the local media to record it. The media came so that more communities across Kenya could learn about it and introduce similar concepts in their individual communities. Both TV and radio stations interviewed Emily and aired the event that evening. ALARM-Kenya brought peace to Eldoret that night, and the media played the role of the angels proclaiming peace across the country.

In East and Central Africa, ALARM is increasingly being requested to execute Jesus' mission of peacemaking. ALARM trains members of parliament, local government officials, civil society leaders, Christian police officers, and Christian lawyers in peacebuilding, conflict resolution, good governance, anti-corruption, biblical forgiveness, reconciliation, trauma healing and servant leadership. In August 2009, President Celestin Musekura even spoke at the Africa Forum on Religion and Government. The Africa Forum on Religion and Government is a biennial conference that brings together government officials and religious leaders from Sub-Saharan Africa. The attendees discuss ways forward that will help bring about true transformation, good governance, peace and development in Africa. Through many such opportunities, ALARM is sharing the message of biblical forgiveness and reconciliation with local, national and regional leaders who are shaping the future of the continent. ALARM is bringing peace to the earth today just as the angels announced Jesus would do all along.

HUMAN SINGERS AND HEAVENLY ANGELS

The angels in Jesus' birth story don't get much attention. If you think about it, most of us pay more attention to what was said than to who announced it. There may be good reason. It may be that the difficulty of singing "Gloria In Excelsis Deo" at Christmastime has fueled the misplaced attention. I personally can't figure out how it can take 18 separate notes to sing a 3-syllable word like Gloria. And why do we sing it in Latin when it's recorded in Greek but probably delivered first in Aramaic? If you are anything like me, I fear singing Christmas songs. It's like they are designed to hit every possible note I can't sing and do it in languages I don't speak.

Christmas songs like "Hark the Herald" and "Angels We Have Heard on High" may be the first thing that comes to our mind when we think of the angels on the night of Christ's birth. However, that wasn't the case for Luke. When Luke has an army of angels taking center stage to sing about Jesus the Savior, he is counting on his audience having a very different association. The singing angels weren't the only chorus in town that sung about the good news of saviors and lords.

Throughout many eastern Roman provinces, the Caesar was honored at athletic competitions and worshipped at imperial temples. At the time of Jesus' birth, temples to the god Augustus and the goddess Roma stood prominently in Pergamon of Asia, Ankyra of Galatia, and Nikomedia of Bithynia.[3] Those names probably mean nothing to you, but it meant that people living in imperial provinces where Luke lived worshipped the emperor like a god.

At the city of Pergamon (one of the seven churches of Revelation located in the Roman province of Asia), organizers named their athletic competition the *Kaisareia* in honor of the Caesar. That would be the equivalent of people in Montana calling a flyfishing competition the *Presidential*. The name would be a play on the grandeur of the most powerful man in politics.

Naming the athletic competitions after the Caesar had a purpose. Every game and competition was supposed to honor the ultimate ruler and victor of the Roman Empire, the Caesar. They were designed to flatter him. These types of competitions were customarily held at all the important cities of Asia.

---

[3] For more information on the imperial cult practices during the time of Augustus, see Steven J. Friesen, *Imperial Cults and the Apocalypse of John* (Oxford: Oxford Univ Pr, 2006), 25-38.

Simon Price writes that these "festivals included competitions, not only in athletics and music, but also in imperial *encomia*."[4] *Encomia* are honorific poems that recount the greatness of a particular character. They don't sound exciting, but *encomia* were a big deal at these games. If you were good at composing these honorary poems, you could make a name for yourself.

Price highlighted one Greek inscription about a famous *encomia* competitor named Coan. The inscription reads: "in all the most distinguished cities of Asia [Coan] won competitions in encomia to the founder of the city Sebaston Caesar and the benefactors Tiberius Caesar and Germanicus Caesar and all their house and to all the other gods in each city." Sebaston Caesar was another way to talk about Caesar Augustus. He got a lot of praise at these local contests while Coan and others showed off their composition skills.

Although the poetry and songs entered into these local competitions do not survive in abundance (which I know disappoints you), we can get a glimpse of their content in the *Odes* of Horace. In chapter twelve of book one, the great Latin poet Horace praises Augustus. He is particularly taken by Augustus's military success against the Parthian threat to the eastern Roman Empire. In the excerpt below, Horace places Augustus atop a list of all the great Roman heroes that "the Sire on high" (or "god") has sent to earth in time of need. Horace implores that the Fates let Augustus continue his reign as second in command to god. It won't all make sense but you'll get the point.

> *Whom praise we first? the Sire on high,*
> *Who gods and men unerring guides,*
> *Who rules the sea, the earth, the sky,*
> *Their times and tides.*
> *No mightier birth may He beget;*
> *No like, no second has He known;*

---

[4] Simon R. F. Price, "Gods and Emperors: The Greek Language of the Roman Imperial Cult," *Journal of Hellenic Studies* 104 (1984): 90.

(A long list of Roman heroes ensues whom are
all considered a distant second to Augustus's greatness)

Dread Sire and Guardian of man's race,
To Thee, O Jove, the Fates assign
Our Caesar's charge; his power and place
Be next to Thine.
Whether the Parthian, threatening Rome,
His eagles scatter to the wind,
Or follow to their eastern home
Cathay and Ind,
Thy second let him rule below:
Thy star shall shake the realms above;
Thy vengeful bolts shall overthrow
Each guilty grove.

So what do these *encomia* honoring Augustus have to do with the singing angels in Luke 2:1-20? Early in Augustus's reign he visited one of Pergamon's celebrations in his honor and heard a chorus of men sing his praises. He was quite taken by their melodic compliments. The gesture of the Asian chorus so pleased the emperor that he ordered the singers to become a permanent fixture in Asia's honorary contests.

To make it feasible Augustus established a special levy to financially support the existence of this forty-person male chorus. The chorus quickly became an elite social club with hereditary rites. They gathered at one event after another to sing the praises of the Caesars. They guaranteed top-quality sycophancy for stroking the ego of Augustus and the emperors thereafter.

When Luke's audience heard about a massive angelic chorus singing the praises of God and his appointed savior, the closest experience would be imperial singers. They had probably been to hear them at a local event.

The instant comparison would quickly become a contrast. Jesus' birth elicited the presence of countless angels from heaven. Caesar Augustus had to pay for a group of men to show up and sing his praises. One of those choruses is clearly superior, and one of those births is more plainly validated by God. This is the impact Luke was looking to make on his Hellenistic audience that had grown up in the *Pax Romana* established by Caesar Augustus. There is a new emperor in town. His name is Jesus.

BEST BUY'S PEACE AND RECONCILIATION

Christmas commercials do the same thing the angels did in the days of Augustus. The angels took the legendary promises of Augustus and applied them to Jesus. Commercials take the stories of Jesus (and Santa Claus) and apply them to retail stores. Sometimes the parallels are subtle like Luke 2, and I imagine most marketing firms have no idea the parallels are there. I can never forget one particularly well-done Christmas commercial for Best Buy.

The scene begins with an adolescent girl on her cell phone—not too uncommon. The pre-teen is complaining about how horrible her parents are while looking out her bedroom window. It is the same old story of a girl who thinks her parents don't get it. They don't understand, and she just wishes they would go away.

In the middle of her rant, her mom pulls into the driveway in a minivan. Her angst is unaffected—at least until she sees her mom take out two presents wrapped in shiny blue and yellow paper. Suddenly her demeanor changes. She hangs up the phone and runs down the stairs. Instead of complaints, she greets her mom with a smile. The estranged mother-daughter relationship is instantly healed. Best Buy has brought reconciliation to one more home on the block. It's a truly beautiful story of peace, love, and electronics.

This commercial advertises the gospel of Best Buy. If you purchase a smart phone or the right TV for your daughter, it can restore your relationship. Strife will turn to peace. Differences can be reconciled. You can have the family you always wanted if you know what to buy.

It is a competing Gospel. At Christmastime, Christ is proclaimed as the bringer of peace and the source of joy for all people. Best Buy is promising peace and joy at your local store. I doubt Best Buy and their marketing initiatives are trying to directly challenge the meaning of Christmas. But that hardly matters. They are doing what the angels did. They are claiming to be the real deal. They are claiming to bring peace to a broken world. It's a smart approach.

Is Christmas Political?

During the 2008 presidential primaries in the United States of America, Christmas became a political tool in the hands of many candidates. Most campaigns released a Christmas-themed commercial in hopes of taking advantage of the season. Those commercials left an imprint on my mind.

It is hard to forget seeing Rudy Giuliani sitting next to Santa Claus defending the quality of his fruitcake or the supposedly simple Christmas wish of Mike Huckabee that became a subliminal message about the cross on account of a white bookshelf in the background. Hillary Clinton's commercial also caught my attention due to the acting performance she gave.

As the commercial begins Hilary is cutting ribbon and wrapping gifts. Each gift for the American people is given a tag with such descriptions as "universal healthcare," "alternative energy," and "middle class tax breaks." Then the camera pulls back to reveal a ponderous Clinton who asks, "Where did I put universal pre-k?" The moment of concern is truly gripping. Thankfully she remembers it is right in front of her, and all is well.

As I listened to feedback on a radio show about these commercials I heard the complaint that Christmas should not be turned into a political affair. A number of people echoed the sentiment. They didn't want the birth of a spiritual savior mixed up with political ambitions. Yet, I am not sure that separating Christmas from the social concerns that politicians address is advisable. The way in which Luke presents the birth of Jesus actually connects it to contemporary politics and its promises of peace and joy for the world under its care.

In that sense Christmas is political, and Jesus' birth should be heard as a polemic against political pretenders promising to deliver what only the Messiah can. As Luke makes clear, Jesus is savior and not some Caesar. His birth is the real good news. He is the one who will bring peace and joy, not Caesar. Jesus' reign reaches the whole world—that is more than Rome's empire. That is why endless angels from heaven sung about Jesus' greatness whereas Caesar had to settle for some dudes he paid. Rome is only a parody of the reality found in Jesus.

So Christmas is the time to remember that Jesus is the one who can truly deliver what the Roman Empire promised. Into our chaos comes Jesus—the long-awaited restorer of order and peace. That proclamation lays claims on humanity. He deserves allegiance and praise. There was none so great before him and none after him will be. Our lives should be ordered around him like the Asians rearranged their calendar around Augustus's birthday to acknowledge that he authored a new world. And his imperial policies should be followed.

The remainder of Luke's Gospel demonstrates that Jesus' kingdom does not change the world through the same means as Rome. He does not bring about a revolution through conquest and fear of reprisal. There is no militant following ready to silence dissidents with the sword or subjugate the nations involuntarily. Into this world of the Caesars, Jesus promises to deliver in a whole new way.

Jesus' kingdom policy involves compassion, suffering to serve others, and the restoration of the oppressed and ostracized. Enemies are loved rather than slaughtered and arrogance is replaced by humility. Social transformation results from personal transformation that leads to public demonstration. Jesus' kingdom is no spiritual escape from the complexities of life in this world and its societal structures. It is designed to reorder it all. It intends to address the same problems for which politicians develop policies and programs. So if that is what is meant by politics, then Christmas is very much political.

HOW CAN JESUS SAVE OUR WORLD?

If you followed the logic of what Luke was doing in his Imperial context of ancient Rome, then the next question is how we can challenge our culture today. We need to find concrete ways to implement the way of Jesus where politicians and power brokers are trying futile methods. In short we must ask: what does it look like in the here and now for Jesus' kingdom policies to bring the peace and joy that other political powers claim to deliver?

The answers to this question are endless, and the potential for productive conversation in response to it would be hard to overestimate. My hope would be that you think long and hard about concrete responses. I want you to talk about it and take action. A little more peaceful order and widespread joy would go a long way.

In the mean time, I am going to provide a couple concrete stories of how Jesus has the power to create peace in situations where human factions have fostered violence. The first example comes from Africa and the second from the Middle East.

JESUS CAN RESOLVE TRIBAL CONFLICT

As food for thought, we would be wise to recount the potential for peace that Jesus' way demonstrated in the tribal genocide of Rwanda back in 1994. According to one eyewitness report, a group of about 13,500 Christians gathered in a small village 13 miles from Kigali to find refuge from the fighting. Although millions sought safety away from city centers during this conflict, this particular gathering set itself apart because of the unique constituency. There were both Hutu and Tutsi.

These tribes were supposed to hate each other. If these Christians had adopted the cultural values of the militants, they would have been fighting one another instead hiding together. This type of mixed gathering was unacceptable to the militias.

Their safe haven was eventually exposed to rebel militia who rounded them up at gunpoint. The rebels demanded that the Hutus and Tutsis separate so that only the inferior tribal people would be killed. In response, the leadership of this Christian gathering proclaimed, "We will not separate. For we are all one in Christ." The apostle Paul would have been proud. He had used that same line to stop senseless conflict between Jews and Gentiles.

The recognition of each person's equality before Christ provided an alternate path to peace that day. The tribal conflict was swallowed up for a moment in the superordinate identity of one true humanity. Unfortunately, that moment did not last long.

The potential power for peace was quickly silenced by the sounds of machine guns spraying bullets and spilling the blood of all those gathered in the name of Jesus. Although Jesus' kingdom policy had resolved the division and conflict between thousands of Hutus and Tutsis, a few men with Romanesque military tactics believed more strongly that violence would relieve their fears and accomplish their cause. The ensuing murderous scene is too horrifying to imagine.

On one hand, the massacre stands out as a sign that Caesars are still promising peace and joy by means of bloodshed and dominance. On the other hand, the shared death of Hutus and Tutsis is a symbol of promise for a world that needs to be saved from more projects of dehumanization and destruction. Jesus can save the world. He can bring peace "on earth" if we embody his new kingdom policies. That is the "good news of great joy" to proclaim to all that have succumbed to the illusory promises of establishing peace through death, joy through terror, and salvation through domination.

QUIET LOVE IN TOUGH PLACES

Jesus has the ability to resolve tribal conflicts in Africa, and he also has solutions for reducing Islamic terrorism in the Middle East. One of the most delicate subjects in the twenty-first century regarding a path to peace is the so-called "war on terror." Many detractors of the western response have rightfully questioned the strategy of killing to stop killing. The concern is: How can killing people in their home countries reduce violence rather than invite retaliation?

The debate about reducing violence from economically suppressed and religiously marginalized populations is profoundly important. However, I want to focus on one organization that has gone beyond debates and has a history of action.

Questscope is an international organization that operates among vulnerable populations in the Middle East. Instead of labeling marginalized youth who are prone to violent and mischievous behavior as problems or enemies, Questscope creates pathways of opportunity. They use non-formal education, mentoring, vocational training, community development, and spiritual formation as tools for bringing peace to the earth.

By replacing alienation with inclusion, Questscope is reducing violent behavior among youth in the Middle East. In fact, Oxford's *Centre for Evidence-Based Intervention* has confirmed it in a recent study of their programs.

In the country of Jordan, alienation becomes permanent for school dropouts. If you don't make it to the tenth grade and obtain your certification, you can't enter the Jordanian vocational training system. You struggle to read and write, and therefore struggle to find professional opportunities. You become an easy target for conniving businessmen or radical religious leaders.

Questscope has created a Non-Formal Education (NFE) process that allows dropouts to obtain the equivalent of a Middle Eastern GED. Jordan has adopted the program, and other countries like Syria are falling in line. Youth that would have become discontent with their lack of opportunity now find renewed hope for the future.

This story of bringing peace to a region through culturally informed activity rather than domination and death is spreading across the region. Similar NFE programs are beginning in Iraq, Yemen, and Sudan. The radicalized notion of finding peace through death and salvation through domination is not the policy that is succeeding. Questscope is bringing peace on earth with policies that look more like Jesus' approach than the Caesars of Rome. If you want to support "peace on earth" in one of the most difficult regions of the world, I'd check out Questscope.

If Jesus has a solution for genocide and Islamic terrorism, what other policy for bringing peace and justice to earth could we emulate on a daily basis? I do want to inspire you with stories of success on a global scale, but I also want to introduce Jesus' paths to peace that you could implement in the mundane affairs of everyday life. So here we go.

Most of us have heard about Jesus' command to "turn the other cheek" (Matthew 5:39). This adage has been mistakenly interpreted as Jesus' support for becoming a doormat underneath the feet of aggressors. We often think the message is to let people beat us up. It verges on religiously motivated masochism.

To take Jesus' advice as a call to compliant capitulation is a dangerous mistake. It is an interpretation that fails to see his cultural context. It is the kind of shortsighted understanding of Jesus that moves me to write this book.

In Jesus' day Roman soldiers strutted arrogantly around Israel. The Jewish land was Roman occupied territory. There was no love lost between the occupying soldiers and the Israelite population. When a soldier decided that he needed a Jew's goods or services, resistance was futile. The Jewish subject better be quick to fetch water, strong enough to carry a load, and ready to give away his shirt or else. If the subject could not perform the request to the soldier's liking, then a quick backhand to the face was not far off. This was the situation Jesus addressed in the Sermon on the Mount.

"If someone slaps you on the right cheek, turn the other cheek toward him." The statement seems to imply that one should invite an aggressor to leave no part of the face out of a good beating. This statement does not sit well among Bible readers who also believe that a man should protect his property and family against aggression. It also does not sit well in the mind of the culturally informed reader.

The culturally informed reader notices an unusually specific reference to the "right cheek" in Jesus' command. Jesus does not just tell someone who takes a fist to the face to expose the uninjured side. He gives clear instruction to expose the left cheek. This leads to a couple important questions. Why would Jesus indicate that the first blow will come to the right cheek? Why would he instruct someone to offer the left cheek to an attacking Roman soldier?

The answer is simple. Roman soldiers tended to be right-handed. When they struck an equal with their fist, it would tend to come in from the right and make contact with the left side of the face. When they struck an inferior person, they swung with the back of their right hand making contact with the right side of the face. In a Mediterranean culture that made clear distinctions between classes, the Roman soldiers backhanded their subjects to make a point. Jews were second-class. No one thought twice about the rectitude of treating a lesser person with less respect.

When Jesus tells his fellow Jews to expose the left cheek, he is calling his countrymen to "peaceful subversion." He does not want them to retaliate in anger nor to shrink in some false sense of meekness. He wants them to force the Roman soldiers to hit them like equals. He wants the Jews to stand up and demand respect. He wants to make each attacker stop and think about how they are mistreating another human being. It is the same motivation behind his command to "go an extra mile" after a soldier asked a Jew to carry water for the first mile (Matt 5:41). It is intended to shame the soldier. How could he treat another human being like an inferior animal? It is designed to play on a person's conscience.

PEACEFUL SUBVERSION

Jesus' command to "turn the other cheek" is ultimately a call to peaceful resistance. It is the mantra of great men inspired by Jesus like Gandhi and Martin Luther King Jr. Elsewhere in the Bible the books of Proverbs and Romans call it "heaping burning coals upon your enemy's head." That expression is an ancient Near Eastern mourning ritual. People put ashes on their head to express deep sorrow or regret. The apostle Paul's call to "overcome evil with good" and thereby "heap burning coals on an enemy's head" is a call to shame evil people into repentance. It is a peaceful plan for change.

Self-professed followers of Jesus have not always taken Jesus' message to heart. Forceful violence has replaced peaceful subversion many times throughout history. Hundreds of wars from the Crusades in the Middle Ages to the Thirty Years' War in the seventeenth century were motivated by Christian theology. Jesus' followers did not shame immoral aggressors for their inhumane acts but rather became immoral perpetrators themselves of rape, pillaging, death, and oppression. The same actions are seen every time an American Christian attacks an abortion doctor, or Nigerian Christians retaliate against the Muslims in Jos.

"Turning the other cheek" is not blanket acceptance of brutality or immorality. It is a plan for change. It is a strategy for motivating others toward lasting repentance. If you meet evil with evil and blow for blow, the cycle of vengeance will never end. The twenty-first century "War on Terror" is going to become the latest example of this forgotten lesson if its strategy remains "slaughter those who slaughter." Violence will beget violence unless someone is strong enough to rise above.

Nelson Mandela knows how "peaceful subversion" works. It doesn't happen quickly. It takes an inordinate amount of courage and character. For Mandela it took 27 years in a prison on Robin Island. But eventually the Apartheid's treatment of black South Africans brought them universal shame. The world could no longer allow the Apartheid to continue its reign after witnessing so many stark examples of extreme brutality and injustice. Mandela and the resistance did not fight back (although he did begin a plan to do so before his arrest). Mandela and the others also did not silently submit to an existence of inhumane treatment. They stood up. They raised their voice. They demonstrated the inequality and inhumanity of their aggressors. An entire country is different because they did.

JESUS' PLAN FOR "PEACE ON EARTH"

"Peaceful subversion" is one among many of Jesus' plans for bringing "peace on earth." It stands in stark contrast to the Roman conquests and imperial policies of oppression. Jesus does not order us to kill all who oppose him. His plans involve the ordinance:

"Love your enemy." The purpose is not to overlook the sin or violence. The purpose is to move them through shame or inspiration to a better way of life—the Jesus way.

In our day-to-day, it means responding with kind and selfless words when a boss has come on the attack with accusatory and thoughtless one-liners. You follow up his attack with a stop by his office where you compliment his demonstrated strengths. You show him how to empower someone thoughtfully so that he sees the contrast between his diminutive assault and your perceptive edification. You don't fire back with a cheap shot. You step back into his space with love. Don't expect it to work immediately. It took Nelson Mandela 27 years in prison.

This plan for peace and joy is rarely the gospel we announce. Too often we settle for a tiny, personalized announcement of inner peace. Or we give up on seeing large-scale peace for all people today and relinquish our hopes to an afterlife or idyllic world to come. I hope these failures on our part only reflect a misunderstanding of Jesus and not our fear to follow him.

Jesus did come to save the world, and he invites you to carry the message and live the dream. He is the only one that can truly do what politicians promise. It is not an easy road, but it is the best path toward peace and joy for all the world. It is the only way to establish lasting peace and order rather than temporarily killing the problem only to have it resurrect with greater destructive power than before.

That's a tall task. It requires patience and discernment, obedience and hope. Are you willing to follow someone whose goals extend to all people in the world and whose method involves your persevering subversion? He wants you to, and it's what the world needs.

Reenacting the Way

1. Do you agree that Christmas is political or do you think Jesus' mission is more personal and spiritual transformation rather than public and social transformation? Explain your answer using the language of "Savior," "Lord," "good news," and "peace" found in Luke's text and Roman texts.

2. Give a personal example of how you have opted to create peace through Romanesque assertion of power over others or a misplaced meekness that turned you into a doormat.

3. How could you shame someone who has mistreated you into realizing the sinfulness of their actions? Be specific about the method and the person whom you will overcome with love and resilience.

CHAPTER 3

WELCOMING OUTSIDERS INTO A COMMUNITY OF EQUALS: WHY JESUS HEALS AND HUGS KIDS

Focal Point: What barriers is Jesus breaking down with each miraculous healing and how can we cross similar lines today so that no one is excluded from a chance at redemption?

A CONTEMPORARY COMMUNITY OF THE EXCLUDED

In southern Ethiopia a vibrant community of HIV-positive individuals gather each week for prayer, worship, and encouragement. The community numbers almost 300 people. If you walked into a gathering one Sunday morning, you would never believe they are all dying. The joy and friendliness is contagious. It's enough to make you wonder how it all started. But that's a question without a happy answer.

In Ethiopia the AIDS population lives in isolation. That is no small population to segregate either—over 1.3 million people are HIV-positive. Once Ethiopian people learn that you've been infected, they want little to do with you. That exclusion knows no bounds. Even Ethiopian churches will force you out of the community.

Since the AIDS population is being forced out of churches, the organization *He Intends Victory* (get it "HIV") has worked with local partners to create an alternate community. That community is called Omo Village Church. In case you're wondering, they chose the name because the Village Church of Irvine in the U.S. helped them get started, and the Ethiopian church itself is located in a southern valley called Omo.

Omo Village Church has no pastor. The congregation cannot afford the $125 per month for a pastor's support. So Ayele Adore, the *He Intends Victory* Country Director, helps the congregation when he can. But funds are limited. During Christmas *He Intends Victory* is able to raise enough money to provide gifts for the children, but the rest of the church's ministry and benevolence has to be funded by the church members themselves.

The church has identified 6 leaders with some church leadership experience who help oversee the congregational needs. Although they lack resources to care for the physical needs, they do everything they can to help. But theirs is an uphill battle. Resources are difficult to find since uninfected Ethiopians deliberately exclude the entire HIV population.

This story of exclusion is depressing because it's real. Victims of rape become victims of AIDS. Children born with AIDS are introduced to a life of suffering. Children who lose their parents to AIDS are introduced to a life of scavenging. And to their suffering is added exclusion. It rips your heart out to meet a girl infected by her male rapist and excluded for life for no fault of her own.

The work of *He Intends Victory* in Ethiopia is noble. They have fostered the creation of a welcoming community. In a society where the suffering are ostracized, the Omo Village Church has become a haven of acceptance. It has become a community of equals. The infected, who have been rejected even by churches, find their place again.

AN ANCIENT COMMUNITY OF THE EXCLUDED

The exclusion of the AIDS population in Ethiopia is reminiscent of Israel in Jesus' day. People with debilitating illnesses were sectioned off from society. Certain extreme disorders had dire consequences. Instead of ostracizing people with HIV, Jewish religious groups discriminated against the paralyzed, the blind, the deaf, the mute, the lepers, the hemophiliacs, and the mentally disturbed. Radical groups like the Essene community at Qumran discriminated against people with these disorders as well as many Rabbis. To put it simply, there was no equal rights legislation for the disabled in Israel.

The documents found in the caves of Qumran (near the Dead Sea) declare that a community of God's true worshippers is not a place for the sick. The Temple wasn't handicap accessible, and the Essenes at Qumran believed God didn't want it to be. One ancient text makes that quite clear: "Neither one afflicted in his flesh, nor paralyzed in his feet or hands, nor lame, nor the blind, nor the deaf, nor the dumb, nor the lepers, nor those whose flesh is blemished shall be admitted to the council of the community" (*1 QSa 2:5-8*). If your body had some type of plainly visible defect, the community of worshippers did not want you. You could participate with a cold or headaches or even irritable bowel syndrome, but you couldn't have disfigured feet or bad hearing. It sounds ridiculous, but those were the rules.

The discrimination did not stop there. In the *Damascus Document* discovered at Qumran (don't worry about the name) we learn that not only are physically and mentally handicapped people excluded but also young people. Notice the last group of people excluded in the following excerpt. "No madman, or lunatic, or idiot, or fool, no blind man, or maimed, or lame or deaf man, and no minor, shall enter into the community" (*CD 15*). Apparently being mentally ill and being 11 years old warranted the same exclusion from worshipping God. On the positive side, that rule would cut down on the need for volunteers to run the children's program, but it also cut kids off from encountering God.

Of course, a historically informed reader may suppose those harsh restrictions were only enforced by one hyper-conservative group that lived in the desert. That's a nice thought, but it's not true. First, an ancient Jewish writer named Philo tells us Essene communities existed in towns and villages all throughout ancient Israel in Jesus' day. Their rules were everywhere. They even maintained an outpost within the walls of Jerusalem itself. Everywhere you went in Israel, you would have found discriminatory communities that considered themselves "righteous" and everyone else "sinful."

Second, Rabbis who controlled access to the Temple at annual worship gatherings practiced the same discriminatory policies described in the Qumran documents above. If you had any of the forbidden physical or mental defects, you were not allowed to enter the Temple. The Rabbis actually told you not to bring an offering to God.

How could they do that? To my surprise, it wasn't hypnosis or censored state TV channels. They were able to make their fellow Jews accept a warped view of God's character without any psychological warfare techniques or mass ingestion of hallucinogenic drugs. It was actually quite simple.

The Rabbis simply added "exception" clauses to laws in Exodus and Deuteronomy regarding Temple access. The additions directly contradicted mandates in the Jewish Law. Here is how one Rabbinic "exception" clause was tacked on to the Law of Moses. The original texts from Exodus 23:14 and Deuteronomy 16:16 read: "All are liable for an appearance offering [before the Lord]." The rabbis added, "except for a deaf-mute, an idiot, a minor, one without pronounced sexual characteristics, hermaphrodites, women, slaves who have not been freed, the lame, the blind, the sick, the old, and one who cannot go up on foot" (Mishnah *Hagigah* 1:1). Needless to say, the Rabbis got carried away with their restrictions. Not only are the mentally and physically disabled barred from worshipping in the Temple, but also women and old people are excluded. I'm not sure how the Rabbis checked for people "without pronounced sexual characteristics," but those guys were out of luck too.

If you weren't a healthy male, first century Israel was a hard place to find a worshipping community that would let you participate. You would either have to worship God on your own or just accept your status as second class. You might just have to give up on experiencing God all together. Or, you may chase down every rumor you hear about a way to find healing and a community of worshippers that accepts children and women. Those were the kinds of rumors that Jesus' ministry stirred up. Those are the kinds of stories we are going to explore.

STORIES OF HEALING, STORIES OF INCLUSION

The Gospel of Mark has often been called the Gospel of Action. In the first eight chapters Jesus is on the move. He is doing tons of miracles and giving few sermons. If you are the kind of person who wants to know more about what Jesus did than what he said, go to the Gospel of Mark. It is more like an "action" film than a "documentary" about Jesus. The pace of the stories is quickened through Mark's repeated use of the phrase "and immediately." One action quickly leads to the next. Most of those activities involve healing miracles.

When the careful reader considers the fast-paced activity of Jesus in Mark 1-8, a striking correlation begins to occur between Jesus' healings and the conditions that caused religious exclusion in first century Israel. The correlations begin in Mark chapter one with a leper Jesus met while traveling around Galilee. Here is the story from Mark 1:40-44.

> [40] A man with leprosy came and knelt in front of Jesus, begging to be healed. "If you are willing, you can heal me and make me clean," he said. [41] Moved with compassion, Jesus reached out and touched him. "I am willing," he said. "Be healed!" [42] Instantly the leprosy disappeared, and the man was healed. [43] Then Jesus sent him on his way with a stern warning: [44] "Don't tell anyone about this. Instead, go to the priest and let him examine you. Take along the offering required in the law of Moses for those who have been healed of leprosy. This will be a public testimony that you have been cleansed."

Jesus completely changed this man's world. He took a man who was on the outside looking in and gave him a chance to rejoin the community of worshippers as an equal. He can go to the Temple again like everyone else. His healing paves the way for a grand "Welcome back!" to the family. The story of Jesus healing the leper is the story that inspires *He Intends Victory* to create worshipping communities that accept HIV-positive people. It is a bold act of restoration.

When Jesus tells the healed leper to take offerings to the nearest priest, he is telling the man to do this one by the book. Leviticus 13-14 provides the regulations for dealing with leprosy. Every healed leper had a priest offer sacrifices on his or her behalf. The offering finalized the atonement for their sin (Lev 14:16, 31). It acted as a declaration before the community and God that they once again were pure, holy, and equal members of the worshipping community. No one needed to exclude them from God's presence anymore.

The change in the way people viewed this former leper was at the heart of Jesus' motivation in healing him. Note Jesus' last words to the man, "This will be a public testimony that you have been cleansed." Jesus knew the man's physical condition cut him off from the community of worshippers controlled by the priest. It wasn't just a physical problem. It was a spiritual barrier. Jesus' healing was a grand reunion—a statement to everyone around him that nothing stood between the healed man and God.

MODERN-DAY EXCLUSION, MODERN-DAY MIRACLES

Have you ever heard of "cleft palette"? Have you ever seen a child who suffers from "clubbed foot"? Do you remember the pictures on TV ads of oversized heads on top of malnourished bodies? The pictures I've seen are almost haunting. The disfigurement breaks your heart and often makes you turn away. The desire to go back in time and fix whatever went wrong runs wild. You really wish you could do something to fix it, but you can't.

To be honest, the deepest suffering of these children has not been captured on television. The deeper pains from the disfigurement cannot be seen in a picture. They take place in the little known dynamics of societies and families afflicted by the disorders. What do I mean? The fact is communities around the world ostracize these children. Many African cultures assume a mangled foot or disfigured face means you're cursed. They fear an evil spirit has targeted the child. So they hide the child from society and potential peers. They abandon the child to die or leave them at an orphanage far away from the rest of their family.

This abuse and neglect creates deeper wounds than we can see. These kids don't just struggle with physical mobility or survival but with social rejection and spiritual darkness. It adds to the sensation of hopelessness I feel when the pictures flash in front of me. To be honest, it makes me want to give up and forget…, but it makes *CURE International* want to get involved.

CURE International is a network of hospitals in underdeveloped countries. Their name says it all. They "cure" physical deformities. In dramatic fashion their surgeons create a whole new life for the people they serve. Disabled children with "clubbed feet" begin to walk again. Plastic surgeons turn a child with "cleft lip" into one more smiling face on the soccer (or fútbol) field. Neural surgeries reduce the swelling in the head for hydrocephalus sufferers and end their fast track to an early death. In fact, *CURE International* does more hydrocephalus surgeries than any other hospital network in the world!

By removing the physical marks that fuel the children's exclusion, *CURE* ushers them back into their communities as equals. They do for kids what Jesus did for lepers. In one instance, *CURE* found a boy whose parents locked him in a closet every Sunday while they went to church. Can you believe that? The parents were afraid to bring a cursed child into the house of God. So week after week, they put him in the dark and did untold psychological damage.

It didn't take long for *CURE* to surgically reconstruct the boy's body when they found him, but that is only part of the problem. The debilitating pain runs much deeper than skin and bones. That is why *CURE* has a spiritual director at each hospital. Someone is needed to begin educating the parents about the disease and correcting their belief that he was cursed. A child's body can change form in a few hours of surgery, but the social and spiritual stigma requires more attention than a surgeon can provide.

The work of *CURE International* is changing children's lives on multiple levels. Children not only regain full acceptance in their families and religious communities, but they also gain new confidence to attend school regularly. They are no longer the disabled or disfigured laughingstock of the class. This reintroduction to the social, educational, and religious life of their communities opens up a whole new world of opportunities. Their role as "beggar" switches to "becomer." They now have the physical and mental capacity to become something greater than they ever could have been before. *CURE*'s work is a modern-day miracle that is dissolving modern-day exclusion. It is Jesus' miraculous work all over again.

HEALING TO MAKE A POINT OF INCLUSION

Jesus didn't do every miracle to make the same point. He had a little more to offer than a one-size-fits-all message about his unusual power. That becomes clear as you read other chapters in this book about water becoming wine, the storm calming down, and the demoniac being set free. Each miracle recorded in the Gospels sent a specific message to people in a particular time and place.

As you will see in the next chapter, the point of feeding 5,000 people with 5 loaves of bread is not the same point behind his healing miracles. Each disease Jesus decided to heal carried a social and spiritual stigma. The diseases he typically healed fell within the categories that warranted religious exclusion in his time.

When you read the Gospels, it is important to notice what ailments Jesus does not cure. Although each Gospel writer adds disclaimers that Jesus healed many more people than they recorded, the types of diseases healed are still limited. He rarely healed temporary aches and pains. Taking away the fever from Peter's mother was the exception not the rule. You won't find stories about Jesus healing broken bones or headaches. He didn't do colds or insomnia or chronic back pain. Jesus healed diseases that made people unclean. Think of leprosy and the hemorrhaging woman. He healed physical defects that hindered mobility and communication. Think of all the deaf, mute, blind, and lame healed by his touch.

The first eight chapters of Mark's Gospel record a string of healing miracles. Jesus heals lepers (Mark 1:40-45), the disabled (Mark 3:1-5), demoniacs (Mark 5:1-20), female hemophiliacs (Mark 5:25-34), and the deaf and mute (Mark 7:30-37). None of these conditions falls into the category of "everyday illnesses." Jesus wasn't healing the flu, acid reflux or tooth decay. He doesn't cure respiratory disorders or athlete's foot. The stories of Jesus' healings in Mark 1-7 consistently relate to disorders and conditions listed as sufficient reason for exclusion from the worshipping community and the Temple itself.

What does all this mean? It means Jesus didn't come just to make people "better." He came to make people "closer." Getting better was really getting closer to God. Jesus came to empower the excluded by removing the barrier between them and the community of God's worshippers. The healing miracles are not simply a demonstration of divine power but rather a grand restoration of those on the outside looking in. The healed can now move from "outsider" status to "insider" status. The stigmas of physical defects, blood discharges, and mental instability no longer sectioned them off from the life of the community and the worship of God.

In a world where religious leaders said people with physical defects had no place in God's presence, Jesus gave them their place back.

THE POWER OF INCLUSION

Most of us understand how important it is to have your place. You've probably experienced what it's like to be on the outside looking in. I can still remember my first year in college when I was forced into the dorms. All I wanted to do was join the "off-campus" crew and free myself from the stigma of on-campus living.

I went to a small college that required students to live on campus in the dorms unless specially exempted. I really enjoyed the community and camaraderie at first. After those 2 days, I wanted my independence. Sitting through meetings where my RA reminded us how to pee without hitting the toilet seat only amused me for so long. Getting in trouble with the security guard for disturbing campus in the middle of the night after a Krispy Kreme donut-eating rampage wasn't acceptable. I could not be caged by dorm checks and lights out laws. I needed the freedom and sanity of an unconstrained life off-campus.

In my third year, I got my chance. A large freshmen class meant I could be exempted from dorm life. I applied for my exemption and won my freedom. I could finally tear myself away from the tyranny of institutionalized living. I could chart my path to personal responsibility and a bigger room.

My dream of self-realization and a life with no boundaries quickly faded. I started looking for off-campus housing in my price range and ran into a problem. I couldn't afford anything better than a 40-foot single wide trailer. It wasn't in the nicest part of town either. And I was going to need 2 roommates to cover the cost. That made for tight and uncomfortable quarters. But that's only part of the story.

On move-in day, it took 2 treatments of carpet cleaner to neutralize the "musky" smell emanating from the floor. I'm not sure what "musky" smells like, but the word was appropriate for how it made your nose feel. The trailer had 2 doors. One worked after trying the key 4 times while the other was chained and padlocked since the locking mechanism couldn't keep the door closed anymore. That drafty door and the 1/2 inch thick walls made for a cold winter. We learned to survive, but it wasn't pretty.

I can still remember the worst moment of the entire "off-campus" experience. I had gone to sleep one night eating Saltine crackers. The bag sat on the 4-inch wide table that separated my bed from my all-too-close roommate. When I began to wake up in the morning, I had an itchy feeling on my left forearm. I found that strange since it rested above the covers in the open air. As I opened my eyes and started to shake it off, I realized the itch wasn't the result of the draft or the musky air. There was a cockroach on my arm.

I jerked my arm so hard the cockroach flew right off. Then I saw another one scamper out of the bag of crackers. I leaped to my feet ready to pounce on the next one I saw but hesitated when I thought of squishing a 3-inch cockroach (or "Palmetto bug" as we called them) under my bare feet.

I had known the cockroaches lived under the house. We had made it a house policy to knock on the bathroom door before entering so that you wouldn't have to see them scatter off the sink and out of the shower upon entry. But waking up with a cockroach on my arm was too much. The off-campus life I had always wanted wasn't all it was cracked up to be. I needed to rethink my path to the good life inside the "off-campus" population.

Needless to say, we switched rentals after one semester. It changed everything. I finally had the privilege of driving my motorcycle on and off campus when I wanted. I had the status of independence and the sought after luxury of avoiding cafeteria food. I also got a home without bugs. I truly had arrived as a major player among the "off-campus" crew. Our pad soon became the host for man nights and a draw for our female counterparts. I realized how good it was to have my own place. I could stand among the "off-campus" students and brag to those still chained to the man and his RA and those uptight security guards. I was on the inside looking out at everyone who wanted to be me. Or at least, that's what I told myself.

THE BARRIERS JESUS BROKE DOWN

Jesus' world didn't care about where college kids lived or the status of "off-campus" students, admittedly because they had no colleges. But Jesus' world did have its stigmas and labels. Those labels gave some people a sense of superiority and gave others the curse of inhumane treatment.

A person with an illness became an impersonal category. A sick woman was called "unclean" and was expected to stay away from crowds and worshipping communities. Once you called her "unclean," you didn't have to treat her like a person anymore. The same was true for people without a Jewish heritage. Jews gave them the derogatory label "pagan." And then they imagined God loved pagans less so Jews could hate them with his approval.

Among the Jews, certain religious men drew another line. They considered themselves the faith's first-class members and went to great lengths to separate themselves from lesser Jews. These religious men joined groups like the Pharisees and Essenes (admittedly not the coolest names for a group). They labeled those who lived outside their lines as "unclean," "common," or just downright "sinners." They put the sick and disabled inside those lines of discrimination (although I personally find them to be the "lame" ones in all the Gospel stories—sorry, bad joke). Their categories gave them a sense of justification and superiority. If you did not say the right prayers, honor the Sabbath, uphold the purity regulations of Leviticus, and keep away from the pagans, you were an "outsider." You needed to tread carefully to say the least. Before them and before God you were considered a second-class Jew.

Jesus' approach to these exclusionary personalities was boundary-breaking. For those that thought youth should not be involved in the life of God's community (including his disciples), he would say, "Let the little children come to me." In a society that dismissed female dignity, he was known for his entourage of female followers (Luke 8:1-3). Every physical healing was a challenge to the tightly knit world of labels and lines that excused inhumane behavior against the afflicted and infected. He didn't recognize the label "unclean," and he invalidated it with his actions. Jesus knew that impersonal categories dehumanize. So he decided to cross the lines, break down the barriers, and remove the labels.

Let's look at how he started his public ministry with this stated goal.

JESUS SAYS: "YOU'RE NOT BETTER THAN EVERYONE ELSE"

In Jesus' first public proclamation at a synagogue in Nazareth, he announced the arrival of the year of Jubilee promised in Isaiah 61. The Jews who believed God focused on them to the exclusion of others thought Isaiah 61 was all about God serving them. They thought Isaiah 61 described a time when they would prosper above all other nations. Jesus thought he needed to turn their interpretation on its head. So he decided to shake up their unchecked self-interest.

To be honest, it's a common problem for all of us who read the Bible and think it is just a love letter to us. We forget that God is not as preoccupied with us as we are about ourselves. His love and interest covers the world, not just our little world.

After Jesus read the passage from Isaiah at the synagogue in Nazareth, he reminds his Jewish listeners of God's special interest in other people. To do so, he uses some forgotten moments in the ministries of Elijah and Elisha.

> But I say to you in truth, there were many widows in Israel in the days of Elijah, when the sky was shut up for three years and six months, when a great famine came over all the land; and yet Elijah was sent to none of them, but only to Zarephath, in the land of Sidon, to a woman who was a widow. And there were many lepers in Israel in the time of Elisha the prophet; and none of them was cleansed, but only Naaman the Syrian (Luke 4:25-27).

These two quick stories hardly mean a thing to us. They seem like random facts from a by-gone era, but they spark mob violence in Nazareth. People immediately march Jesus out of town to a nearby cliff and attempt to throw him down to his death.

Why? Why such displeasure? Because Jesus was crossing lines and invalidating labels. Instead of the Jews alone receiving God's attention, people from Sidon and Syria are blessed. Instead of Jewish males being the apple of God's eye, females and unclean foreigners get his attention. Even the widows and lepers of Israel are overlooked.

The violent response of the crowd to Jesus' stories in Luke 4:25-27 is not surprising. In the midst of a three and a half year famine, Jesus says Elijah was sent "to a woman" in a foreign land. How could a pagan woman rouse the compassion of God over all the Israelite males? And how could a leprous, unclean Gentile man be cleansed in place of an Israelite sufferer? These stories cut deeply into the world of labels and lines that Jesus came to revolutionize. They were fightin' words.

The ethnicity, gender, and physical health of Zarephath and Naaman were supposed to place both people in unsympathetic categories. It was supposed to excuse Jews from any compassionate concern. Who cares what happens to some pagan in Syria or some woman in a Gentile country?

That is how it worked in Jesus' day. If a first century Jew in Israel could identify someone as pagan, unclean, or even female, one no longer had to sympathize as though they were fellow human beings. That is how their world of dehumanizing categories operated. That is the world that Jesus encountered again and again. That is also the world he came to change. His opening interpretation of Isaiah 61 set the momentum for his ministry—a ministry that sought to dismantle every label and category that excused ungodly behavior.

How We Dehumanize Each Other

Each one of us inhabits a sub-culture that categorizes people to excuse insults, exclusion and unkindness. What does that look like? It looks like Democrats who relish in the defeat of Republicans. It looks like members of the religious right finding joy in the denial of marriage ceremonies for homosexuals. It looks like atheists finding pleasure in the exposed homosexual exploits of Ted Haggard, and evangelicals attributing natural and terrorist-induced disasters to such homosexuality. I know. I'm walking right into the fire with these examples, but that's exactly what Jesus was doing when he healed lepers, hugged children, and hung out with women. He was pressing people's buttons. He was tackling the issues that cut people off from access to God and his people.

Dehumanizing categories can also be seen today when a Palestinian rejoices over a rocket that hits a human Israeli target. Israelis then return the same desensitized response by finding relief in the number of Palestinians slaughtered in the latest Gaza Strip operation. Each one of these groups uses labels to excuse them from following the "Golden Rule." It works like this: You denigrate the opposition with a label and then condition yourself to relish in their pain and dismiss yourself from basic human decency.

I do not pretend to have simple explanations or answers to the complexity and history of issues like these and those that you experience. No chapter in a book or magical motto will resolve the tensions. But I do believe that each example of unsympathetic aggression is rooted in the names we give people. We turn each other into categories and all hell breaks loose. People become political opponents. Men become the enemy. Women become the problem. And all along we show our children how to destroy our common humanity.

So how do you plan to reverse the dehumanization and serve and love and guide those whom you have cut off from contact? Let's go to China to see what it looks like there.

SEGREGATED CHINESE MIGRANT WORKERS

In China, migrant workers that move to Beijing and Shanghai for low-wage jobs are given "outsider" status. Their ID cards give away the fact that they are from rural China. So local authorities exclude the immigrants in every way possible.

The immigrant children are not allowed to attend public schools. The adults have limited economic opportunities and get no help from government-funded services. These families who struggled to survive in rural settings now struggle to survive in shanty-towns on the outskirts of China's biggest cities.

Government authorities permit their presence near cities because the migrants work jobs no one else will, but that is where they must stay. They are "migrants," and they better not try to rise above their lower-class level.

The *Thornston Educational Fund* has decided to do what the Chinese government will not do. Motivated by the life and teachings of Jesus, this organization has turned their attention to the ostracized migrant communities of Beijing and Shanghai. They have built them schools. They have put on job fairs. They have hosted marriage enrichment seminars. They are giving the migrant workers a chance to live and to advance.

The *Thornston Educational Fund* sees the migrant workers as human beings. They cross the lines, drop the labels, and welcome them as equals to an alternate Chinese society. The educational and economic empowerment provides a path out of second-class status. The Christian community is ultimately reconnecting people to society and the God who loves them.

Jesus took away diseases that excluded Israelites from the community. The *Thornston Educational Fund* takes away the "outsider" status that leads to the discrimination of Chinese migrant workers. It may be taking place far from Israel and 2,000 years later, but it is the healing ministry of Jesus all over again.

THE FIRST TIME I GOT KICKED OUT OF CHURCH

Most of us have not experienced painful levels of inhumane treatment or exclusion. I'm no different. My worst experience of exclusion from God's people probably came on a Super Bowl Sunday in 2007.

I was living in Chicago at the time and the Chicago Bears happened to make it to the Super Bowl. The whole town was brimming with excitement about the opportunity to regain the title "World Champions" since the legendary 1985 Bears brought it home.

On a sidenote, I'm still not sure how two U.S. teams playing in a "National" Football League can be "World Champions." I can guarantee you no team from another country in the world could ever become the NFL's "World Champions." At least Major League Baseball (MLB) and the National Basketball Association (NBA) have the decency to include a few Canadian teams in their battles for the "World Champion" title. Sorry for the rabbit trail.

With that being said, let me return to Sunday morning at my church in Chicago the day of the Super Bowl. Since I grew up in Knoxville, TN, I was cheering for Peyton Manning's Indianapolis Colts (a University of Tennessee standout and future Hall of Famer who was robbed of the Heisman by a defensive back from Michigan… ahh the injustice!). That meant I couldn't wear my usual clothes to church. I had to be authentic. I had to wear a Peyton Manning Colts jersey.

When I entered the auditorium, I was wearing a winter coat. After the service began, I took off the coat and unveiled a beautiful blue and white football jersey. I couldn't have been more proud.

During the first break in the opening music, my disposition quickly changed from pride to shame. The worship leader (whom I knew quite well) stopped the music and pointed me out in front of the entire congregation. He rebuked me for wearing the blue and white colors in Bears' territory and instructed me to leave the building. Soon the lead pastor took notice and seconded the motion to have me excommunicated for the day. I couldn't believe it. I had never been kicked out of a church before.

Needless to say, no one stuck up for me. My football allegiances had excluded me from the church. I was a Colts fan, and people had no love for Peyton Manning supporters. It didn't matter who I was. On that day, I was the enemy. Of course, later I began to theorize that the worship leader used the jersey as an excuse simply to remove my off-key voice from the room. I do like to sing loud even if I don't know the words, or what a "key" is for that matter.

My story of exclusion makes no serious comparison to what people that CURE serves face today. It also pales in comparison to the lines and dehumanizing labels that Jesus had to confront in his day.

JESUS REDRAWS THE LINES

So much could be written (and it has) about the ways in which Jesus aimed to end the abuse propagated by categories of rich and poor, Jew and Gentile, male and female, clean and unclean, and righteous and sinner. We will limit ourselves to two moments where Jesus proclaimed "peace" and reconciliation to a person when others only saw "unclean" categories.

In Luke's Gospel Jesus tells only two people to "go in peace." It should be no surprise at this point that both are "women." Females were particularly subject to inhumane treatment and unchecked segregation.

STORY ONE: REHUMANIZING A SINFUL WOMAN

The first person granted "peace" is labeled both a "woman" and a "sinner" by the religious elite (see Luke 7:36-50). The story takes place in the home of a Pharisee—a home built on the principles of exclusionary labels and lines. The story's drama begins when Jesus comes into physical contact with a "woman" who is labeled a "sinner." Simon the Pharisee cannot believe Jesus lets it happen. His thoughts of disgust swirl in his head.

Luke 7:39 captures Simon's thoughts about Jesus' failure to recognize the boundary lines. "If this man were a prophet he would know who and what *sort of person* this woman is who is touching him, that she is a sinner." His thoughts are particularly revealing. All Simon can see is a certain "sort of person"—a person categorized by the labels "woman" and "sinner." She fits all the categories for being excluded.

Jesus sees something else. He sees someone who needs restoration not exclusion. He sees an opportunity to redraw the lines. So he confronts Simon. Jesus points out how she has washed his feet and anointed him with oil. He doesn't call out her sin. He forgives her sin.

His public proclamation of forgiveness and his public acceptance of her hospitality make a statement. He is rehumanizing the woman before a crowd of those who have labeled her a second-class citizen. He didn't forget what "sort of person" the woman was. He deliberately welcomed her as an equal to the dinner table. He is challenging the idea that only certain "sorts" of people could be there.

In Luke 8:43-48, another woman touches Jesus. She grabs the corner of his garment. We explained why she grabbed the corner of Jesus' prayer shawl in chapter one. She was reaching out to be healed by the Messiah, but the crowd would have interpreted her action quite differently.

Any informed Jew would insist this woman contaminated everyone she touched. Her reach was an unwelcome attempt to pollute those who were clean. She was like an Ohio State fan trying to walk through a section of Maize and Blue Michigan fans at the Big House or the guy at your office with strep throat that doesn't know when to stay home from work. I've been that guy. You get no love.

Why was this woman contaminating everyone else? Essentially her menstrual period never fully stopped. So she would emit blood frequently. According to Leviticus 15:19-33 the blood discharge made her unclean and put everyone else around her in danger of falling into the same category. Her illness made her a liability to the crowd instead of a person to be helped. As Craig Keener describes,

> If she touched anyone or anyone's clothes, she rendered that person ceremonially unclean for the rest of the day (cf. Lev 15:26–27). She therefore should not have even been in this heavy crowd. Many teachers avoided touching women altogether, lest they become accidentally contaminated. Thus this woman could not touch or be touched, was probably now divorced or had never married, and was marginal to the rest of Jewish society.[5]

Knowing these tense dynamics within the Judean culture of Jesus' day exposes the significance of Jesus' reaction to this "unclean woman." When she grabs him in hopes of being healed, she crosses lines that should not be crossed. Jesus should have avoided her like the plague.

---

[5]Craig S. Keener, *The IVP Bible Background Commentary: New Testament* (Downers Grove, Ill.: InterVarsity Press, 1993), Lk 8:44.

Instead, the discovery of who touched him leads to restoration. He does not tell her to bug off or go back to her hole so everyone else can live in peace without concern for her contaminating presence. Rather he ends her discrimination and tells her to "go in peace." He heals her hemorrhage and removes the barrier between her and God's people.

This is how Jesus' kingdom works. Those who have been labeled and pushed outside the lines are welcomed back. Discrimination dissolves and dignity is restored.

WHEN DOES JESUS USE LABELS

If you are familiar with Jesus' whole life, you may wonder how I can so frankly denounce the use of labels and categories. Didn't Jesus himself call the religious teachers of his day "hypocrites" and "vipers" and even "sons of hell?" He definitely did. When someone began making up rules for pleasing God that everyone couldn't follow, Jesus went after them. When a bunch of corrupt salesmen started hindering people from worshipping God at the Temple, he called them "thieves" and kicked them out.

But do you see why Jesus called people names and kicked them out? It's the same reason why he erased other labels and crossed lines. Jesus had no use for people that made it hard for others to find and follow God. Jesus had all sorts of names for people who put up barriers. Jesus' labels were designed to warn the rest of us about people who did the exact opposite of what he wanted to do. Jesus came "to seek and save the lost" not to section them off.

Jesus' mission to go after the sick rather than the healthy, the sinners rather than the righteous explains why he sectioned off the exclusionary religious elite. It also shows us that his boundary-breaking actions didn't negate his recognition of sin. Jesus is no poster child for universal toleration and acceptance.

Remember how most of Jesus' encounters with the "sinners" and "segregated" ended. Jesus didn't tell the audience at a prostitute's attempted stoning to accept her way of life. He didn't heal the lame man at a pool near the Temple and tell him to go do whatever he wants. He didn't stop by the house of Zaccheus and say he accepted him even though Zaccheus had stolen money from everyone in town. Jesus did break down barriers to connect with all these people, but he also told them to "go and sin no more."

In our postmodern world, tolerance has been mistaken for approval of everyone and everything. Those two actions must be kept separate. You can be tolerant without giving approval. Jesus exhibited tolerance when he embraced rather than excluded. But he did not dole out approval. And there's good reason for it. How could anyone approve a lifestyle that discarded God's design and thereby introduced more pain into this world? Jesus couldn't. If messed up ways of living reap destructive consequences, Jesus couldn't love people and approve everything.

Jesus' boundary-breaking actions had a purpose. He crossed lines instead of cutting people off so they could have a chance. Rather than piling on rules and requirements for who could and could not be around him, he embraced people where they were at. He went to great lengths so that no one missed an opportunity because of their label or stigma.

That is what we will do today to follow him. We will not approve of everyone's lifestyle just to get along. I certainly don't approve when my son chooses to hit another child, run in front of cars, or use my laptop for a sled. All those choices bring harm. But I do accept him and love him deeply while guiding him toward a better way of life. That is the kind of boundary-breaking love Jesus exemplifies. If we follow him, we will find ourselves around people whose choices we don't approve but whose common need for redemption moves us right through barriers to be with them.

THE FIGHT FOR EQUALITY IN INDIA

The history of India has been marred by rampant discrimination caused by the Caste system. Hindu Law teaches that human beings were formed out of the body parts of the god Brahma. The most privileged class known as the Brahman priests were formed from his head. Other Castes were formed from his shoulders and thighs and feet. Somehow, a few classes of people were made by accident apart from the will of the god Brahma. One of those Castes is the Dalits.

The Dalits are considered lower than animals. Their entire existence is a mistake and their presence pollutes the purity of India. Consequently, this belief has dehumanized the Dalits and cut them off from society.

In the majority of India's villages, non-Dalits have historically avoided eating or drinking with Dalits to preserve their purity. Traditionally, when Dalits entered a tea shop and requested a cup of tea, they were served in a clay cup rather than a glass or metal cup that others received. Non-Dalits did not want to risk contamination by drinking out of the same cup even after it had been washed. After drinking their tea, Dalits were expected to crush the cup on the ground so that no other person risked being polluted by it.

Today, clay cups are commonly used in many parts of India and are no longer exclusively limited to Dalit use. However, Dalits are still rarely served in glass or metal cups—which could carry their "untouchability." The long history of discrimination still lingers.

That's why the Dalit Freedom Network ("DFN") exists to undo centuries of this inequality. The Dalit Freedom Network advocates for Dalits internationally in Washington, DC, London, at the United Nations, and at major conferences on human rights and religious liberty. DFN seeks to raise awareness, advocate for change, and find relief funding for Dalits across India.

In theory, the Indian constitution guarantees equality, justice, and human dignity for all people and bans discrimination based on one's Caste. However, slavery and oppression excused by the Hindu Caste system are very much alive in India, especially in rural areas. The Dalits are still excluded from educational opportunity and respectable jobs despite government legislation.

So DFN is on the ground working to bring an end to Caste-based discrimination and the resulting oppression the Dalit community has experienced. As part of this effort, DFN has partnered with the *All*

India Christian Council to launch 1,000 Dalit Education Centers where poor children can receive an English-speaking education. Historically, the upper Brahmin Caste has had exclusive access to English-speaking education and therefore the best economic opportunities. The Dalit Freedom Network wants to change all that.

Joseph D'Zousa leads the efforts of the network, and Jesus' example leads him. Joseph D'Zousa believes passionately that we are all equal in Jesus and deserving of proper, humane treatment. So he is determined to combat the dehumanizing lines in his homeland. He knows that Jesus himself fought the same fight in first century Israel, and he is determined to follow Jesus' example of breaking down discriminatory barriers. Although advocating for Dalits looks nothing like healing a woman with a hemorraging problem, Joseph's mission is the same mission. He lives with the same purpose Jesus had behind Jesus' healings.

THE WESTERN HISTORY OF DEHUMANIZATION AND DEATH

Western history is just as full of discriminating labels that have led to inhumane acts. Think of Adolf Hitler who conceived of a superior Aryan race. He categorized the Jews as inferior members of the species and thereby excused himself from treating them as equals. Hitler declared during the war that peace would come when the strong rule the weak. That required the destruction of inferior Jews who had usurped power in society.[6] We must see that such categorization is an exercise in dehumanization, and dehumanization desensitizes people. It becomes difficult to engage in sympathetic or even empathetic evaluation of how you treat those who fall within the "inferior" and "enemy" categories.

Religious people have failed to act much better throughout history. For the Christian crusaders "Muslim" was a label that made the enemy "other" and therefore made decency and diplomacy unnecessary. When seventeenth century Lutherans in Germany sung

---

[6] Gunnar Heinsohn, "What Makes the Holocaust a Uniquely Unique Genocide," Journal of Genocide Research, vol. 2, no. 3 (2000): 416.

"A Mighty Fortress is our God" as a fight song on their way to kill Catholics, they did not think twice about the justness of their cause or the violence of their actions. Any person called "Catholic" lost their bid to be treated with justice and compassion. They were simply the "enemy."

The fact is people lose their humanity when they become a label in the mind of a competing faction. Many western nations have experienced this first hand in the early twenty-first century. For example, the United States of America has become the "Infidel" in the minds of certain Islamic extremists. The USA now endures the hostility of those who no longer see their common humanity. European nations have suffered the same fate. Contemporary labels are still leading to discrimination and death.

This list of lines and labels that lead to disorder and death could be elongated to lengths I can hardly imagine nor want to imagine. Think of second-century European people slaughtered by Romans who simply saw them as "barbarians." Envision the Native American chests riddled with musket balls because they were simply "savages" living on good land. Turn to the central Asian headlines today that show acid-burned faces of young Afghan girls because Islamic men see them crossing a line by getting an education. All of these violent actions go back to our tendency to turn people into categories—categories that excuse inhumane treatment. It was dangerous to use labels like "unclean" in Jesus' day and it's still dangerous to create new ones today.

DEHUMANIZING LABELS AND CHRISTIANS KILLING CHILDREN

So-called "followers of Christ" have failed to follow Jesus' path of erasing labels in Nigeria. In the Nigerian city of Jos, employment in civil services has been determined by one's label as a "settler" or an "indigene." The "indigenes" are given preference because of their historic claims to the area. The "settlers" are excluded even if they are the more qualified candidates for a job. The Christians with political power have both perpetrated the "labels" and the exclusionary practices.

The economic injustices springing from this policy led to the deaths of almost 1,000 people during violent clashes in 2001. The problem has persisted and violence has flared up periodically ever since then. However, the problem runs much deeper than a debate about "indigene" and "settler" status. There are ethnic and religious labels that divide.

The largest ethnic group in northern Nigeria, the Hausa-Fulani, are generally Muslim. The Hausa-Fulani are considered "settlers" while the self-proclaimed "indigenes" in Jos are mainly Christian. The Muslims and Christians in Jos do not mix. One resident Nanreh Dauda knows the religious labels and boundary lines quite well. She says the unwritten rule is: "If you are Christian, you have to be where Christians are and if you're a Muslim, you have to be where Muslims are."

These labels and lines led to another round of violence in January 2009. A disputed local election in which a Christian candidate defeated a Muslim aggravated the conflict. The Muslims lashed out after hearing the results, and the Christians retaliated in kind.

In one instance a "Christian" mob attacked the Muslim Al-Bayan school. You can hardly believe what they did. The mob came throwing stones, shooting arrows at kids, cutting up teachers with blades, and setting buildings and school children on fire. Yes, a "Christian" mob killed kids and set people on fire with gasoline and torches. Sometimes we pretend "Christians" have advanced beyond such atrocious behavior, but that only reflects our lack of information. People bearing the name of Christ literally ran an arrow through an 8-year old's body and set him and his school on fire.

Each religious and ethnic group in Jos seeks justice and economic opportunity, but the labels "Christian" and "Muslim," "settler" and "indigene," blind them from a sympathetic concern for the other. People in Jos don't see everyone else as people. There are people like me and then categories to kill. When a human being becomes a hated category, you even find self-proclaimed followers of Jesus killing young children without remorse.

I wonder what life in Nigeria could be like if Jesus broke down these lines and labels. Could it stop a Christian neighbor from becoming a Muslim boy's worst nightmare? Could it transform policies of exclusion into practices of inclusion regardless of origin? What would really happen if the dehumanizing categories that turn people into "problems" disappeared?

THE DANGER OF GIVING UP LINES AND LABELS

According to the apostle Paul the deadly tradition of lines and labels is nullified in Jesus' community where there is "neither Jew nor Gentile, neither male nor female, neither Greek nor barbarian, neither slave nor free." Any label designed to dehumanize and excuse senseless maltreatment goes away. Any class system that would have cut someone off from access to Christ's redemption disappears.

What Paul teaches in these words, Jesus embodied. The Gospels bring it to life in story after story. Jesus feels compassion for the Gentile and the Jew. He does not validate the divisions of righteous and sinner. He does not praise the Pharisees and Priests while lambasting tax collectors and prostitutes. Instead, he warns the rich of their inhumane treatment of the poor and tells every story he can imagine that might make them sense their shared plight.

But beware. Jesus' revolutionary streak did not win him a wealth of friends. Few leaders who benefited from the labels and lines of first century Israel applauded his commitment to mercy and justice. Those whose categories cracked under the weight of his life and teaching labeled him a "friend of sinners" in a dehumanizing scheme that coincided with plans for crucifixion. They placed Jesus on the other side of the lines and labeled him in such a way that their conscience did not cringe at his death. Who cares about killing a "friend of sinners" and a "blasphemer"? In the end, the very lines and labels that Jesus came to invalidate were used to justify his execution.

When you threaten the categories that keep certain men in positions of righteous power, the system will protect itself. It will fight to protect its labels and lines. If you plan to follow Jesus down this road, you better prepare yourself for name-calling and antagonism from others. Remember that Jesus encourages those who follow his way with these words, "Blessed are you when men hate you, and ostracize you, and insult you, and scorn your name as evil" (Luke 6:22). That's not a blessing most of us pray for.

Jesus had no illusions of grandeur. He knew the road he traveled and the lines he crossed would not be well received. So don't be caught off guard. When you start redrawing lines in your community or country, you will be ostracized and branded in offensive and demeaning ways. Don't be shocked if following Jesus ruins your reputation with powerful people who make a living off putting others in condescending categories.

CROSSING OUR LINES

What does it look like in your world to break down the barriers and labels that cut people off from God and his community of worshippers? The answer to that question is dynamic. You will have to pay attention to your culture, to your headlines, to punch lines, and political jargon. You will have to open your eyes and see all people as people. You will have to see where others are blind. You will have to re-focus on people that have been relegated to the backdrop of your life.

For most of us, we won't have to add new places to go. The people we have excused ourselves from loving often still walk around us. They sit next to us at soccer games. They work at nearby cubicles. They drop their kids off at the same school. They work where we shop. We walk on the same sidewalks, exercise at the same gym, and sometimes even stop by the same church. The problem is we don't treat them like everybody else. We have positioned them in another category in our minds and therefore cut them off from an opportunity to experience the God we know.

When you stop trying to put yourself in the best class, you can begin to care about people you labeled "second class." You will see through the name-calling that turns people into "problems" and "others," "idiots" and "enemies," and the "awkward" and "unneeded." Then you will realize that your categorical discrimination only cuts people off from your community and the God you try to serve. Once you remember that human beings lie behind the labels, you will be ready to welcome outsiders as equals. You will be ready to reenact the purpose of Jesus' healing miracles.

In my world, it means you don't use the adjective "gay" to describe something that is abnormal or stupid. Just ask the kid in one of my classes who blurted it out to make fun of his friend. I gave him a good lecture in front of the class about how his language would create anger, pain and division between he and anyone that wore that label. In my world, crossing lines also means I refuse to vilify all Muslims because of violent men who come from Islamic cultures. I don't want to destroy their chance at redemption because of indirect or direct associations with sinful men. That's not how Jesus did it.

What does it look like in your world? Have you separated yourself from obese people? Do you avoid time with mentally or physically handicapped folks? Do you prefer to mock the wealthy rather than befriend them? Do you write off lower class people as less important? The religious elite in Israel did. Jesus didn't. The path to follow is clear.

Remember. If you do it right, you'll pay for it. People who have carved out spaces of power will retaliate, even today's religious leaders. They will not be comfortable with your engagement of people they prefer to write off. They will think you are stripping them of their righteous place in the world. They will start calling you names or just stop inviting you to big conferences where important people climb the ladder to the top of Christian clubs. It happened to Jesus. To those he healed, he became the welcoming arms of God. To those he disturbed, he became a category that justified his death. Don't think following Jesus will win you a Nobel Peace prize. It may just ruin your life.

So who still wants to follow him now that you know what he was doing?

Reenacting the Way

1. What categories, labels, and lines of separation do you use to brand others and cut them off from the opportunity at redemption you could share? Identify categories from your life and subculture not already mentioned in the chapter.

2. Give an example of one way you have freely insulted or belittled a person in one of the categories without a cringe in your conscience because they are merely an opposing "label" rather than a fellow person in a shared plight.

3. Describe a specific way you could cross a boundary line. Could you change your language in conversation, the place you eat lunch, the people with whom you socialize, etc.? Remember the purpose is not blanket toleration but rather the ability to cross all lines to invite people into God's ways.

CHAPTER 4

LOAVES, FISH, AND WALKING ON WATER: EMBODYING THE MESSAGE

Focal Point: What do a walk on water and multiplied loaves and fish tell us about Jesus' mission and how we must demonstrate who we are before declaring it?

BEING WHAT YOU SAY

Shane Claiborne has stirred up some controversy and condemnation for his blend of politics and faith. Just read his book *Jesus For President* and see how well it sits with you. You might be inspired or just offended. In any case, you'll get one man's take on what it means to embody the message of Jesus in today's social realities.

Regardless of whether you read one of Shane's books (or listen to it as an MP3 download as I prefer), his values can be understood quite clearly. For example, you don't have to read a 300-page book on Shane's theology of the poor to figure out what he thinks. You could have learned that by serving alongside him and Mother Theresa among the poor in Calcutta. You also don't need to engage him in a debate about war to discover he is an active pacifist. Just observe his work for 10 weeks as a member of the Iraq Peace Team. Each visit he made to meet and pray for Iraqi victims rather than pray for victory through death makes the point. Similarly, Shane Claiborne doesn't need to write an ethics book to explain his position on materialism. A visit to his residence and neighborhood in Philly tells the whole story. He lives simply and purposefully among the middle class… by choice not by default.

On Good Friday in 2009 Shane Claiborne was arrested for trespassing. He and about 20 others were praying next to the property of Lockheed Martin, the world's largest arms contractor. They had read the Passion narrative and walked through the stations of the cross in memory of Jesus' suffering. They were remembering how Jesus suffered on our behalf and praying that the rampant suffering in war-torn countries would cease. As they stepped onto Lockheed Martin's property to recite the Lord's Prayer, the police apprehended them.

Why do I bring it up? Because his actions make a point. You will know Shane is serious about alleviating the suffering of war victims when you look at his police record. He embodies what he believes. That's why one of his books bears the title *Becoming the Answer to Our Prayers*.

Whether or not you agree with Shane, you can't be confused about who he is and what he stands for. He makes that clear with his actions. If you read one of his books or skim his blogs, it is simply a commentary on his way of doing life. It is the talk that follows a life of action.

SHOWING PEOPLE WHAT YOU THINK

Paypal co-founder Peter Thiel is walking the same road alongside Shane Claiborne (well, a much more profitable one). Peter is forcing kids to quit college to make a point about education. The Thiel Foundation is paying two dozen of the brightest minds at schools like Harvard, MIT, and Stanford to drop out of college. Sounds strange, right? His Foundation has selected 24 students under the age of 20 to receive $100,000 to get business ideas off the ground. He doesn't want the next best thing to stall out while sitting in a classroom.

You don't have to interview Peter Thiel to know what he thinks about the state of higher education. He sees problems. He sees kids coming out of school with massive debt and no means to act on their best business ideas. He sees an education system that isn't setting up its graduates for success. So instead of charging these kids tuition, he is paying them to test their entrepreneurial potential for a couple of years.

I must confess. I wish he would have come up with this idea before I invested six figures into a Bachelor-Masters-Doctorate combo punch of degree debt. But oh the lessons I have learned clawing my way out of an upside down balance sheet! I know how to replace my own brake lines, to create 3 different meals out of bread and beans, and craft a tight budget with the best of them.

Peter Thiel's decision to encourage college dropouts is designed to make a statement. It stands out in a sea of funders who pour billions of dollars into college scholarship funds each year. His counter-cultural initiative has definitely caught people's attention. His new program has been highlighted in every major news publication across the U.S. He is showing people what he thinks without having to say a thing.

This kind of newsworthy and symbolic exploit is the same approach we see Jesus taking in Mark's Gospel. Sometimes the best way to show people what's inside is by making headlines with your actions on the outside.

JESUS WEARS HIS HEART ON HIS ~~SLEEVE~~ ACTIONS

In the Gospel of Mark, Jesus' sermons take a back seat to his actions for the first 8 chapters. Whereas the Gospels of Matthew and Luke fill in Mark's action-packed outline with all sorts of additional sayings, Mark just sticks to the action. When you first notice the absence of sermons and sayings and parables in Mark 1-8, it makes sense to ask: Why? Why all the scenes in motion with so little monologue? What is Mark trying to tell us about Jesus?

Mark's take on Jesus shows us a guy who demonstrated who he was rather than simply declaring it. Jesus didn't just come out of the Messianic closet at age 30 and start flinging around terms like "Son of God" and "Savior." He didn't get a patch sewn onto his tunic that said: "I know the Lord. It's me!" He started doing things that no one else would or could do. He started bucking trends in the religious world. He rolled out his identity with countercultural and eye-catching exploits.

You didn't have to ask Jesus if he thought that all sinners should be stoned (I mean with actual stones). You just watched him hang out at parties with prostitutes and other people who had been put in the "sinner" category of humanity. He never threw a single rock!

You didn't have to wonder about his opinion of the religious leadership at the Temple. You could watch him flipping over tables and running bird salesmen out of the courts. That outburst gave away what he really thought inside. You also didn't need to ask Jesus if he supported the movement to corral and ostracize lepers. He blew up that idea every time he touched one.

A fundamental part of Jesus' plan was: "Demonstrate who you are. Don't just declare it." Life isn't a debate where you fight to get your point across. It's not a word game where you just need to find a sexy slogan. Jesus put substance behind every slogan. His words were commentary on his demonstrations. That is what happened when he healed lepers and cleaned out the Temple. That is also what happened when he turned a few loaves and some fish into a feeding frenzy for thousands.

SOUNDS LIKE I'VE HEARD THAT STORY BEFORE

If you carefully read the account in Mark 6 of Jesus feeding 5,000 people from a few loaves and fish, it sounds like an old familiar story. Which one? Try to guess.

First, Jesus tells the disciples in Mark 6:8-9 to follow some specific instructions when they go out to imitate his ministry. "He instructed them that they should take nothing for their journey, except a mere staff—no bread, no bag, no money in their belt—but to wear sandals; and He added, 'Do not put on two tunics.' " I'm not sure why he's hating on the double-popped collar, but these instructions seem to be the opposite of good planning. It sounds too similar to the way I prepared for road trips in college. It is purposefully putting the disciples in a position to struggle with hunger, warmth, and comfort. The only apparent positive would be improved safety during travel. Who is going to mug a guy with no food, no luggage, and no money?

When you think about why Jesus gave these instructions, the most obvious answer is a lesson in faith. The disciples would have to depend on God to provide daily sustenance. That explanation makes complete sense. I don't think there is any more suitable reason for the travel restrictions. However, I do believe the specific instructions go deeper.

The instructions to take one set of clothes, one pair of sandals, and no food or money re-creates the experience of the disciples' ancestors. It is a reenactment of the Israelites in the wilderness.

Just read the summary of the wilderness experience in Deuteronomy 29:5-6. "I have led you forty years in the wilderness; your clothes have not worn out on you, and your sandal has not worn out on your foot. You have not eaten bread, nor have you drunk wine or strong drink, in order that you might know that I am the LORD your God." The disciples are going through the same 40-year lesson in trusting God that the ancient Hebrews experienced. Thankfully they only have to do it for a few days. Jesus is ordering the disciples to re-live the wilderness experience from Israel's first Exodus out of Egypt.

The connections to the Israelite wilderness experience don't end there. Check out the connections to the Exodus (**in bold**) after the disciples return from doing ministry with no bags or back up clothes.

> The apostles gathered together with Jesus; and they reported to Him all that they had done and taught. And He said to them, "Come away by yourselves **to a secluded place** and rest a while." (For there were many *people* coming and going, and they did not even have time to eat.) They went away in the boat to **a secluded place** by themselves. *The people* saw them going, and many recognized *them* and ran there together on foot from all the cities, and got there ahead of them. When Jesus went ashore, He saw a large crowd, and He felt compassion for them because they were

like sheep without a shepherd; and He began to teach them many things. When it was already quite late, His disciples came to Him and said, "**This place is desolate** and it is already quite late; send them away so that they may go into the surrounding countryside and villages and buy themselves something to eat."

This passage from Mark 6:30-36 puts the disciples and all the hungry Israelites in an isolated place that has no food resources. Then it describes them as "sheep without a shepherd." Sound familiar? The description of a desolate place is reminiscent of Exodus 16 where the Israelites are in the wilderness without any food sources. The additional reference to the Israelites being "sheep without a shepherd" is the same language Moses used to describe Israel's need for another prophetic leader after he's gone. Numbers 27:15-17 recounts:

> Then Moses spoke to the LORD, saying, "May the LORD, the God of the spirits of all flesh, appoint a man over the congregation, who will go out and come in before them, and who will lead them out and bring them in, so that the congregation of the LORD will not be **like sheep which have no shepherd**."

If that connection to the Exodus experience isn't enough, Mark gives more details that connect Jesus' feeding of the 5,000 to the Israelites in the wilderness. In Mark 6:40, Jesus divides up the people into groups of "hundreds and fifties" for a more manageable distribution of food. Why does Mark provide such a random detail? The simple answer is: it's not supposed to be taken as "random." It is a detail that connects back to Moses' decision to divide up the people of Israel into divisions of thousands and hundreds and fifties and tens (see Deuteronomy 1:15). Mark is throwing in any part of the story that will make the reader think about the Israelites' first experience in the wilderness.

Of course, the blatant connection comes between Jesus miraculously feeding 5,000 people and the miracle of providing manna in the desert. In Exodus 16 the Israelites needed food in the Sinai wilderness. They had no available resources to feed so many people. So God provided it. In the desolate place where Israelites had gathered around Jesus, the same hunger existed. So Jesus provided it.

What does all this mean? It means that Jesus was reenacting the Exodus with his disciples and the Israelite people. It is a dramatic new scene in redemptive history. He is leading his followers on a new Exodus. In the same way that God brought his people out of Egypt to establish a holy nation, Jesus was forming a new community of God's people through similar Exodus experiences. He was creating a new community of people who would embody his ways on earth.

Moses was concerned that the Israelites would be like "sheep without a shepherd" when he was gone. Jesus was answering that concern. He was taking up the role of Moses. Jesus was becoming the new leader of God's people who could guide them and provide for them. There was nothing accidental or incidental about his actions. They were sending a message about who he was and what he was all about.

DEFINING THE NOW FROM THE PAST

When Mark makes Jesus' story sound like the story of the Exodus, he's using a common literary technique. It's an allusion. Allusions bring in greater significance to the story at hand.

It's like when Abraham Lincoln gave the Gettysburg address and described the founding of the United States in the King James language of the biblical creation story. "Four score and seven years ago our fathers **brought forth** on this continent a new nation, **conceived** in liberty, and dedicated to the proposition that all men are **created** equal." Lincoln not only affirmed that God had created men, but his language implies that God also created the United States of America.

The verbs "brought forth" and "conceived" represent the same language found in the early chapters of Genesis. "Brought forth" depicts the creation of the earth and all its inhabitants in Genesis 1 and 2. The verb "conceived" described the first acts of procreation in Genesis 4. Even the language of "four score and seven years ago" seems to be styled after similar language in Psalm 90 about God's role as Creator of humanity (and as American historians will tell you, this is not the only time Lincoln eloquently alluded to the Authorized Version of the Bible).

Lincoln's allusion to the creation language of Scripture draws in greater significance to the story of the United States of America. The nation was not a historical accident but the deliberate act of God. God wouldn't create this nation so it could fall apart a few generations later. That raised the importance of a future resolution to the civil war. Lincoln's implied message said: You better not mess up this beautiful thing God created. That's quite a loaded message. I may not buy his argument for God's special favor on the USA over other countries, but it has powerful implications.

Jesus' implied significance to the miracle of feeding 5,000 people had similar grandeur to it. Whereas Lincoln implied that God had performed another great act of creation with the founding of the USA, Jesus claimed a brand new Exodus was underway. He was calling out a new community of people to follow him. The allusions to the first Exodus made it undeniable.

BLENDING MOVIE SCRIPTS WITH REALITY

I personally don't find the allusions too surprising. It reminds me of a very good friend (who shall remain nameless) who constantly creates allusions to famous films. In his best deliveries, they come as complicated tapestries full of layered meaning. In the weaker moments, his allusions display themselves as incoherent one-liners.

For example, I might happen to disagree with some opinion he spouts off. So he boisterously responds, "You can't handle the truth (reference to *A Few Good Men*) in your thick candy shell (reference to *Tommy Boy*)!" Or else I might ask him what pastry he ordered at a coffee shop, and he'll sarcastically reply, "I got worms (reference to *Dumb and Dumber*). It's the second breakfast of champions (a strange mixed reference to *Lord of the Rings* and Wheaties cereal)."

This guy's addiction to weaving film references into real life knows no bounds. For example, we might be engaged in a serious discussion about my upcoming trip to Kenya when he interjects, "I had a friend once who drove his motorcycle around the world so he could 'do the bull dance' in 100 different countries. He returned with a new tattoo that read: the Burninator. Now every time I hear a motorcycle after 7pm, I scream: Tragdor comes in the night!" You'd have to watch *Billy Madison*, *Long Way Around*, *Happy Gilmore*, and a random internet cartoon called *Homestar Runner* to decipher where that imaginative story originated. It seems that fictitious movie scripts and cartoons have actually blended into his real life.

He's got so many cinematic allusions wrapped up in those statements I normally try to pretend it didn't happen. Because you'd have to get a subscription to Netflix, rent nightly movies from Redbox, and scour the internet for cartoons just to start peeling the quotation layers apart. And I still wouldn't know if he had any bigger point to make than to confuse me!

Although the movie, cartoon, and commercial references keep me guessing and laughing, they also remind me of Abe Lincoln and even Jesus himself. Abe brought a whole new level of significance to U.S. history by making references to the biblical depiction of creation. Jesus revealed a whole new level of significance to his actions by connecting them to the biblical account of the Exodus. The allusions make a much bigger point.

Jesus wanted his disciples to interpret his actions through the lens of the Exodus story. God formed the nation of Israel by bringing them out of Egypt and through the wilderness. Jesus was forming a new community of faithful followers and every reference to the Exodus story reinforced that point.

WHY WALK ON WATER?

Have you ever wondered why Jesus took walks on the Sea of Galilee? You're not alone if you have. I know at least one other person who has, but he prefers to remain anonymous. When you keep reading after the miraculous feeding of the 5,000 in Mark 6, you bump into one of the times Jesus decided to walk on water.

Most of us just think it's one more random example of Jesus showing off his divine powers. The reasoning goes: he's God so he can do that. However, the story has much more nuance. The disciples hadn't quite figured out exactly who Jesus was at this point in his life. And walking on the water was designed to fix that. If you pay attention to the story's details, you will find that his walk on the water is one more purposeful allusion to the past.

> Immediately (after feeding the 5,000) Jesus made His disciples get into the boat and go ahead of *Him* to the other side to Bethsaida, while He Himself was sending the crowd away. After bidding them farewell, He left for the mountain to pray. When it was evening, the boat was in the middle of the sea, and He was alone on the land. Seeing them straining at the oars, for the wind was against them, at about the fourth watch of the night He came to them, walking on the sea; and **He intended to pass by them**. But when they saw Him walking on the sea, they supposed that it was a ghost, and cried out; for they all saw Him and were terrified. But immediately He spoke with them and said to them, **"Take courage; it is I**, do not be afraid." Then He got into the boat with them, and the wind stopped; and they were utterly astonished, for they had not gained any insight from the *incident of* the loaves, but their heart was hardened. (Mark 6:45-52)

Whatever they were supposed to learn from the loaves' miracle, the disciples didn't get it. That confusion left them scared of ghosts when Jesus came walking on the water. They were not interpreting all the allusions the way Jesus wanted.

Why did Jesus come walking on water? One could argue it's as simple as why the chicken crossed the road. He wanted to get to the other side. But if that was the case, why not just teleport to the other side or leap the entire sea in one fell swoop. That would have been just as divinely impressive. It could have even made a bigger impact if he parted the Sea of Galilee and walked across on dry ground like the first Exodus through the Red Sea. He would have definitely caught the disciples' attention with that stunt. The real question is: what point was he trying to make that the disciples didn't get?

The answer to that question lies in the clauses I highlighted in the passage above. First Mark says, "He intended to pass by them."

What? Why? Mark says Jesus began to walk out to the disciples because they were struggling to paddle through a nasty storm. How is it helpful to walk out to them and then decide to pass right by? It seems a bit cruel to just want a closer look at 12 guys trying not to drown in a rickety boat (I'm assuming the boat was rickety for the sake of increased dramatic effect! Are you feeling the suspense?).

If Jesus purposefully intended to pass by them, he must have had a reason that exceeded their immediate safety. And he did. The reason can be found in the Exodus story. The intention to "pass by" the disciples and Jesus' subsequent words "Take courage; it is I" are a combined allusion to Exodus 33 and 34.

In Exodus 33:18, Moses asks to see God's glory. That's a pretty bold request. God tells him, "I Myself will make all My goodness pass before you, and will proclaim the name of the Lord before you" (Exodus 38:19). God further explains to Moses what will happen when he is "passing by" (Exodus 38:19-22) and then the actual event is recorded in Exodus 34:6. "The Lord **passed by** in front of him and proclaimed, '**The Lord**, the Lord God, compassionate and gracious, slow to anger, and abounding in lovingkindness and truth.' " God passed by Moses and introduced himself.

The same sequence of events takes place on the Sea of Galilee. Jesus passes by the disciples and then boards the ship and proclaims: "It is I." The phrase "It is I" could also be translated: "I AM." We don't know for sure what expression Jesus used in Aramaic or Hebrew when he first spoke to the disciples on the sea. But the Hebrew word translated "the Lord" in Exodus 34:6 can be translated in Greek as "It is I" or "I AM." If Jesus identified himself as "the Lord" using the expression "I AM," then both God's passing by in Exodus 33-34 and Jesus' walk on water have the same sequence. There is a "passing by" that leads to a revelation of identity. Jesus is imitating a divine move.

The allusion to the Lord's passing by on the first Exodus puts it all in perspective. Jesus didn't walk on the water to catch up. He caught up and passed by to make a statement about who he is. Instead of just saying it, he was demonstrating it. He gave the disciples an experience that would leave them asking: what kind of person would walk by your boat on the water and then turn to you and say, "I AM"? He wanted the disciples to see him through his actions. He wanted them to reflect on all the references to the Exodus and what that meant about Jesus and his mission.

This paradigm for how Jesus lived his life should not be overlooked. He wasn't just the mouthpiece for God's love and justice. He wasn't just a great expositor of who God is. He was a symbolic actor.

Jesus knew that words were not enough. People won't figure out you are any different if you don't show them. Jesus went way beyond a good political campaign that paints a clear picture of a candidate's values through consistent messaging. He became the message. He caught people's attention because he didn't live the average Israelite life. He started a whole new movement of God's people by embodying God's ways. Now that's a paradigm for us to put into action.

DEFINING YOURSELF IN ACTION

In 2008, evangelical churches, an evangelist and a gay mayor came together to solve problems facing the city of Portland. I know it sounds like a new sitcom, but it's not a joke. It's going on as I write. For years the church community had played an active role in meeting needs in the community. But in the summer of 2008, Portland churches along with the Palau Association began to think about how they might multiply their impact in the city of Portland. The realization came quickly that more could be accomplished together than apart.

These leaders decided to try something bold: bring the church, civic and corporate communities together to serve the region as never before. Several Christian leaders visited with the Portland Mayor to discuss the needs without dictating the agenda. They simply asked, "What do you need?" and "How can we help?"

Out of that meeting the "Season of Service" was born. By the end of the summer more than 27,000 volunteers from hundreds of churches served the city in areas recommended by civic leadership:

hunger/poverty, homelessness, education/schools, neighborhood revitalization, health and wellness, and human trafficking.

But the desire was not just for one season of serving the city. No one needed another temporary flash of compassion. The churches wanted to make a long-term impact. So the Season of Service has become an annual affair and churches are beginning to ask, "What does Portland look like 20 years from now if we continue loving and serving together?"

In the very liberal city of Portland, an openly gay mayor and evangelical churches are working together breaking down walls, debunking stereotypes, and proving that what we have in common is much more than anyone imagined. The business, civic, and church communities have found common ground in the common good. It's an unprecedented display of unity. And most importantly, needs have been met making a positive change in the city of Portland.

The Portland story is now one part of a larger "Season of Service" movement around the country. As this model has expanded to include San Diego, Arizona, Sacramento, and more, the nation is taking notice and cities are experiencing positive transformation. USA Today has dubbed this model "Evangelism 2.0." Instead of talking, church leaders are taking action. By the time community members show up at a Palau Association event, they already have a sense of what the love and justice of God looks like. They've seen or heard of Jesus' people feeding the hungry and fighting to prevent sex slavery.

Reader's Digest named the Season of Service the "Best Group Service Project" in the country back in 2009. More suspicious of the motives, the *Willamette Week*—a local newspaper in Portland— called it "Undercover Jesus." Whether or not you like it and no matter what you call it, it will catch your attention.

The Palau Association's Season of Service demonstrates what churches are all about before describing it. As school campuses improve and people receive free healthcare, it stands out in a struggling economy where budget cuts are reducing services and site maintenance. Certainly a good number of citizens will misinterpret the church's compassionate action as the disciples did with Jesus' miraculous actions. But embodying your message first is a trail that Jesus blazed. It makes sense for us to follow his lead today.

DON'T STOP ACTING IT OUT

The Season of Service in Portland didn't stop after logging 26,000 hours of volunteer service in its first year. Despite a mixture of responses, they hope to keep it up for decades to come as an unflinching testimony to the city.

Jesus didn't stop after feeding the 5,000 either. Even though his disciples didn't figure out what it said about him, he kept demonstrating who he was and symbolically acting out his mission. He moved from land to sea. If 12 baskets of leftover bread didn't mean anything to the disciples, then maybe a walk on water would do it.

Unfortunately, Jesus' walk on water made another point the disciples didn't understand. As Mark 6:52 states, "They had not gained any insight from the *incident of* the loaves. Their hearts were hardened." The disciples' density didn't change Jesus' methods. He didn't give up and try some other approach. You might expect him to back off the symbolic actions and dumb it down to a few simple statements about his identity and mission. But he refused. People needed to experience Jesus not just hear words about him. So he took his disciples to the southeastern part of the Galilee region to feed a different set of 4,000 people in another symbolic display of what he was all about.

That determination is what we often lack. It's too easy to give up after you try to demonstrate what you're all about and people don't get it. No one comes up to you and says, "Ah ha! You want me to join in a movement to re-create the world around communities of justice, love, and humility whose leading example is a self-sacrificing servant named Jesus. I'm in!"

Since that just doesn't happen even when you blow people's minds with miracles like Jesus did, we tend to stop acting with much intentionality. We go back to focusing on declarations rather than demonstrations. Debates take the place of demos. The logic goes: even if people disagree, at least we get the satisfaction of knowing they understand. The only problem is: Jesus thought crafting experiences for people to see who you are were more important than just telling them what you meant.

I think we need to take note here. Jesus' way is not an easy way. It is much easier to stay in the realm of beliefs. We can tell people what to believe, and then chock it up to their rebellious hearts if they don't consent. However, Jesus' way requires an embodiment of the message. You don't just talk about it. You do it. Then you make sense out of it along the way with those who care.

Just imagine if Jesus' whole ministry was a message. What if he walked around Israel just telling people how much God loves them? What if he called other people to a life of humility and service but never died in shame? Jesus' words about God's intertwined love and justice only gain a hearing because of the way he put them into action. Throwing crooks out of the Temple, hanging out with the dregs of society, and then giving up his life for the cause all made a point that words alone cannot. He showed us what love and justice look like.

Jesus didn't settle for explaining universal truths. He put on a dynamic revelation of who he was by doing things that caught people's attention. We're still talking about them 2,000 years later. So don't give up too soon on his approach.

Saving Our Youth Takes Time

You know who doesn't give up too soon? Save Our Youth mentors. Save Our Youth (SOY) is the industry standard for how to mentor at-risk youth in American urban centers. SOY is a Denver-based ministry that recruits Christian adult mentors, matches them with at-risk youth, and then monitors and supports the match. SOY staff support mentors so that they are well-prepared to pour into the life of a young person.

What happens to youth who get off the SOY waiting list and into a mentoring relationship? First and foremost, they get *someone* they would have never had. Youth get access to a caring adult who listens, values them, and is trustworthy. SOY mentors share time and special experiences that no other adult has offered to these kids. SOY mentors advocate for their mentees and encourage, guide, and teach them how to navigate life.

As a result, the youth develop positive coping skills to process their emotions. They grow spiritually with Jesus Christ and get connected to a local church. They graduate from high school and pursue a college education. That's no small feat for kids who come from neighborhoods with 40-70% dropout rates and a better chance of going to jail than graduating college.

Why does the Save Our Youth mentoring model work better than your average program? Because Save Our Youth mentors don't stop reenacting the way. They don't quit after a few months when it fails to change a kid's life. SOY mentoring relationships last an average of 4 years while the national mentoring average is only 9 months. Those long-term relationships provide the best opportunity to positively impact a life spiritually and emotionally.

If you ask Save Our Youth's director Luis Villarreal what the hardest part of SOY's work is, his answer might surprise you. It's not raising money (although I'm sure he appreciates every donation he gets). It's not finding kids who want a long-term mentor. SOY always has a waiting list full of kids who couldn't want anything more than a consistent, caring adult in their lives. The hardest part is finding adult mentors.

If we are asked to drop off food in the church lobby or at a food pantry, that's no problem. If we are asked to come volunteer at a soup kitchen for a couple hours once a year, we will probably say "yes." But when it comes to showing a kid what the love of God looks like week in and week out, that's no simple request. It's a huge time commitment. It's also a huge risk. What if I spend 3 years loving a high school boy, and he still fails. What if I embody the love and wisdom of Christ, but he never gets it.

That is the kind of risk Jesus took when he embodied what he was all about rather than simply talking about it. Think about it. What if Jesus spent 3 years pouring into some young guys and they don't get it? That happened with Judas. But Jesus still knew it was worth it.

Jesus took the risk. He created experiences for his disciples to figure out who he was. He didn't quit even when his best man turned on him the night before he was crucified. SOY mentors do the same thing. They don't quit showing the character of God through consistent demonstrations of love and support. SOY gives every adult mentor the resources, advice and assistance they need to stay in there for the long haul. And it pays off. Embodying the way of Jesus for years on end is saving our youth in Denver.

FEEDING 4,000 GENTILES CHANGES EVERYTHING

The feeding of the 4,000 is often an afterthought. Most people hype up the feeding of the 5,000 but don't know what to do with the slightly smaller scale miracle a couple chapters later in Mark 8. You might say it's like trying to sell a stripped down Camaro after you finish describing the SuperSport package on the performance edition. It just seems less impressive to do the same miracle but for 1,000 less people.

Some revisionist scholars of the Bible have suggested that the feeding of the 4,000 is a revised version of the feeding of the 5,000 that transcribers added to the Gospel in later editions. This theory shows how confusing the significance of the second miracle can be. People either ignore it or start making up wild explanations about why it's there.

The key to understanding its significance lies in the change of venue that occurs between the feeding in Mark 6 and the feeding in Mark 8. The transition happens in Mark 7. In Mark 7, Jesus heals a Syro-Phoenician woman in Tyre. Then, he heals a deaf and mute man in the Decapolis. If you are trying to figure out where those people lived, that's the point. Wherever it is, it ain't in a Jewish town.

You might ask: why mention these "in-between" stories? First and foremost, you need to see what's similar about the two miracle stories in Mark 7. Both healings target Gentile people in Gentile lands. Jesus has moved from a context of Israelites to the world of Gentiles.

In Mark 8:1-10 Jesus performs the feeding miracle for a crowd of 4,000 Gentiles. That's an important difference. The miracle takes place in the Decapolis—a Roman province located to the east of the Sea of Galilee and the Jordan River. The location and audience have to be considered carefully if you want to understand the symbolic meaning of the second feeding miracle.

So what's the symbolic meaning of feeding Gentiles? To my surprise, it has nothing to do with Jesus' love for bacon and why I should consume it too (although I desperately wish Jesus would justify my obsession with swine belly meat). The answer lies in the number of baskets that the disciples filled with bread after everyone was full. Mark 8:8 says "7 baskets" were filled with leftovers. It seems like a random fact of history at first, but there's more going on here.

Now you might think I'm crazy to find meaning in the number of baskets. You've probably heard enough television prophets predict the end of the world using symbolic numbers from the Bible. I have too. And I promise not to make up something based on an impulsive connection to news stories or the potential for me to make money by creating fear in my audience. Of course, no one would do that (…at least no one with a conscience).

The reason I know the number of baskets has a deeper meaning is because Jesus told me so. No, he didn't tell me in a dream or in a trance-like state I experienced on a mountain somewhere while eating angel food cake. I didn't see 7 baskets under a picture of Jesus at a fourth of July party and take it as a message that God will feed the whole world from American farms just like the 4,000 Gentiles. Actually Jesus told us all the 7 baskets were important in his follow-up comments to the disciples after the second feeding miracle.

In Mark 8:14-21, Jesus gets frustrated with his disciples for not figuring out the symbolic meaning behind the leftover baskets of bread. After the disciples miss another metaphorical reference to bread, Jesus castigates them and drops a couple of leading questions.

"Why do you discuss the fact that you have no bread? Do you not yet see or understand? Do you have a hardened heart? Having eyes, do you not see? And having ears, do you not hear? And do you not remember when I broke the five loaves for the 5,000, how many baskets full of broken pieces you picked up?" They said to him, "12." "When I broke the 7 for the 4,000, how many large baskets full of broken pieces did you pick up?" And they said to him, "7." And he was saying to them, "Do you not yet understand?"

Jesus wanted to make sure the disciples knew exactly how many baskets were left. They did. Jesus also wanted them to understand the significance. That they did not.

What is the significance of 7 baskets? First, let's figure out the significance of the 12 baskets. As we already figured out, the first feeding of the 5,000 Israelites was a reenactment of the manna miracle during the Exodus. All the clues leading up to that feeding miracle connected Jesus' actions to a time when God was making a people for himself by bringing the Israelites out of Egypt. The 12 baskets left over recall the 12 tribes of Israel. That's the significance. In the same way that God's people were originally made up of Israel's 12 tribes, Jesus was demonstrating that his new kingdom would include Israelites. Jesus wanted people from all 12 tribes to follow him.

However, Jesus' invitation diverged from the first Exodus at this point. At the end of the first Exodus, God instructed the Israelites to go into the Promised Land and destroy all the Gentile nations. There were seven of them. Deuteronomy 7:1-2 records these words from God.

When the Lord your God brings you into the land where you are entering to possess it and clears away many nations before you, the Hittites and the Girgashites and the Amorites and the Canaanites and the Perizzites and the Hivites and the Jebusites, **seven nations** greater and stronger than you, and when the Lord your God delivers them before you and you defeat them, then you shall utterly destroy them. You shall make no covenant with them and show no favor to them.

Under God's first covenant, the seven Gentile nations were excluded from his people and his favor. God's explicit instructions were: defeat them and utterly destroy them. Yikes! Not exactly the "hope for all nations message" we prefer to hear.

Jesus' new covenant flipped that policy on its head. The remaining seven baskets of bread signified that Jesus' new community would include the Gentiles and the Jews as one. There would be no exclusion or destruction of other nations. Jesus' words would feed the Israelites and non-Israelites just the same.

The feeding of 4,000 Gentiles cemented Jesus' commitment to include them among the new kingdom he was forming. It was a powerful message that he had to put on display for his Jewish followers. The miracle for the Gentiles showed that God validated Jesus' new all-inclusive movement. That is what he wanted his disciples to understand.

WAITING FOR SOME MIRACULOUS BREAD

You might wonder: how could Jesus expect the disciples to figure that out? I can't say that I have a simple answer to that question. There is much we don't know of Jesus' ministry. Maybe they played charades a lot. Maybe he dabbled in telepathic communication. Maybe it was one of those youth group games that led a few gullible kids to believe in aliens. Regardless of those unimportant games on the side, I can tell you that some Jews in Jesus' day were waiting for a king to reenact the manna miracle.

An old Jewish apocalypse about God's next great intervention in history describes the reenactment of the manna miracle. The Messiah, or God's anointed king, would prove he had arrived when the miracle happens. The *Apocalypse of Baruch* reads:

> And it shall come to pass when all is accomplished that was planned for that time period that the Messiah shall then begin to be revealed. …And it shall come to pass at the same time that the

treasury of manna shall again descend from on high, and they will eat it in those years, because these are they who have come to the consummation of time. (2 *Apocalypse of Baruch* 29:3-8)

The Messiah was scheduled to appear, and then the manna miracle would happen all over again. This timeline of events captured the imagination of enough Jews to make its way into a document that we were able to recover centuries later. It surely doesn't represent the opinion of every person in Israel, but it gives us one idea of what some people were expecting. Some were expecting the Messiah to show up and feed people just like God did during the Exodus. Jesus seems to expect his disciples to put 2 and 2 together in this way. The leftover baskets were supposed to tell them that he is the Messiah, and his new kingdom will include Jews and Gentiles.

GETTING INTO THEIR WORLD

Students and readers always ask me: why would Jesus fulfill a prophecy from a book that's not in the Bible? They ask because it makes them feel uncomfortable. They wonder if the *Apocalypse of Baruch* is a book that should have been put in the Bible. They don't understand why Jesus wouldn't just stick to some clearer Old Testament prophecies. I think the answer is plain and simple. Jesus did what he needed to do to relate to the people around him.

Too much of the time professing followers of Jesus want everyone to enter their world instead of the other way around. We want people to speak Christian lingo, go inside churches, and ask questions about spiritual things. We want them to read the Bible and ask for our interpretation. But that wasn't Jesus' way. He pursued people.

Jesus figured out the way first century people in Israel experienced the world and entered into it. He talked about farming with farmers and baking with bakers. He fit himself into the hierarchy of ranking officers when a Roman centurion needed his help. And he miraculously helped his disciples with fishing because they were fishermen. He got into their world. So when people were waiting for a Messiah to reenact the manna miracle, he started making tons of bread for Jews and Gentiles to eat.

I admire those who follow in Jesus' footsteps. That's why a church in my hometown of Colorado Springs called Woodmen Valley Chapel has earned my respect.

It all started when I heard about a motto the church's senior leader believed in. It goes something like this: "If our church disappears this week and the only people who miss us are confused church members who can't find the building next Sunday, then we've failed to follow Christ in our community." That pastor knows what it means for a church to follow Christ. A church that fails to get into the community at large is a church that fails completely. That knowledge and those words have turned into action time and time again at Woodmen Valley Chapel.

In a recent budget crisis for the city of Colorado Springs, municipal leaders decided to close four city-run community centers. The money just wasn't there. Community members lamented the decision and complained. But that got us nowhere. All the centers stayed on course for closure until one church stepped into action.

Woodmen Valley sent in one of its strategic ministry branches under a separate LLC to run the community center. You can bet what happened next. No one said "thank you." Community members complained about the center becoming a church. They didn't want a community center turning into an evangelism center. Despite the objections, no one else offered to fund or to operate the center and all its programs.

After some lively city council debates, Woodmen Valley was given the right to run the center for the next few years. A number of church members now volunteer in the center to keep its services available to the west side neighborhoods. And it isn't a center for evangelism, but it does embody the loving engagement that Jesus practiced.

Closing the community center's doors would have affected low-income families the most. Woodmen's willingness to invest money and human resources into the center prevented that from happening.

Instead of staying inside their church building and sending out invitations to attend, Woodmen got involved. They walked right into a local neighborhood. They entered someone else's world. And they have been doing it month after month after month.

That is what Jesus did. He caught people's attention with some radical actions that carried a symbolic message. That is our example to follow.

The Attention and Intention of Embodying the Message

Here is a reality check for all of us who like to teach. If I have to go to a conference or a class and hear you speak to know what you're about, then all you're about is speaking. Words—without a corresponding way of life—leave me no other conclusion. Your actions are the real message. If your only activity is a "talk" about what to do, then you'll teach other people to talk. That's the harsh reality of it all.

Jesus wasn't all talk. He wasn't the embodiment of divine intelligence floating around with timeless lectures to deliver. He was an actor who demonstrated who he was before declaring it. He showed everyone that God cared about the irreligious classes and unchosen ethnic groups when he spent time with them. He got people thinking he could forgive sin because they saw him heal the diseases people attributed to sin. He caught the attention of people looking for God to send a Messiah because he performed the Manna miracle all over again. He grabbed people's attention with the intention of embodying the message.

When someone analyzes the details of your behavior, does it reveal your mission? It definitely does, but does it reveal the mission you say you care about? Do your friends know you believe in the justice and mercy of Jesus because they've seen it? Has your family been able to figure out what humility and grace look like because of your character? Are people surprised and even perturbed when you return good for evil? Do you catch their attention with the intention of embodying the way of Jesus?

I don't think we can call ourselves followers of Jesus if we just agree with him on the answers to spiritual questions. We've got to be what we want to communicate. That's his way.

HERE'S WHAT IT LOOKS LIKE

Let me interject with a personal question. I have had to wrestle with the implications of Jesus' embodiment of his message just like you do. I have had to ask: what does that look like *for me*?

For starters it means I put my heart and soul into forgiving people instantly. I want my wife to know what I believe in. So I do it. I don't fly off the handle or fight fire with fire when I'm wronged. I muscle all the self-control I can find because I've got a message to send.

What's that message I believe in? I don't expect people to be perfect. And I don't write you off when my expectations come true. That's not the world that Jesus embodied for me, and I want to act out the same message for you. It does me no good to define the nuances of "grace" with theological techno-jargon. I need to grab your attention because I'm gracious to you. That's what Jesus did.

Jesus didn't show up one day and start talking about a new exodus he was starting. He didn't wear a T-shirt that said, "Yeah, I'm the Messiah. Join my movement." He didn't write Papyrus pamphlets that explained his mission and then distribute them at Falafel eating contests. He acted out who he was.

We need to swallow the fact that the extent of our beliefs go no farther than what we embody in action. Don't think you are on some valiant mission if people can only hear about it. When you reenact Jesus' way, people see it.
So let's do it. Let's make people wonder who we are and what we are doing. Let's demonstrate our identity with the way of Christ before we declare it to the disbelief of those looking at us.

We can't ask people to join us until they see where we are going. That's where so many Jesus followers get stuck. All they can think to do is invite people to church because that is the main action they perform to follow him. Yes, I said that.

When we start being intentional about the way we go, we have a path to invite others to follow. So put your head together with some other sojourners and figure out what symbolic actions you could take to embody the message where you're at. Start surprising people with the way you live. Those actions will give you the platform to have a conversation with people like Jesus did with his disciples. You will be able to ask: do you understand why I live the way I do? That's when you know you are reenacting the way.

Reenacting the Way

1. Do you know any other examples of people who embody the message they believe in? Think of current examples of Jesus' followers as well as other examples of people who have caught your attention with their intentional living.

2. What part of your behavior normally surprises, confuses, or amazes people? The answers to this question could keep you talking for a while.

3. How could you catch people's attention with actions that embody what Jesus was all about?

CHAPTER 5

CALMING STORMS, EXORCISING DEMONS, AND DROWNING PIGS: DON'T FEAR YOUR IMAGINATION

Focal Point: What did Jesus teach us about challenging imaginary divine powers when he calmed storms, exorcised demons and drowned pigs?

THE DEVIL IN THE MOUNTAIN

In the highest city of the world stands a "mountain that eats men." The longer you inhabit its hallways the shorter your life becomes. Those who enter its cavernous caves to mine its metallic resources have a life expectancy of forty years. They don't advertise it that way, but each miner knows the fate he has been assigned. The mountain is going to feed them and their families for a time, and then it is going to eat them alive.

This mountain may simply be an old pile of rocks to an outside observer, but it is the home of the devil himself for all who enter. It is a place of darkness and death, of fear and deceptive fortune.

Such statements seem more fitting for a description of middle earth in Tolkien's fantasy world than a depiction of the real world. But in fact, that mountain is no myth. During the Spanish colonial period from 1545 to 1825 it is estimated that over eight million Black and Indian slaves died as a consequence of mining its silver. It is a mountain to be feared, but its promise of rare metals and great riches continues to attract local miners to an early death. The tally of taken lives grows every year.

That mountain is known as Cerro Rico (or "rich mountain"). It towers symmetrically like a pyramid over downtown Potosí in southern Bolivia. The city rests at an elevation of 4,090 meters or 13,500 feet giving Bolivia claim to both the highest elevated capital city of any country in the world (La Paz) as well as the highest incorporated city.

In its heyday the city of Potosí rivaled London and Paris with a larger population than either European city. Its wealth and success fueled the entire Spanish empire. The city is so full of irreplaceable architectural wonders from the colonial period that UNESCO in 1987 declared it a "world heritage site." However, its legacy of fear and death far outweighs its historical value for the local population.

The silver has virtually disappeared from the mines. The former boomtown is now just one more place where people struggle to get by each day. For a while the mountain was mined mainly for tin, but these days zinc produces the most profit. But whatever metal comes out of its caves does not determine whether miners will go in. The prospects are too inviting. For even though a miner is expected to contract silicosis pneumonia within fifteen years of exposure to the fine dust, dangerous explosions, and mercury, people continue to brave its deadly crawl spaces. The promise of better pay leads to more dynamite blasts every day. Those prospects motivate workers to kill themselves slowly and hope that they last longer than the guy next to them.

In these tough working conditions, the miners have found a way to manage. The workers turn to "alcohol potable" for escape, coca leaves for energy, and El Tío for protection. The alcohol provides escape on the weekends while the coca leaves function like caffeinated coffee or tea to energize the workers during long shifts of manual labor. As for El Tío, he is their divine protector and destroyer.

According to local myth El Tío rules the underworld where miners risk their lives everyday, and so they seek his goodwill. They bestow gifts and offerings upon his altars spread all throughout the maze of 20,000 tunnels. These daily offerings typically include the most prized items that a miner can acquire—coca leaves, alcohol potable and cigarettes. I know. With that diet El Tío should have died years ago. I can't even imagine how awful it is to be one of these miner's wives who has to kiss them at night. Nothing says "I love you" like a smoky nicotine-enriched alcoholic leafy taste on the lips.

At regular intervals, the villagers of Potosí offer a sacrifice to this devil in the mines, ritually slaughtering a llama. They smear the animal's blood on the entrance to the mine and on one another in hopes of satiating El Tío's bloodlust that has claimed so many of their ancestors.

El Tío is their hope and their worst nightmare. He preserves life and takes it away. Although local Catholics believe Jesus rules above the ground, El Tío controls the underworld of Cerro Rico. So the people of Potosí live in a culture of fear and fruitless appeasement of a god who is no greater than the deadly mining conditions that no one is addressing.

Potosí is no exception, not in the world today and certainly not in the history of the human race. Natural and unnatural forces have often been deified and given deceptive powers to wield within the minds of men.

Modern-day Bolivia with its mythical fear of El Tío is strikingly similar to the southeastern Galilee region of Jesus' time. In the ancient Mediterranean world, religions, rituals, and the myths that made them necessary could be found everywhere. When we read the Gospel narratives of Jesus' actions we must always be ready to find him challenging the powers that be and the tales that told people to fear them. The sequence of stories in Mark 4:35-5:20 is one such challenge.

WHO IS THIS?

In Mark 4:35-41 the disciples find themselves in a relentless storm on the Sea of Galilee. The wind and waves are threatening their buoyancy but failing to rouse Jesus from his nap. So they take it upon themselves to wake Jesus and complain, "Teacher, do you not care that we are about to die?"

From our perspective, the disciples look like blithering idiots. How in the world could they ask the man who is going to die for them whether or not he cares what happens to them? But if we put ourselves in their position without the knowledge of what Jesus is going to do and going to show himself to be, their question born out of immediate fear makes sense. People who sleep through you drowning in the sea could be reasonably blamed for not caring.

The text provides no verbal response from Jesus to their sensible question about his concern. We only know that he rose and told the wind to cease and the waves to calm down. The response of the wind and the waves to Jesus' words is no surprise to the familiar reader of the Gospels. They listened to what he said, and the storm stopped. For us the miracle seems like one more moment in a string of repetitive miracles that rarely captures our amazement.

For the disciples the experience was overwhelming. Their fear of the storm quickly turned to fear of the man who controlled the storm. Storms were to be expected, but men who can control storms with their words would scare you half to death.

It reminds me of the time four thieves broke through a window into my house sending my wife and I into a panic. They rushed down the hallway through our kitchen and towards the family room. However, before they could begin collecting valuables, our pet turtle came to the rescue. He jumped out of his aquarium and spit four rocks at lightning speed into their foreheads knocking them unconscious instantly! It completely changed our frame of mind.

When we first started hearing the cracking glass and stomping feet, we feared the men. But our fear quickly transferred to the mutant turtle in the kitchen that had leaped out of his aquarium with lethal rock-spitting skills. When a turtle's power outmans four men, you fear the turtle. OK, that never happened, but you get the point. The disciples would have been afraid of Jesus after he overpowered a storm.

The disciples never could have expected Jesus to pull that stunt. So the text says, "They became very much afraid and said to one another, 'Who then is this, that even the wind and the sea obey Him?'" (Mark 4:41). This question that summarizes the disciples' reaction to Jesus' shocking feat is a key to understanding the story. In fact, it is a well-placed question in Mark's narrative designed for the audience to consider the possible answers. Who did people in the pagan areas of the Galilee believe could control the wind and the sea? And what did Jesus' actions say about that powerful figure?

Although one Christian preacher after another has focused on the question of which metaphorical storm in your life Jesus wants to calm (please stop doing that), Mark wants us to focus on his climactic concluding question. What type of person is this that controls the storm clouds and the raging sea? Of course, we might want to blurt out the answer, "It is the Son of God!" Isn't that the answer Mark intends?

Although Mark does begin and end his Gospel with an affirmation that Jesus is the "Son of God" (Mark 1:1; 15:39), it is more important in Mark 4:35-5:20 to identify what that means for different sections of the population around Israel. People had diverse ideas about the gods that had been passed down for centuries. In the Galilee region, there were many different gods that claimed to have varying levels of power. Mark wants us to see how Jesus outclasses one particular god—the god of the storm.

The answer to our question—"Who can control storms?"—lies in centuries-old myths that circulated in the ancient Near East. Specifically, the stories of a god named Baal (recovered from the city of Ugarit north of Canaan—think Syria) will tell us what people would have known in ancient Galilee. The stories describe the divine struggle that led to Baal ruling over the waters above and the waters below. I think we can all understand how important it is to compare Jesus' calming of the storm to a god thought to rule over the seas and rains and storms.

The Ugaritic myths of Baal betray striking similarities to the content and structure of Mark 4:35-41. So we are going to survey sections of the ancient myths and compare them to Jesus' actions. It may just tell us the point Jesus was making so we can stop turning it all into a metaphor. But please don't worry, you do not have to know how to pronounce Ugarit or know where it is located to get the point. And I will try to keep the Ugaritic quotes about the pantheon of gods to a minimum. That may disappoint the 7 English-speaking Ugaritic scholars in the world, but all the rest of you can thank me right now. You're welcome.

BAAL AS THE "RIDER OF THE CLOUDS"

In the Ugaritic myths, the god named Baal is also called the charioteer or rider of the clouds—which makes a fairly accurate mental picture of what people believed he did. When the rider of the clouds approached, his presence was announced by thunder in the heavens and lightning streaking down from the sky (see picture of Baal to the right where a lightning bolt was originally in his hand). These ancient words about his arrival in the rainy season summarize it well: "And now the season of his rains may Baal indeed appoint, the season of his storm-chariot. And the sound of his voice from the clouds, his hurling to the earth of lightning-flashes" (KTU 1.4 V 6-9).

The logic goes: if a storm moves in, then Baal is at work. We might say,

"When it rains, it pours." But they would say, "When it rains, Baal roars." For storms are not the result of the water cycle or jet streams or high and low pressure systems. They are the sound and fury of the most high god Baal.

BAAL AS THE "RULER OF THE SEA"

In the stories about him found at the city of Ugarit, his domain far exceeds the storm clouds above. Although he initially is limited to the sky, he reaches down to extend his authority over another part of the world in his quest for power. To do so requires an attack on the gods who had claimed power in the world below. According to the myths he had the right friends in the right places to wage this war. They provided the weapons Baal needed to achieve eventual success.

With the encouragement of the divine assembly, Baal first challenged the god of the sea named Yam. Baal was fighting for control over the waters below. Two messengers from the assembly named Kothar and Hassis (these names are not recommended for your children) came to Baal and authorized the fight:

> 'Indeed I say to you, O Prince Baal,
> I repeat, O Charioteer of the Clouds,
> now your foe you must smite;
> now you must destroy your adversary!
> Take your everlasting kingdom,
> your eternal dominion!' (KTU 1.2)

The messengers not only delivered the command to fight, but Kothar created two special weapons for Baal to use in the battle with Yam. Those weapons proved effective. Here is the story in its ancient poetic form.

> Kothar fashioned two maces, and he pronounced their names: 'You, your name is "All-Driver." All-Driver, drive Yam away, drive Yam from his throne, Nahar from the siege of his dominion! (*Note*: "Nahar" is another name for Yam because it connects him to "rivers") You must leap from the hand of Baal, like a falcon from his fingers. Strike the skull of Prince Yam,

the brow of Ruler Nahar! Let Yam collapse in a heap, and let him fall to the ground!' Then the mace leapt from the hand of Baal, like a falcon from his fingers. It struck the skull of Prince Yam, the brow of Ruler Nahar. Yam collapsed in a heap; he fell to the ground. His joints trembled, and his visage was discomposed. Baal gathered up and drank Yam to the dregs; he exterminated Ruler Nahar. ...Yam is indeed dead! Baal will rule. (KTU 1.2)

The mythical battle of Baal and Yam established Baal's rule over the storms above and the waters below. The dangerous seas and the flooding rivers answered to him, and anyone in need of relief from their threatening power knew they had only to invoke his protection. This legend had a huge effect on religious practices. People worshipped Baal to secure much-needed rains for crops and to protect themselves from flooding rivers and stormy seas. Naturally Baal became an important deity for fishermen and sailors on the sea.

Unfortunately, he developed a reputation for sleeping on the job. Since Baal's presence manifested itself in rainstorms, he became an absent god in droughts and dry seasons. Where was he when your crops needed some timely irrigation? The logic also followed that out-of-control stormy seas were to blame on an inattentive Baal. A little rain was wonderful; too much was just mean. Most fishermen and sailors had a love/hate relationship with Baal. His finicky assistance earned him a reputation for not always paying attention to your safety.

JESUS IS THE REAL BAAL

Reading the story of Jesus' calming the storm on the sea takes on fresh meaning against this backdrop of the Baal and Yam myths. When the disciples seem to mistake Jesus for sleeping through their destruction on the stormy sea like Baal, he asks them to rethink what they believe about him. "Why are you afraid? How is it that you have no faith?" (Mark 4:40). He isn't like the god all the fishermen know.

When Jesus rises up and does what only Baal should be able to do, he is challenging the very substance of Baal's authority. Jesus is now the one who controls the waters below and the waters above, and he does not sleep through the death of his loved ones. He is the bigger God. And he is the better one too.

In the bigger picture, the calming of the raging sea and the stilling of the storm are theological counter-claims. Jesus is taking aim at a long history of mistaken faith in gods that are no gods at all. Jesus is proving himself to be the true Lord over all the waters in the world. Any thought that Baal controlled the stormy seas needs to be dismissed in the face of Jesus' demonstrated authority. Jesus is everything that Baal wishes he could be.

DO YOU BELIEVE IN GERMS?

How you answer the question—"Who's in control here?"—is an unbelievably significant question for all areas of life. In the Galilee region it determined to whom you turned when a storm swept in while you were at sea. For my friends who served as community developers in Bangladesh, it determined how sanitary their house was and how sick their kids got.

How did faith affect the health and sanitation of my friends' lives in Bangladesh? First of all, it has nothing to do with having the faith to never get sick. Please don't mistake me for a "name it and claim it" healing preacher. My point is much more mundane than that.

In the culture where they served it is commonplace to have a house helper who cooks and cleans with the lady of the house each day. So finding a suitable helper becomes an important factor in the quality of life that the family experiences. You either eat well and enjoy a clean home, or you may endure improperly prepared foods and unsanitary conditions that wreak havoc on you and your children's health.

Over the course of a year, my friends informed me that they were having trouble with their house helper. When I inquired about the reason, they told me it had to do with her belief system.

Immediately I was concerned. Did they attempt to speak about Christ with her in a way that insulted her Muslim faith? Did she respond negatively to their Christian witness and decide to speak to government authorities about their "conversionist" desires? Or maybe she just took too many breaks during the workday citing her "religion" as the excuse? I didn't know, but as their friend I wanted to know why and offer any suggestions that might help. I thought my former studies in world religions and cultural anthropology could help.

What they told me left me speechless. Later on, it even made me laugh. I know. I shouldn't. This was serious business causing serious health problems. But I couldn't help myself. You see the problem with the house helper's faith had nothing to do with Islam or Christianity, Hinduism or Buddhism. The problem had to do with germs.

That's right, germs. Their house helper did not *believe* in germs. She didn't care if a little worm and some nitrates added flavor to their food from the dirt floor where the vegetables had been stored for the day. She also saw no problem preparing the food with unwashed hands—which made for especially awkward moments when she returned from the toilet only to go back to handling the fruits and vegetables. Yikes!

How in the world can you trust someone who does not believe in germs to prepare your food? And what concept of "clean" can a house helper have who does not even conceive of the same medical and scientific notion of "sanitary" and "unsanitary" conditions? It's not easy to start a conversation about why we don't store foodstuffs on the bathroom floor when someone doesn't believe tiny little organisms and bacteria exist.

I did eventually receive good news that they moved to a new location and found a house helper who shares their faith in germs. Unfortunately, that move came after a string of emails recounting the diarrhea, fevers, and stomach aches that they and their children may have been able to avoid. If only their former house helper could have believed that germs were in control of the family's health, the last year of their life could have been different. If she would have believed that germs caused and controlled those illnesses, more pain could have been avoided.

So the question of who is in control must be seen in all its significance. Whether it is germs or Jesus (not typically two interchangeable entities), knowing who is in control behind the scenes will determine what course your life takes. It will inform what you do when things go wrong. Returning to our story in Mark we could say that being ignorant to the existence of germs is like assuming Baal controls the storms and the seas. It is a delusion that could get you killed. That's why Jesus has to take such dramatic steps to demonstrate the truth of his control. People needed to drop their delusions of Baal's divine authority.

JESUS AS THE ROPE

The importance of addressing regional religious delusions should not be underestimated. That is why T4 Global uses stories about Jesus recorded on MP3 players to release people from false fears all the time. They are trying to follow Jesus' first century example in a twenty-first century world.

The Samburu people of central Kenya are oral learners steeped in a culture of fear. According to the worldview of the Samburu, the gods responsible for the accidental creation of the world are hard to figure out. They are in turns mean and then kind; quick to anger and then patient and understanding. They have, for example, blessed the Samburu men with cattle – but then turned right around and given the mixed blessing that is woman (…if my wife is reading this, please know I do not endorse this Samburu belief). The Samburu gods are hard to understand, and given their immense power, one must tread lightly and wisely when dealing with them.

All is not lost, however. The gods did provide a rope to heaven. When seeking to discern the will or leading of the gods, all the Samburu have to do is climb the rope and seek the counsel of the gods. Problem solved.

But, as is always the case in a world where men walk about, a certain family grew angry and indignant with some news received from the gods. And so, the rope was cut. The path to communication and understanding was destroyed.

How have the Samburu coped with the loss of direct contact? Each village possessed wise men who had made numerous trips up the rope, so with the path destroyed, the people looked to these men. Over time their wisdom was handed down from father to son (or daughter) and these individuals found themselves in positions of great power and influence in their villages.

Where one had to be careful of angering the gods before, now the problem doubled. Everyone must also guard against offending the wise man in your village. The destruction of the rope has turned a difficult task into an impossible one. Now, the Samburu must cater to the whims of the gods, the wise men, *and* the witch doctors. I don't know how those last guys inserted themselves into the religious power structure, but they scare the Samburu just like the other two groups.

To address the disconnect from God in Samburu culture, T4 Global's indigenous partners turned to John 14:6 where Jesus says, "I am the way, the truth and the life. No one comes to the Father but through me." In Samburu terms, Jesus is calling himself the rope. Where the anger and sin of man had destroyed the rope to the gods, Jesus is offering a way to get back. No longer do the Samburu need to fear the whims of the witch doctors because Jesus can get them access to truth and life. What was lost has now been found. People can have direct access to God.

When shared this way, a people that have known fear now discover the joy of the gospel. Anxious inquiries into the will of the gods have become fervent prayers in Jesus' name. They have found the truth of Jesus, and that truth has set them free from all sorts of oppressive personalities in their village.

T4 Global is making these types of relevant connections in recorded stories for dozens of cultures and languages around the world. They are doing today with stories on MP3 players what Jesus did through miraculous actions on the Sea of Galilee.

ISRAEL'S BAAL WORSHIP AND MARK 5:1-5

Jesus' challenge to Baal did not end after the storm stopped. In Mark 5:1-5 a crazed man emerges from the tombs whose reputation for superhuman strength, screaming all night long, and blood-letting precedes him. He is not exactly the kind of character you want to meet out on a country road—or in a convenience store or in a cave or even in a very crowded room for that matter. However, he is the kind of character you would expect to meet in a story that confronts Baal.

One does not have to go far beyond Elijah's confrontation with the prophets of Baal or Isaiah's rebuke of Israel's participation in Baal worship to figure that out. Some of you probably remember Elijah's confrontation with the prophets of Baal in 1 Kings 18. The land of Israel was facing a three-year drought, and Elijah was trying to prove to his people that God is the one who can help them and not Baal. So he set up a contest with the prophets of Baal to prove once and for all that the God of Israel controls the rains and should be sought for relief.

The challenge of whose God could send fire down from heaven made sense to all the people. After all, Baal was the "Lord of fire." In the statuettes and stone reliefs of Baal that we have recovered from archaeological excavations, he is constantly depicted with a lightning bolt of fire in one of his hands. It is one of the chief means through which he makes contact with earth. So for Elijah to propose a competition where the first God to send a bolt of fire from heaven wins is theoretically to play to Baal's strong suit. Too bad he actually didn't exist.

As the story goes in 1 Kings 18, Baal fails to respond with fire after a day-long invocation of 450 desperate prophets. Elijah finds Baal's silence worth taunting. "It came about at noon, that Elijah mocked them and said, 'Call out with a loud voice, for he is a god; maybe he is occupied or relieving himself, or is on a journey, or perhaps he is asleep and needs to be awakened'" (1 Kings 18:27). Elijah's mockery taps into Baal's reputation for sleeping on the job. He accuses Baal of not responding due to his preoccupation with some other task or a possible day-long nap. Elijah encourages the prophets to be a more flamboyant if they want to get his divine attention.

The prophets take Elijah's advice to add a little more drama by launching into an extreme mourning ritual. "So they cried with a loud voice and cut themselves according to their custom with swords and lances until the blood gushed out on them. When midday was past, they raved until the time of the offering of the evening sacrifice; but there was no voice, no one answered, and no one paid attention" (1 Kings 18:28-29).

Think for a minute about the particular actions in this mourning ritual. Who else do we know that resorts to loud shrieks and blood-letting? The parallels between the prophets carrying out their mourning over the absence of Baal and the demoniac's actions in Mark's story are undeniable. Read Mark 5:5. "Constantly, night and day, he was screaming among the tombs and in the mountains, and gashing himself with stones." It is hard to argue that a man drawing his own blood with stones and screaming loudly in the mountains does not reflect the worship of Baal exemplified by the 450 prophets who competed against and lost to Elijah and his God.

The parallels to Baal worship do not end with 1 Kings 18. We can also begin to make sense of the demoniac's residence in the tombs by looking at an indictment of Israelites who worshipped Baal at night. In Isaiah 65:3-4a, Yahweh denounces the Israelites for being "people who continually provoke me to my face offering sacrifices in gardens and burning incense on bricks [and] who sit among graves and spend the night in secret places." This denunciation depicts typical Baal worship. The Israelites' participation in the regional worship of Baal drives them to dark places and tombs where they can perform their sacrifices.

This location for Baal worship reveals further affinity with the demoniac in Mark 5:1-5. The connection between the demoniac and the tombs could not be more adamantly asserted. In Mark 5:2 he is called "a man from the tombs." In Mark 5:3 the narrator reiterates, "[H]e had his dwelling among the tombs." And in Mark 5:5 he is described as doing much of his "screaming among the tombs." We are obviously not meant to miss this point. Such thematic repetition in a narrative doesn't happen on accident. In fact, if my wife reminded me that many times of things I was supposed to remember, the trash might actually make it to the road every Wednesday morning!

But why does Mark highlight the connection between the demoniac and the tombs? In general, the ancients often associated demons with death and identified tombs as a common haunt for evil spirits. However, the connections to mourning rituals performed by Baal worshippers stands out. So it is good for us to ask what unique connection Baal had with demons and death that might explain why the demoniac of Mark 5:1-5 acts like other Baal worshippers during mourning rituals?

BAAL THE BELOVED SON OF EL AND JESUS' EXORCISM

We noted above that Baal battled with Yam the sea god and came out victorious. That victory gave him free reign over the waters above and below—a reign that Jesus challenges in his mastery of those forces on the stormy Sea of Galilee. According to the Baal myths recovered from Ugarit in Syria, Baal's lust for power was not satisfied with his dominance of Yam.

After his father El, the most high god, granted the construction of Baal's temple in the sky, Baal issued a challenge to another god named Mot who ruled the underworld. Baal was angry over Mot's privileged place as the god whom El favors. It just goes to show how important it is for parents not to play favorites with their children. It can lead to intergalactic battles to the death (at least in the case of sibling deities). Here's how the Baal and Mot battle got started.

> Will either king or commoner establish for himself dominion in the earth? I shall surely send a messenger to divine Mot, an envoy to the Beloved of El, the hero. Mot may mutter to himself, the

Beloved may scheme in his heart, (but) I alone it is who will rule over the gods, who will fill gods and men, who will satisfy the multitudes of earth! (KTU 1.4 vii 43-52)

Baal's arrogance led to a battle with Mot that went back and forth without a clear victor. Baal went down for a while, but he was never out. In fact, Baal's persistence eventually robbed Mot of his established position as the favored god. Baal now became El's beloved and obtained a position of superiority over Mot. Baal was the favored son of the most high god El.

We see this new-found authority manifest itself in various ways throughout the stories recovered from the city of Ugarit. For example, although Mot reigned over the evil spirits of the underworld, the texts testify to Baal's authority over those same spirits. The clearest example of this spiritual authority can be seen in an exorcism text where the "spirit of Baal" is invoked for power to expel a demon. It reads, "May the spirit of Baal expel you, may it expel you so that you come out at the voice of the exorcist, like smoke through a chimney, like a snake into a green tree, like goats to a summit, like lions to a lair" (KTU 1.169 1-4). I'm not sure why you needed so many analogies to expel a demon. I've personally never considered evil spirits to be literary artists who respond better to similes than concrete speech. But what do I know? The actual power of the incantation rested on the belief in Baal's authority over evil spirits, and such a belief intersects fittingly with the exorcism of the demoniac in Mark 5:1-20.

When Jesus performed the exorcism, he was not just casting out a bunch of demons to demonstrate his own authority. He was challenging the mythical authority that Baal claimed to have acquired over the inhabitants of the underworld. Jesus is showing himself to be the true Lord over all in place of Baal.

This interpretation of the events comes straight from the words of the demons themselves. In the verbal exchange between Jesus and the legion of demons, the demons call Jesus "Son of the Most High God?" (Mark 5:7). The full title "Son of the Most High God" is an unparalleled expression in the Gospels and the New Testament as a whole. That's right. You can't find it anywhere else. It stands out and suggests a unique significance specific to this context. The title given to Jesus counters directly Baal's identity as "Son of the Most High God," or Son of El. The demons are in essence witnessing to the fact that Jesus is the beloved Son of God and not Baal. There is a new boss in town, and all spiritual powers must recognize him not Baal.

A LITTLE LESSON IN HUMILITY

Every now and again I get students who come into my classroom and communicate in not so many words that they know more than everybody else. They expect to get high scores on everything, and if they don't receive an A, they either challenge me on the grade or explain it away by the fact that they didn't try on the assignment. In their minds, they knew just as much about the course subject as I did the day they walked into the room. Their arrogance is easy to spot because I possessed the same mentality during my college days.

For some of these students they are right to think of themselves as intelligent and gifted. For others, delusional or wishful probably represents a better description. Whichever category they fit, they could all use a little lesson in humility.

One day I decided to create an environment that could feed these students a piece of humble pie. All I needed was a racquet, a ball, and a sealed room with a 25-foot ceiling—all items that our college sports complex possessed when I was a full-time professor. I decided to challenge a few of them to a racquetball match. They did not hesitate to accept.

In their minds some old professor who spends his every waking hour reading books about ancient Near Eastern culture and analyzing the Greek texts of the Gospels had no shot against the sheer supremacy of their youthful athleticism. In my mind, I was hoping they were thinking exactly that. I wanted to meet them on their turf and get them to think twice about how naturally gifted they are.

This plan could have backfired on me, but thankfully they proved themselves to be just as mistaken about their racquetball skills as they were about their naturally-infused knowledge. So the games began. At first I watched how they played and hung back until I could read their tendencies. Then I let them experience the confusion of being beat by a card-carrying nerd that they wholeheartedly believed could not outplay them. To watch the frustration mount and to force them to deal with it right in front of their Bible professor was probably an adequate sanctifying experience in and of itself. However, I would not let it stop with back-to-back-to-back losses.

At a certain point I would sense the need to have some sort of false compassion. So I'd start playing with my left hand instead of my right. It kept the games closer, but the outcome remained the same. After one rather thrilling kill shot, one student remarked about my swing, "I didn't know you were left-handed." I simply replied, "I'm not." The little lesson in humility had been served and received. I know it seems cruel and a bit cocky, but it was all done in the spirit of character development.

I imagine Jesus' actions with the demoniac in Mark 5 were intended to have the same impact. All the locals who heard the story and saw the demon-possessed man restored to sanity knew Jesus was feeding Baal some humble pie. Jesus was showing up in Baal's territory and saying, "I'm the real deal, not you. I whooped you at your own game." If Baal's strength was supposed to be his control over storms and his power over demons, Jesus was humiliating him on his own turf. Baal was just one more delusional persona claiming skills and authority he did not in fact possess.

WHY DROWN THE PIGS?

The demons did not acknowledge Jesus' identity as the true "Son of the Most High" and then disappear. They specifically asked Jesus to be thrown into a nearby herd of pigs. And that brings us to our next critical question: Why pigs? Of all the random details that the Gospel writers could be sure to include, why is it so important that every writer mention the demons are sent into a nearby herd of pigs? And then why do the demons drive those swine into the sea?

The typical explanation for the significance of the drowning pigs is inadequate. In commentaries and sermons alike, the question of "why" the pigs were drowned is side-stepped. Instead, interpreters opt for a discussion about how the dead pigs affected the locals. They jump ahead to the comments about the people's fury and link it to the lost swine. As the typical explanation goes: the economic toll of losing 2,000 pigs drives the people to anger and to ask Jesus to depart.

This is a reasonable explanation for the locals' fear and request for Jesus' departure in Mark 5:15-17. Although the dead pigs could be retrieved from the Sea of Galilee for ample bacon breakfasts and ham sandwiches (and yes, it makes me hungry too just writing it), the herd would have included sows with valuable farrowing capabilities. The herders and their local clients in nearby cities could have been perturbed over the loss of costly livestock. However, it does not explain why the demons chose the pigs as their next inhabitants and then proceeded with mass murder of those same swine in the Sea. Good interpretations must make sense of all the data.

What if the people were frightened of Jesus' exorcism and motivated to demand his departure because he had undone a regional plan for coping with systemic fear? I know. That was a mouthful. But what if the demons drowned the pigs as a statement against the very god who claimed to rule the demons, the pigs, and the sea? What if the people's concern had nothing to do with economics? These "what if" questions may seem like out-of-the-blue bolts of half-baked hypotheses, but literary data from Ugarit may in fact demonstrate the greater viability of this picture over any generic commentary on the economic impact of the exorcism. Stay with me. It's about to get good …and a little strange.

BAAL'S FAVORITE FARM ANIMAL

In the Ugaritic Baal myths, there are stories of Baal's death or disappearance into the underworld and then his return to life. Quite possibly the stories reflect the seasonal cycle where the rain (and by association the rain-god) disappears for the dry season into the underworld and then returns in a storm. In any case the myths recount Baal's procession into the underworld and all the associates that succumb to the same deathly fate, including his favorite farm animal. Take special note of all his companions on the way to the underworld in the following ancient text.

> Mot commands Baal after the fall rains:
> "And you, take with you your clouds,
> Your wind, your thunder-bolts, your rains;
> (Take) with you your seven attendants,
> And your eight swine;
> (Take) with you Pidriya daughter of mist,
> (Take) with you Taliya daughter of showers,
> Then your face you will surely set,
> Toward the cavernous mountain." (KTU 1.5 v 6-12)

Most of Baal's associates make plain sense. The clouds, wind, lightning, rains, and daughters of mist and showers are all natural friends of the storm god. They should all disappear into the netherworld when the dry season or a famine commences.

However, there is no meteorological explanation for the "eight swine" that accompany Baal. I, for one, have never seen any pigs flying around in a storm (but then again I do not live in Tornado territory). Folks in the heartland may be more accustomed to seeing a stray cow or pig swirling around a category five.

So why are pigs traveling around with Baal? Honestly we can't answer that question with certainty. Ancient Near Eastern evidence does suggest that wild boars were often the target of great hunters, and Baal claimed to be one such great hunter. So the subservience of these boars may be a symbol of his hunting prowess. We just don't know for sure.

In any case, the pigs are special servants who follow Baal wherever he might go. For example, when Baal arrives at a feast of the gods recorded just prior to the procession described above, it is specifically mentioned that "Baal appeared [with his seven divine assistants], with his eight [boars]" (KTU 1.5 iv 8-9). This connection between Baal and his pigs did not only appear in ancient literature.

His unusual fondness for them had a counterpart in his ritual worship ceremonies.

In ceremonies designed to honor Baal, pigs were used in sacrificial worship as an offering and a meal. Killing and eating pigs somehow made Baal happy. I'll be honest. I probably would have worshipped Baal in those days if it meant I could get a late night BLT. I have a weakness for bacon. I could have never made it as an observant Jew.

This practice of offering and eating swine is legislated against in the Torah of the Jews, yet those prohibitions did not stop Israelites from participating. In fact, Isaiah 65:4 pointedly condemns contemporary groups of Israelites "who eat pig's flesh." The temptation to placate rival gods always existed for the Israelites, and some Jews involved themselves in the worship of Baal by consuming swine's flesh after it had been sacrificed. They had the same fears about inadequate rains for their crops, oppression from evil spirits and safety at sea. So they wanted to appease the local god. Or I guess they could have just wanted a late night BLT too.

JESUS DROWNS BAAL'S PIGS

The role that pigs play in Baal's myths and worship should redirect our understanding of the drowning pigs in Mark 5. By drowning the pigs Jesus was crippling the regional worship of Baal. People could no longer use those pigs in sacrificial ceremonies aimed at gaining Baal's favor. That created a big problem.

Naturally, these actions would elicit a negative reaction from people. Jesus was responsible for destroying their means of worship. The worship of Baal, the god who provided them safety from death and evil spirits and who provided them with water for their growing season, had been interrupted. The regional religion that people employed for protection and provision was shaken.

How now would they deal with their fear? The demons had drowned their futile program of worship in the sea. It is no wonder why Jesus commanded the healed demoniac, "Go home to your people and report to them what great things the Lord has done for you, and how He had mercy on you" (Mark 5:19). They needed to hear that a new more powerful and merciful boss was in town. They needed to hear exactly what the demons knew. This is the actual "Son of the Most High God."

UNDERMINING THE SYSTEMIC FEAR OF BAAL

If all the connections described above are considered together when observing Jesus' actions in Mark 4:35-5:20, then the sequence of events becomes a targeted attack on a regional religion that held its adherents in fear. Jesus is boldly taking over Baal's role. He is questioning his power and hindering his worship in the Decapolis region. His actions are an intentional challenge to a cultural myth. People had fears, and they needed faith in someone who could help. But they had identified the wrong helper in Baal. Jesus is the one to worship and to trust. He will not fail to protect them or provide for them in their hour of need. That is the whole point of his actions on the sea and on land.

When these cultural dynamics are seen in the story, it invites us to ask an intriguing question for today: How many more regions of the world are still waiting to be freed from their mythical fears and mistaken deities? Could we in fact do today what Jesus was doing in first century Galilee?

I believe that many people still live and die in endless cycles of fear and misguided practices of appeasement. Regional myths have trapped people in cycles of pointless pursuits aimed at alleviating that fear, but it is not working. So for those of us who want to reenact the way of Jesus, we must identify those regions of the world and support the cause of culture-specific redemption.

UNDERMINING SYSTEMIC FEAR IN BOLIVIA

As we noted above in the opening story about Potosí, Bolivia, the locals live in fear of El Tío, their divine protector and destroyer. He rules the underworld where miners work, and they bestow gifts and offerings upon his altars. They offer a blood sacrifice to this devil in the mine a few times each week. El Tío is their hope and their worst nightmare. The people of Potosí live in a culture of fear and fruitless appeasement of a god who is no greater than the deadly mining conditions that no one is addressing.

But what if we addressed them? What if we could change the mining conditions and the options that local Bolivians face when choosing where to work? What if we took Jesus as our example and acted boldly to question El Tío's control and lead people out of their cycles of fear? I believe there is a way to follow Jesus into the highest city of the world and undermine its fear and death. It requires very specific action. But taking targeted action is exactly what Jesus to free a region of people captivated by Baal.

MISSION TRIP FOR MINERS

First, a group of miners from West Virginia or Colorado (or wherever else you might be) could organize a mission trip to Potosí, Bolivia in conjunction with local government officials, churches, and miners. The trip's mission would be making the mining conditions safer for the workers. Money would have to be raised for mining equipment to be purchased, rented, and/or shipped, and the project would probably require months of time with crews rotating in for a couple weeks each. But it could be the first "Miners without Borders" mission trip that changes the history of death and devil worship in Bolivia.

Being that I am no miner myself, I am unsure of the exact process needed to create a safe ventilation system. Providing a permanent solution for clean air and new access to affordable explosives that do not release dangerous compounds into the air would be essential. If these health hazards could be reduced within the mines, the life expectancy of the miners could drastically increase while the fear decreases. In the process of renovating the mines with better ventilation, the miners on this mission trip could also teach safer techniques to prevent collapses and accidents. With the right people and strategic planning, the experience of the underworld of Cerro Rico could be radically changed.

This mining renovation trip would naturally be accompanied with the proclamation of a God who relieves fear and also rules underground. Church groups could join local churches in providing meals for the miners and simultaneously introducing them to the one whose example has led them to the highest city in the world. As the reasons to fear El Tío are lessened, new reasons to hope in Christ could be introduced.

Teams that have regularly traveled to this city to do ministry such as Teen Mania summer teams could join the effort. Doctors and healthcare professionals could add a key component to analyzing the health of miners and recommending the best course for a healthy future. If all these teams worked together at different times through the summer months, the fear of El Tío could be relieved while the worship of Jesus increases. As I think about its possibility, it is an enormous dream, but it is also a sensible step for us to take in following Jesus.

EDUCATING CHILDREN FOR NEW OCCUPATIONS

A documentary called *The Devil's Miner* has specifically highlighted the plight of children who are being drawn into the mines of Potosí. Since an experienced miner makes better money than just about anyone else in town, it is hard to resist the temptation to join the cooperative mining efforts. That temptation even reaches down to children.

Although child labor is technically illegal in Bolivia, it is not feasible for many families to pay for their child to go to school. They cannot give up the chance to increase their income even if it means illegal work in the mountain. So a number of children can be found working in the hazardous conditions and being exposed to the alcoholism and devil worship of the miners.

However, we can help. Even if you are unable to invest in the project of making the mining conditions better and thereby replacing the fear of El Tío with the hope and love shared by selfless Christ followers, you can invest in children's lives. Particularly, two organizations are doing notable work in Potosí, Bolivia. First, a

German aid organization called *Kindernothilfe* (KNH), translated *Help the Children*, is providing better living conditions and alternative sources of income for the children of Potosí. Over 400 young people receive medical care, healthy food, school lessons, and school materials, and their parents are given opportunities to learn how to read and write and develop other vocational skills than mining.

Second, CARE is working to reduce child labor in Bolivia's silver mining regions by improving access to education and preparing children for jobs outside the mines. They are focusing their efforts and resources specifically on improving the quality of education that students receive at the two technical training centers available for children of mining families in Potosí. A restricted donation to either CARE or *Kindernothilfe* could help to redirect one more child from a mountain in Potosí that trains its inhabitants to live in fear and beg the devil for mercy.

VAPOR TAKES ON VOODOO

Bolivia isn't the only country captivated by deceptive religious traditions. In July 2012 staff members from Vapor Sports (an international ministry to impoverished kids) found an abandoned, malnourished, and deathly ill girl in Togoville—a rural village in West Africa. It was no run-of-the-mill starvation story. This girl's family had purposefully sent her away from home. Rather than directing her to an orphanage or hoping for her safety, her mother actually prayed that the local voodoo god would punish her. Her mother carried out a ritual to invoke god to take vengeance against her.

How could a mother pray for divine help in taking revenge against her own daughter? No excuse could be enough, but her mother attributed it to the loss of about $250. The girl had been entrusted with the money to run an errand, but unfortunately, she squandered it. That was the last straw for her mom. This girl needed to be turned over to god to have him deal with her directly.

In Togoville the practice of voodoo and witchcraft runs rampant. Villagers turn to voodoo gods for justice. This girl's case was fairly standard. Her mom invoked a divine curse and left her for dead. No one in the family or community stepped up to help out of fear the curse could fall on them. So a little girl faced a divine death penalty rather than a more fitting lesson in financial responsibility.

Vapor's staff members in Togoville wouldn't accept the religious status quo. They did what everyone else feared doing. They intervened. They ran to her when everyone else was running away. They squared off against voodoo spirits and in more concrete ways than they expected.

"When we found her, she could not eat or drink," Vapor's staff reported. "She was suffering from all sorts of sores." So they took her to a nearby hospital in Lome, and they prayed. When they started praying over the girl, a voice that was clearly not her own came from her and demanded for an animal sacrifice to be made. The voice named itself and declared that life would be lost if he was not appeased. Vapor's staff members cried out to God for help. "We prayed and prayed and finally... a loud shout. Something came out of her. Then she fell into a deep sleep." Vapor's staff faced off with voodoo's god, and Vapor's God won.

Vapor's staff members ministered to the girl once she woke. "The first thing we did was tell her that she should trust in Jesus who died for her and who will never forsake her." The suffering girl embraced the gospel and trusted in the grace of Christ. It was a welcome message in a vengeful world.

The next day she started eating and drinking, but it was too late. The abuse and neglect had taken its toll. Her body gave out, and she passed away. Vapor's staff mourned her death but not without hope. This little girl had lost her life but gained her soul. She had been set free from the oppression of voodoo's demons.

In her death, the service of Vapor's staff has become a testimony to the community. A statement has been made. Vapor does not fear wicked spirits or voodoo curses. Vapor's imagination is not captivated by witchcraft and gods of vengeance. Vapor follows

Jesus, and Jesus is the way out of fear and oppression. Jesus is the real deal, and his justice does not come at the agony of children. That testimony will follow Vapor's work in that community for years to come.

I'm not sure what you think of this story, but it disturbs me. The fact that Vapor has to take a stand against voodoo is depressing. How can there still be people in such spiritual darkness that they abandon children and turn them over to "god" for divine retribution?

When Vapor shared this story in Togoville, one native of Togo commented in French: Pourquoi des togovilois pourrissent le nom de Togoville? Many West Africans speak French if you didn't already know. It means: why would a native of Togoville spoil the name of Togoville? This man was more concerned about Togoville's reputation than the health and well-being of a child. He was more concerned about a negative representation of Togo's traditions than fighting against the inherent wickedness of its practices. Thank God Vapor is bold enough to stand against the cultural pressure.

Vapor's everyday work involves sports, humanitarian assistance, and discipleship. In Togoville many of the children who participate in Vapor's discipleship leagues come from families entrapped in voodoo and witchcraft. In the midst of soccer, educational opportunities and clean water, they hear about Jesus. The children have a chance to break out of the cycle of curses and vengeance. They have the chance to let Jesus replace the religious fear that has trapped them for centuries. They have the chance to experience exactly what Jesus did for Baal worshippers in the land of the Gerasenes.

UNDERMINING SYSTEMIC FEAR EVERYDAY

Reenacting Jesus' decisive blow to Baal's supremacy need not be so far from home or done on such a large scale like sending miners to Bolivia. Rituals are all around us that people employ to manage their fears. Sometimes it is more difficult to identify them because of our passive participation. From an insider's perspective bankrupt approaches to managing fear just seem like everyday life.

However, we have the opportunity to discern what misguided "fear" management systems look like in our neighborhoods, our families, and our sub-cultures. We have the opportunity to follow Jesus in challenging the empty paths towards peace and mistaken attempts at control. When we find a moment where we can expose myths and redraw reality with Jesus at its center, we can free ourselves and others from the cycles of fear and fruitless alleviation that we so easily identify in the lives of Bolivian miners. So let us open our eyes and take action with the culture-specific care of Christ.

I'd encourage you to ask this question: Which pigs could we drown? Yes, that is not a typo or a joke. Well, it is kind of a joke because I find it funny, but I ask the question that way so you can see the connection between Jesus' action and our imitation. In Jesus' day certain Gentiles around the Sea of Galilee sacrificed pigs to gain the favor of Baal. They thought making bacon might protect them from harmful weather patterns and even death (on a lighter note I do feel that a few pieces of bacon each morning keep my muscles lean, hair shiny, and heart happy but that has no relevance here). In our contemporary world, we have different schemes for self-preservation and protection from the fear we feel and the dangers we encounter.

That is why we must think long and hard about this question: Where might Jesus be liberating us from patterns of control and fear that we use to manage life? Most of us do not worship another spiritual being or appease some underground force for protection. We do not use the stars to warn us of harm like astrologists or wear an amulet to guard ourselves from spiritual evil. If you or those around you do, then Jesus is here to replace fearful habits with calm redemption. If not, then your response probably has more to do getting involved with those like Vapor or T4 Global who are freeing those who do.

In the U.S. we are more readily found seeking security in long-term financial planning, a brick home outside of a flood zone, a car with high safety ratings, life and fire insurance, the predictions of meteorologists, the latest study on what causes cancer, and reducing one's carbon footprint. None of these examples directly correlate to the use of pigs in Baal worship around the Sea of Galilee or to the offerings made to El Tio in Cerro Rico, and we shouldn't force it. However, they do demonstrate that we, like the ancient Gentile

Galileans, have to address our fears somehow. So we must take a careful look at our lives to identify how we calm our fears and where Jesus' authority has been usurped by an untrustworthy impostor.

If Jesus' pattern of redemptive action is continuing, then he will be found "drowning pigs" and drawing people into a place of peace and service. He not only wants to communicate his unique position over all, but he wants you to experience peace and to work to bring that peace to the world. That is what happened to the demoniac. That is what will happen with us if we continue the mission Jesus began on a boat in the sea and by the tombs in Baal country.

Reenacting the Way

1. Do you know any other examples of people who live in fear from false gods or try to protect themselves through pointless practices? Examples may come from other countries or from superstitious people right in your own social network.

2. Which actions of Jesus have reduced your fear of life's unpredictabilities and death? Which fears do the general population have that you don't have because of Jesus?

3. How could you take action to make the point to others that they are playing pointless games to deal with their fear? Be specific about the method, the location, and the target audience. Actions are louder than words.

CHAPTER 6

TURNING WATER INTO WINE: CELEBRATING THE TRUE SOURCE OF LIFE

Focal Point: Do the good things of life remind you to celebrate God's benevolent presence or credit some secondary figure?

IS JESUS THE "LIFE OF THE PARTY"?

I will never forget the first and only chapel message I ever heard on Jesus being the "life of the party." I was a Bible teacher at a Christian academy. My job was to teach Juniors and Seniors how to interpret the Bible correctly. We spent weeks on interpretation projects that required detailed analysis of words, grammar, cultural backgrounds, and literary context. I expected my students to learn the process and use the tools necessary for interpreting any passage in the Bible correctly. Little did I know chapel speakers would undermine my objective.

The first warning came when I found out an upcoming chapel message was called "Life of the Party." We probably should have stopped that one before it started, but hindsight is always 20/20. The chapel message began with a photo. On a 100 inch x 100 inch video screen the guest speaker projected Ben Stein's head. My mind immediately went to his role as the boring science teacher in the movie *Ferris Bueller's Day Off*. I imagined his monotone voice and repetitive calls for "Bueller, Bueller, Bueller." While I rehearsed old movie lines in my head, the speaker interrupted my nostalgia with this statement: "Many of you think Jesus is like this guy."

I, for one, did not identify with his statement. I agreed intellectually that both Ben Stein and Jesus were Jews, but that is where the comparison ended. I had seen enough movies to know that Jesus always wears a purple sash. Ben Stein has no sash. Jesus also has long silky hair and sandals. Ben Stein probably gave up the hippie clothes and longer hair length in the 1970s.

The point of the speaker's comparison centered on our perception of Jesus' likeability (*if that is even a word?*). His suspicion was that most people think Jesus is boring. If you are going to hang out with him, you better sit down, shut up, and wipe the smile off your face. If you want to pray to him, you better take off your hat and use King James language. The speaker wanted to challenge that perception. He planned to use the story of Jesus turning water into wine to do it.

After he recounted the water-to-wine miracle (and embellished parts about getting toe jam in the stone water pots), he came to his conclusion. He brought the picture of Ben Stein back up on the screen and asked: "Is the Jesus in this story boring and strict?" It was a rhetorical question. The obvious answer was no. Jesus had created huge bottles of fine wine to keep a crowd of people celebrating at a 7-day wedding party. That is not the action of a killjoy.

The speaker put up another picture to make his final point. This time he showed us Ruben Studdard – American Idol runner-up from 2003. Ruben was wearing a pin-striped suit and sporting some oversized sun glasses. He was the definition of cool. What was his point? He wanted all the kids in the room to see that Jesus is more like Ruben Studdard than Ben Stein. What!? This is where his interpretation of Jesus' actions got kind of fuzzy. He wanted us to see that Jesus is the "life of the party." He doesn't come to rain on our parade but to throw us a parade. He doesn't come with a list of rules. He comes with barrels of wine.

His point seemed to imply that Jesus likes to get people a little tipsy and have a good time—at least that is how all of my high schoolers understood it. Needless to say I was not pumped to have a spiritual authority imply that Jesus would bring 3 kegs to a party if he were here. That's not the message a bunch of underage kids needed. But who could blame him or them? How else could you understand the character of a man who miraculously produced vats of alcohol for a party?

As the Bible teacher, I had a few ideas. And I spent the rest of the day undoing what the chapel speaker did. I had to go all the way back to why John chose to include the story in his Gospel and what associations his first readers would have made with miraculous wine-making. Let me tell you. It has nothing to do with being the "life of the party." He was not trying to front his superior social status with deeper reds and more subtle oak and cherry finishes. Now I'm not saying Jesus is boring, but he had a very specific point to make and it had nothing to do with how cool he is.

WHY JOHN TELLS UNIQUE STORIES ABOUT JESUS

We often miss the point of Jesus' miracles because we think they all make the same point in the first place. The logic goes something like this. Jesus did a miracle. So Jesus has divine power. So Jesus is divine.

This logic is simple and has an element of truth to it. However, it has a couple flaws. First, many stories circulated in the first century about people who performed miracles. Doing miracles did not mean a person was divine. The ability to perform miracles only demonstrated some type of divine favor. You wouldn't call the Apostle Paul a divine being because he did miracles in Ephesus, would you? Second, making every miracle a statement about Jesus' divine power flattens out the meaning of each action. Jesus' miracles were meant to deliver specific messages to specific audiences. To ignore the specific meaning of each miracle is to disrespect both the Gospel's author and main actor. It means you are dismissing the particular reason he did it in favor of a quick cookie-cutter explanation. That's not an approach I want to take.

At the end of John's Gospel he makes a profound statement about Jesus' actions. *"And there are also many other things which Jesus did, which if they were written in detail, I suppose that even the world itself would not contain the books that would be written"*

(John 21:25). This statement makes the content of John's Gospel all the more important. If Jesus did millions of amazing things, then John had to choose carefully what to include on his scroll. He had plenty of material. He just had to choose the most pertinent stories. As any good author does, John would have made sure that each event had a timely message for his audience.

THE RIGHT STORY FOR THE RIGHT AUDIENCE

I use the same selectivity when I go to teach students at a local Torchbearers center in Colorado. By way of background, Torchbearers International is a worldwide network of one-year Bible training centers. They provide dynamic teaching, serving opportunities, and mentoring relationships all focused on experiencing the sufficiency of Christ. I highly recommend spending a year with them.

It happens that my roommate from college is now the director of a Torchbearers center near Winter Park, CO. So he invites me to take time off work and teach a class or two for the students. It is an absolute blast and also a great opportunity to share stories that don't get the same laughs elsewhere.

Over the 12 years of our friendship I have amassed a litany of stories about Dan that I readily embellish at his expense. Although my stories about cliff jumping and poor driving don't connect with the average audience, the students at Timberline Lodge love it. They know Dan, and hearing stories about how we hazed him the night before his wedding warrants complete and total attention from every student. When I tell the story about first meeting Dan during a sacred men-only tea drinking ritual where he was knitting, they love every punch line about how he reminded me of my grandmother. When I talk about how his girlfriend in college changed him from a man's man to a folksy, sweet-talking, whipped boyfriend, they start rolling on the floor. When I share how that same girlfriend switched him from Rock and Punk music to high-pitched male vocalists and female hippie artists, the guys in the room can't wait to hassle him.

The reason these embellished stories attacking Dan's masculinity work so well is simple. My audience in that mountain center knows Dan and the pride he takes in being a rugged, tough mountain man. They know how strong, skilled, and indefatigable he is. He is a mountain climbing, snow boarding, hockey playing bloke. That is the inside knowledge that makes every story about his granny-style driving and ballerina slippers so powerful.

In general, that is the kind of inside knowledge every good speaker should share with his audience and use to his advantage. It makes your message hit home in more personal and lasting ways. That is why John used the same kind of shared inside knowledge when he wrote his Gospel to its first audience.

WHO WAS JOHN'S ORIGINAL AUDIENCE?

Before we can figure out the unique meaning of the water-to-wine miracle, we have to know something about the people John first wanted to hear it. That first audience had a unique connection to Jesus' mysterious miracle. No other Gospel writer besides John saw reason to include it. So what about John's audience was different than the audiences of the other three Gospels? Why did John choose to begin his string of stories about Jesus with this water-to-wine wedding miracle?

As every good scholar has to say, "Many scholars disagree about the exact nature of John's audience." Having provided that disclaimer, let me tell you what I have concluded from the evidence available. John's audience was primarily a group of Hellenistic Jews and Gentile God-fearers who lived in Asia Minor (modern-day Western Turkey). What I mean is John's audience either involved Jews who grew up in a Greco-Roman world or Gentiles who had developed an appreciation for elements of the Jewish faith.

What's important for you to know is that this group of folks in Asia Minor made pilgrimages to Jerusalem every year. They would consistently go to the Temple to celebrate major festivals on the Jewish calendar. So on the one hand they knew Jerusalem very well, but on the other hand they knew all about Greco-Roman religious life in Asia Minor.

Understanding these basic characteristics explains a lot about John's Gospel. John does not tell many stories about Jesus' ministry in Galilee because it was unfamiliar territory. The fact is almost no one in John's audience had ever been to Galilee. That's why John focuses on events that happened around the Temple during festival times. Think about it. John is the only Gospel writer to describe Jesus' actions and words during the Feast of Booths and the Feast of Dedication in Jerusalem. All the other Gospel writers limit Jesus' ministry in Jerusalem to his final days around Passover.

John also refrains from recording parables with farming illustrations from the land of Israel. People who grew up in Asia Minor would not relate. Instead he includes long speeches that use religious language popular in Asia Minor—expressions about light and darkness, truth and lies, spirit and flesh, the world and the eternal, and spiritual oneness and spiritual knowing.

JESUS' WORDS AFTER A WATER CEREMONY

Why does it matter that you know this? Take for example one of the many cryptic statements in John's Gospel. In John 7:37, Jesus says, "If anyone is thirsty, let him come to me and drink." That is a strange statement… unless Jesus had an eternal CamelBak under his tunic that never ran out of water. (That would be cool and quite useful during Israel's hot summers, but that has nothing to do with the passage or the point Jesus was trying to make.)

In the beginning of John 7:37 we are told how to figure out the point of Jesus' statement. John tells us that Jesus made this statement at a specific time: "on the last day of the feast, the great day." There is something about the last day that explains Jesus' invitation to drink from the water he is providing.

The feast mentioned in John 7 is *Sukkoth*, or the Festival of Booths. It is the time set aside to remember how God led his people through the wilderness to the Promised Land. To relive the experience,

Israelites were instructed to set up tents as their ancestors did in the Sinai wilderness. The 8-day ceremony gave space for God's people to reflect on his intervention in the past and stir their longing for his intervention in the future. Each day of the festival was full of ceremonies and sacrifices commanded in the Jewish Law (Num. 29:12-40).

One daily ceremony involved pouring out water. While the morning sacrifice was being prepared, a priest accompanied by a joyous musical procession would exit the Temple and draw water with a golden pitcher at the Pool of Siloam. The priest would then return to the Temple for a ceremonial pouring of the water on the altar while the sacrifice was burning. When the priest reentered the Temple, he would walk through the 'Water-gate' (which makes complete sense when you think about it). He would ascend the steps of the altar, turn to the left, and pour out the water into two silver basins.

This water pouring ceremony was not prescribed in the Jewish Law. The Law only called for the wine of the drink-offering to be poured out at this festival. However, some time prior to the first century the water offering was combined with the wine offering and both were poured into basins on the altar.

Why pour water on the altar? The water offering had three purposes. First, God's people were saying thanks for the previous year's rain. Second, it was a petition to God for more rain. Third, the water pouring out of the golden pitcher illustrated the great outpouring of God's Spirit for which his people longed (Ezekiel 36; 47; Joel 2; Zechariah 14). It had both a natural and supernatural meaning.

With all these layers of meaning wrapped up in the water ceremony, it is easy to understand how it became a time of great rejoicing and expectation. It actually gained quite a reputation. The Rabbis describe the excitement surrounding this water ceremony in an ancient set of instructions for the Festival of Booths called *Tractate Sukkoth*. Believe me, it's a real page-turner.

In *Tractate Sukkoth* one Rabbi claims: "He who has not witnessed the rejoicing at the water-drawing huts has, throughout the whole of his life, witnessed no real rejoicing" (Sukkah 53b). This ceremony captured the hopes and dreams of the Jewish people. God has redeemed them once from slavery in Egypt. Now they were waiting for him to act again and pour out his salvation in a fresh way. That got them excited.

The last day of the feast reached a climax in the people's expectation for salvation. The priests would circle the altar seven times singing with a loud voice a song of redemption and salvation. The song comes straight from Psalm 118. *"Save now, I pray, O LORD; O LORD, I pray, send now prosperity. Blessed is he who comes in the name of the LORD"* (Psalm 118:25-26).

Imagine thousands of people joining the priests and singing this song. It is the last day of the festival. They have thanked God for his provision of rain. Now they are begging him to send a Redeemer who can bring salvation and a fresh spiritual experience. The frenzy of anticipation would be hard to imagine. The emotion would be running high.

This is the kind of morning people had experienced the day Jesus offered them the water of new spiritual life. Put this picture of longing and hoping and pleading in the background of your mind as you read John 7:37-39.

> Now on the last day, the great day of the feast, Jesus stood and cried out, saying, "If anyone is thirsty, let him come to Me and drink. He who believes in Me, as the Scripture said, 'From his innermost being will flow rivers of living water.'" And this He spoke of the Spirit, whom those who believed in Him were to receive.

God had promised in Isaiah 44:3, "I will pour out water on the thirsty and streams on the dry ground; I will pour out My Spirit on your offspring." The 8th day of Sukkoth was the time to ask God to make good on this promise. And Jesus was telling them that their prayers had been answered. He is the One who had come "in the name of the Lord." Jesus was announcing that a new day had dawned, and the hope of salvation symbolized by the water ceremony had materialized in him.

If you read Jesus' offer to pour the water of life into the souls of the thirsty as just another spiritual metaphor, you miss the point. His words were meant to resonate with the songs still ringing in their ears from the morning celebration. His words were infused with the meaning of eight days' worth of water ceremonies. His words were supposed to be received as the response of God to passionate prayers for an outpouring of salvation and fresh spiritual life. We miss their meaning if we miss this context.

"CUTEST GUY IN THE CLASS"

I'll never forget the first girl who told me I was the cutest guy in the class. It was the sixth grade. I had moved into town about a year before the experience. I was the new guy without a strong social network, but I planned to build one starting with the ladies. So I found the cutest girl in my class that didn't already have a serious, committed relationship with another 11-year old and asked her to be my girlfriend. Her name was Stephanie, and she said, "Yes."

I can never forget how I felt when she said, "Yes." It not only meant I had a girl to call on the phone and sit by at lunch, but also I had tapped into a cooler clique than my "new" status had previously allowed. She ran with all the cool kids. And I was now gaining access to their ranks.

Our relationship progressed fast. I asked her in Science class to be my girlfriend (and by "asked" I mean "wrote a note with 'yes' and 'no' boxes to check with her answer"). In Health class I received my first love note from her. It started out, "Paul, you are the cutest guy in the whole class." Wow. What a rush! I wasn't the only one who thought so. Stephanie had seen the light of my face as well. I couldn't wait to read more.

Although the letter started with an outrageous compliment, I was on the verge of depression by the end. It was a "Dear John" letter. After 45 minutes of pure relational bliss, she was breaking up with me. I no longer had a girlfriend. More importantly, I no longer had access to the in-crowd. I had lost everything an 11-year old could desire (except my favorite Batman T-shirt and Nike Jordan shoes).

The self-inflating power of her initial compliment quickly slipped away when I realized she was just buttering me up before a big let-down. Context was everything. A few kind words don't mean much when their real purpose is to dissolve a blossoming relationship.

At the ripe old age of eleven I was experiencing what linguist's call the illocutionary force of language. What a text says does not create meaning. What an author does with words in a specific situation creates the meaning. Stephanie was using words to end the best 45 minutes of my life up to that point. They might have said I was cute, but what they did was break my heart (for about 2 hours until it mended itself and I was back in the game).

ACTIONS + CONTEXT = MEANING

My experience with kind words in a break-up letter is not much different than the way people originally experienced Jesus' water-to-wine miracle. The action taken alone is confusing, mysterious, and somewhat misleading. Why would Jesus make a bunch of wine for a wedding? You need more information than you read in the story. The meaning is locked inside the context in which John recorded it. To figure it out, we have to identify the purpose John had in telling the story to his first century audience.

To be clear John didn't tell his audience in Asia Minor about Jesus' water-to-wine miracle to encourage drunkenness. John wasn't trying to make Jesus' image more appealing to social drinkers. He told the story to an audience that already knew what miraculously making wine meant. He told the story because it resonated with the world they knew. John's audience was deeply enculturated in Greco-Roman religious traditions, and Jesus' one action made a clear statement in that context.

GREEK LEGENDS OF THE GOD OF WINE

When John completes his brief story about Jesus turning water into wine, he makes an important concluding statement. "This was the beginning of the signs Jesus did in Cana of Galilee and it manifested his glory" (John 2:11). The conclusion tells us the point of the story. The miracle revealed Jesus' "glory." In John's Gospel, "glory" is a characteristic of the divine Father. And somehow changing water to wine pointed out a characteristic that Jesus shared with the Father. Specifically, it showed their common divine greatness.

Why did making wine demonstrate Jesus' unique reflection of the Father's glory? You may first think Jesus is reenacting an ancient miracle that God performed for Israel. However, in the Jewish Scriptures you will not find any stories of God turning water into wine. There is no ancient poem or prophecy where Israel's God demonstrated his divine greatness that way.

Jesus did do other miracles that reenacted God's historic treatment of Israel. We saw a detailed example in chapter 4. The provision of food for 5,000 had multiple connections to the provision of manna in the wilderness. In contrast, the miracle of turning water into wine has no counterpart in the Old Testament.

Jesus' miracle only makes sense when you place it in a Greco-Roman context. In the Greco-Roman world they told stories about how wine was created. The details changed, but the main actor remained the same. The god Dionysus created wine.

Legends are told that vines full of thick clusters of red grapes grew from the ground where Dionysus's blood fell. Other legends describe the first time Dionysus taught humanity how to create wine from grapes. For example, Achilles Tatius in *The Adventures of Leucippe and Clitophon* recalls how a kind farmer and herdsman, Icarius, set a meal before the god Dionysus and gained access to the god's wine recipe.

As the story goes, humanity had no good refreshments in those days. They drank the same water as their oxen. So Dionysus thanked the herdsman for his hospitality by giving him a cup to drink. Instead of finding water, Icarius found the god's own wine. In his excitement he begged the god to know how such fine drink was made, and Dionysus told him. According to legend the manufacture of wine spread from there, and a festival was established to honor the god's gift to humanity.

Rooted in these legends is an enduring association of Dionysus with vines, grapes, and wine. The appearance of grapevines and wine became one and the same as the appearance of Dionysus the god himself. The *Homeric Hymn* 7 recounts how the sudden appearance of a vine proved the presence of the god. In the midst of a fearful situation on the water the Homeric narrator interjects, "Then in an instant a vine, running along the topmost edge of the sail, sprang up and sent out its branches in every direction heavy with thick-hanging clusters of grapes, and around the mast cloud dark-leaved ivy, rich in blossoms and bright with ripe berries." The vine meant the sailors could relax in the knowledge of Dionysus's nearness. He would take care of them.

In other parts of the Greco-Roman world, the miracle of "one-day vines" became popular and supposedly occurred at multiple ancient sites for Dionysus worship.[7] Sophocles in his *Thyestes* records that in Euboea one could watch the holy vine grow green in the early morning. By noon the grapes were already forming, and by evening the dark and heavy fruit could be cut down and a drink made from them. Pretty impressive stuff.

DIONYSUS'S MIRACULOUS WINE-MAKING

Miracles demonstrating the presence of Dionysus became a mainstay at annual festivals. According to Pausanius, people celebrated the feast of Dionysus at the beginning of every year. It was a rollicking, raucous event of the sort you might expect to be linked to a deity that makes wine in abundance and represents the renewed fertility of the earth.

At many temples, legends circulated about the miraculous appearance of Dionysus during the New Year festival. The traveler

---

[7] The one-day vines "flowered and bore fruit in the course of a few hours during the festivals of the epiphany of the God" (Walter Otto, *Dionysus,* 98).

Pausanias recounts a curious phenomenon in the city of Ellis that happened during an annual Dionysian festival. People believed it proved Dionysus's attendance. Pausanias recounts the phenomenon in first person.

> Three pots are brought into the Temple and set down empty in the presence of citizens and of any strangers who may chance to be in the country. The doors of the building are sealed by the priests themselves and by any others who may be so inclined. On the morrow they are allowed to examine the seals, and on going into the building they find the pots filled with wine. I did not myself arrive at the time of the festival, but the most respected Elean citizens, and with them strangers also, swore that what I have said is the truth. The Andrians too assert that every other year at their feast of Dionysus wine flows of it's own accord from the sanctuary.[8]

Two other ancient historians Didorus Siculus and Pliny the Elder talk of fountains of wine that flowed by themselves from the ground and of spring water from Dionysus's temple which had the flavor of wine on festival days.[9] No matter how the wine appeared at these festivals, the presence of wine meant the presence of the god. The one who brought fertility to the ground, who made thick clusters of grapes grow on vines, and who taught humanity to make wine was among his people. Everyone knew when water turned to wine or tasted like wine, god was there. That is precisely what John's audience knew when they heard the story of Jesus' miraculous wine-making.

JESUS' ACTIONS IN A GRECO-ROMAN CONTEXT

So what would Jesus' creation of wine out of water have meant to John's audience? The answer is simple and clear once you know what John's audience knew. They lived in a Greco-Roman world that associated miraculous wine-making with the benevolent

---

[8] Pausanias, *Description of Greece* 6. 26.1-2.

[9] Didorus Siculus, *Library of History*, 3.66.1-2; Pliny the Elder, *Natural History*, 2.106, 31.13

presence of the god Dionysus. Stories circulated every year about where and how it happened at New Year festivals. Although Jesus' first Jewish audience in Israel would connect the new wine to OT prophecies of God's saving presence returning to his people (Isaiah 25:6-9; Hosea 14:7; Joel 2:18-27; Amos 9:11-15), John wanted his audience also to see that Jesus replaces the legends of Dionysus.

In the water-to-wine miracle, Jesus' actions attack the claims that new growth in the vineyards and fresh wine is a manifestation of Dionysus's benevolent presence. The legends of Dionysus's wine-making at special New Year festivals cannot rival the reality of Jesus' water-to-wine miracle. Jesus was doing what Dionysus's followers claimed their god did. That is why John says making wine appear displays Jesus' divine glory. The message to everyone who would hear what he did was: God is here.

TRACES OF SOMEONE'S PRESENCE

Jesus turning water to wine is not much different than hosting friends and family who leave unique signs of their presence. Whenever my mother-in-law spends time at our house, small miracles occur in my kitchen. I know it's probably not smart to use my mother-in-law as an illustration, but I can't help myself.

Now she doesn't turn water into wine, but she does turn Cokes into Diet Cokes. A few days into her visit I will reach into the fridge for a refreshing soft drink and find that every option begins with "Diet." Sugar doesn't stand a chance in her presence. Even my Mountain Dew transforms into Diet Mountain Dew. I can't even imagine the reason for drinking that yellow jolt of 13-minute energy if it isn't for the 400 grams of sugar!

Her miraculous powers also affect the refined sugar in our cupboard. When I go to put sugar in my coffee, I suddenly find a stash of sugar substitutes in little yellow packets stuffed into its place. It's like she has some moral conviction against the sugar cane. Maybe she had a bad experience with a jar of sugar when she was younger. I don't know. I do know she has the "Midas touch," but everything turns to sucralose instead of gold. One day I imagine she will show up at my house in a flex fuel car that only uses Splenda-based ethanol rather than sugar cane ethanol because it's a "lighter" fuel.

In any case, you get the point. Sometimes we know people are around because they leave traces of their presence. That was the case with Dionysus. When water started tasting like wine or when grapes grew out of a vine in one day, you knew the god was near. When Jesus created wine out of water, he was making the same point. God was near.

PLANTING TREES AND REVEALING GOD'S BENEVOLENT PRESENCE

Since 1984, over 250 villages in six different countries have seen the presence of God in tree saplings. Yes, planting tree saplings is not always a sign of earthy environmentalists who refuse to shower in order to save tree roots and whales named Willy. An organization called *Plant With Purpose* has planted over 5 million trees with the expressed purpose of reversing deforestation and ending environmentally fueled poverty. Tree-planting actually restores the genius of what God created.

In thousands of rural communities around the world, people are digging their way down to new depths of poverty. They strip the land of trees in an effort to fuel wood stoves and unwittingly unleash erosion that destroys farmland and pollutes water sources. *Plant With Purpose* identifies these rural communities and reverses the process that has led to rampant starvation and malnutrition.

Plant With Purpose provides the tools and resources needed to sustain a higher quality of life. They introduce more fuel-efficient stoves to address the cause of deforestation. They train local farmers on agricultural and agri-forestry techniques that produce enriched soil and larger harvests. They plant trees near water sources to promote natural filtration processes. They create savings and loans groups so that farmers can purchase better seed and local businesses can expand services.

Plant With Purpose does all these activities in partnership with local churches. The goal is to demonstrate the tangible goodness of God through the restoration of the land. With each improved harvest and cleaner water source, people can experience the presence of God in fresh vegetation. It re-creates the goodness of God's "good" creation.

Plant With Purpose is doing with trees in the developing world what Jesus did with wine in a Greco-Roman world. They are sending signs of God's benevolent presence. The restoration of the earth at the hands of Jesus' followers makes a statement: God has not forsaken them. He is near, and they can taste it.

The tree-planting initiatives may not be turning water into wine, but they are bringing life out of barren land. The produce of God's good earth is being enjoyed once again. That activity is sending a message to local communities that resonates like the Cana wedding miracle in first century Asia Minor.

THE ANCIENT CHURCH VERSUS THE WORSHIP OF DIONYSUS

Why is John the only biographer to include the water-to-wine miracle in his Gospel? The simple answer is John's audience needed to hear it. Inhabitants of Asia Minor had a cultural proclivity to celebrate Dionysus's appearance each New Year. While crushing grapes or attending festivals, people wore masks of Dionysus's face and sang praises to his name. The connection between fertile soil, grapes, and wine and the god Dionysus had been cemented over centuries. It wouldn't be easy to break such a deeply ingrained tradition. So John told the story to point Jesus' new followers toward the real source of life and refreshment.

Unfortunately, cultural practices in Asia Minor were not transformed after John wrote his story to the audience in Asia Minor—not even among the believing community. Church documents from the Eastern Roman Empire tell us that the problem persisted for at least 600 years. At the Council of Constantinople in 691 CE, the Church still had to forbid Christians from honoring Dionysus's name while wine making. The Council had to decree that wearing satyr masks and singing songs about Dionysus while they worked honored the wrong god. Worshipping Dionysus while making new batches of wine was a deeply entrenched cultural habit.

To confront the problem, the Church created an alternate celebration at the beginning of the year. On the same day Dionysian festivals took place around the Hellenized world, the Church decided to celebrate the appearance of Jesus. The church calendar calls this celebration Epiphany.

Epiphany simply means "appearance." According to ancient lectionaries, churches were to read passages about events that signaled Jesus' manifestation to the world (e.g., Jesus' baptism or the visitation of the Magi). One particularly relevant passage that ancient Greek lectionaries scheduled for Epiphany was John 2:1-11. The water-to-wine miracle was a particularly meaningful epiphany of the one true God to every person familiar with the legends and worship of Dionysus.

In the same way that Christmas was placed on the day Romans celebrated the rebirth of the sun-god Mithras, Epiphany was placed on January 6th when people celebrated the re-appearance of Dionysus. The Church wanted to change people's theology. They wanted to replace popular theology with the claims of Christ. Dionysus did not make the soil fertile that gave life to grape clusters for wine-making. Jesus does that. Jesus is the one that brings fresh vegetation and all its fruits each year. That is what his followers needed to remember on the day when everyone else was praising Dionysus. Jesus is the divine provider of all the good things in life, symbolized by wine. That timely message for an ancient Greco-Roman audience may need to be re-casted for our day and culture.

THE BLESSING OF THE WATERS

As part of Epiphany, the Greek Orthodox Church has long celebrated a ceremony called the "Blessing of the Waters." As the tradition goes, a congregation will gather by a significant body of water near the beginning of the New Year. A priest will take a sanctified object and throw it into the water. Parishioners then jump into the water to retrieve the object. The first parishioner to get the object is awarded a special blessing from the priest.

The ceremony is a poignant experience (especially for Russian Orthodox parishioners who experience mild hypothermia after jumping into the water in the dead of winter). The point of the ceremony (not to say that all Orthodox priests do the ceremony for this one purpose) is the recognition of water as God's gift of life to the earth and all its inhabitants. It is a time to remember who is responsible for the fruitfulness and verve of our planet. It reconnects the new life after the dead of winter with the God who makes it all possible and reveals God's presence in its goodness.

It would not be a bad idea for all of Jesus' followers in every tradition to have a venue for reflecting on God's provision of all that is good in life. Our appreciation for each year's new growth could be enhanced if we stopped each winter to remember that Jesus is the source of what the spring will bring. It could change the way we experience the deadness of winter and the new life in spring. It could challenge the way we give credit to the wrong source for new life in our culture.

For many of us, we probably fail to credit anyone in our scientific age for the goodness and source of life. Or else we credit the companies that sell the new produce or products. So we miss God in the water cycle and mistake him for the business plan of food companies. They receive our praise, our trust, and our allegiance whether or not they are life-giving.

Although Dionysus's worship is no longer a force in any contemporary context today, Jesus' ancient challenge suggests that rhythms in our culture—which credit another source for life and vegetation—vie for our attention. I'd recommend taking time each New Year to expose the pretenders and recognize Jesus as the divine supplier of new life. Maybe a trip to a garden or farm after the "blessing of the waters" would be a good start. Everyone could bring a frozen TV dinner and burn it symbolically as a way to remember that our food is not supplied first by a grocery store but rather by the one who gave us soil and sun and water (please post pictures if you do this!).

For us to find the motivation to reenact tangible experiences of God's benevolent presence for those who are missing out, we must be acutely aware of the blessing ourselves. Unfortunately, many of us look over the goodness of things baked into our everyday experience. That's not what God wants for us. Ecclesiastes 3:12 commands us to "eat and drink and enjoy the fruits of our labor, for these are gifts from God." The verse is a bit of an anomaly. Such a mundane, earthly path to joy seems out of place in the Bible. Aren't we supposed to be focusing on spirituality and the eternal, not the temporary satisfaction from good food, drink, and successful work?

In my life, I am constantly harassed for slow eating. Workmates, friends and even family members want to get done and get on with it. But that's not me. I want to savor each bite and each different part of the meal. I don't want to miss the gifts that God has put right on my plate.

Every time I'm harassed for savoring a meal, I get concerned that the other party is missing something. I have found in the modern cultures of most industrialized nations that our economic strength and our personal weakness is a focus on the future. We are always thinking about the next thing, the next meeting, the next outing, or the next year. Positively, that makes many of us planned, prepared, and successful. However, the backlash is an unfortunate avoidance of the beauty in front of us. I believe rampant discontent in life is driven by constantly overlooking the goodness of things right under our nose. We forget to savor the food, the drink, the music, and the day's work. We keep driving toward the next thing and never really taste the goodness of present things. Is that true of you?

There is divinely baked beauty in the everyday mundane that is available for our satisfaction. Ecclesiastes 3:12 clearly states that "these are gifts from God." It's not earthly or unspiritual to derive satisfaction from a good southern meal. Tropical fruit smoothies or a job well done are gifts from God for us to enjoy. That's part of the everyday pleasures God built into the world.

This message in the Bible starts at the very beginning. In Genesis one, the biblical beginnings of humanity are structured poetically to climax with the arrival of man and woman. All the stars in the sky and the ocean waters, all the birds in the air and the plants on the ground create a beautiful backdrop for humanity to enter. Days one to three and then days four to six move from the heavens above to the closest surroundings of humanity on land. What does that mean? It means the Bible views the formation of the universe as fundamentally an anthropic story. OK, what does that mean? Put simply, humanity is the centerpiece of the universe and served by all the other parts. This framework for our existence is life-changing. The world was designed for humanity to properly oversee and enjoy everything it has to offer.

So embrace it. If you have the luxury of eating good food everyday, don't forget to enjoy yourself. If you have music that makes you smile, play it while you drive. If you have the privilege of a job that pays a fair wage, be proud of the work you do when you go home. If you have a good friend, treasure your years of living life together (see Ecclesiastes 4:9-12). Take in a sunset or a sunrise (if you're a morning person). Have fun playing ball in the park with your nephew or even playing catch with a dog that God created for you enjoy.

There are so many ways to do the good gifts God gave us in the world. In my younger days, I'd have a secluded place by a local lake to read and take motorcycle rides on sunny days. In my mid-life years, I make sure to celebrate every child's achievement and each major milestone at work. None of these everyday joys fall outside the sacred. These are not the base desires of human beings. These are God-intended joys built into our existence.

It is true that we must be careful here. I'm not telling you to become obsessed with personal pleasure. Ecclesiastes 7:4 cautions, "The mind of the wise is in the house of mourning while the mind of fools dwells in the house of pleasure." Enjoying God's goodness in life is not pursuing endless pleasure. That will never work. That road leads to discontentment. As Ecclesiastes 5:10 reminds us, "He who loves money will not be satisfied by it." That's true of any other path to temporary pleasure. What Ecclesiastes encourages us to do is appreciate the goodness of God that is right in front of us whatever our place in life may be. It is not something else to chase into the future. The everyday joys of life are not supposed to turn into another self-indulgent obsession that creates more discontent than fulfillment. God's gifts of food, drink and work are something for us to savor wherever we may be, in whatever lot "God has given us" (Ecclesiastes 8:15).

The meaning of everyday pleasures is skin deep without more to the story. That's why Ecclesiastes 2:24 asks, "For who can eat and drink and find pleasure in their work without Him?"" Experiencing life's pleasures without a sense of recognition that someone personally built them into the fabric of life for you will strip them of their value. But when you know that someone designed great pleasure into the small things for you to enjoy, it couldn't be more special. It's like when my wife surprises me with my favorite Latte in the middle of the work day or when I bring home her favorite ice cream for a snack after the kids go to sleep. Savoring little things from one who loves you can fill many mundane moments of life with joy. Don't let that beauty pass you by because you keep looking over God's everyday pleasures at some idyllic future you may never reach.

GOD'S GIFT OF WATER

Beyond remembering the source of life's goodness ourselves, we should think of what action we can take to imitate Jesus' miracle and demonstrate his life-giving presence to others. Specifically, how can we reenact the purpose of the water-to-wine miracle in our context today?

If Jesus showed himself to be the source of life and vegetation by providing wine at a wedding, how could we re-create the same dynamic? I have thought long and hard about this question. I think a number of options are available. I will only mention one here to give you an idea of how to respond faithfully to John 2:1-11. Remember, an appropriate response to the actions and instructions of Jesus always involves both fidelity and creativity. We must be *faithful* to the point of his choices and words, but we must be *creative* as we find ways to reenact them in our own time and place. One of the most prevalent ways to reenact the purpose of Jesus' water-to-wine miracle is creating clean water in communities where there is none. Clean water is both life's basic building block and a missing ingredient in the lives of almost 1 billion people.

If you have grown up in an industrialized nation, it is difficult to imagine life without water. Every time you turn on the faucet, it just comes out. Your only concern about water is not how sanitary it may be but how good it tastes. We use filters and infuse berry flavors to make it more appealing to our taste buds. For almost 1 billion people they would be ecstatic to have stale tap water. They would even be happy with a water hole less than 4 miles away that wasn't full of mud and human waste.

To provide a local source for clean water in the remote areas of Africa can have the same effect that Jesus' miracle had on John's audience. It can be a sign of God's presence that every community member tastes. It is a real opportunity for us to reenact the purpose of Jesus' miracle around the world. Instead of turning water into wine, we can create clean water out of disease-infested water. Where dry climates leave people thirsty, we can drill deep wells that provide year-round access to water. People who were cut off from this basic necessity can experience God's blessing of life one drink at a time. That one compassionate action can mean more than a thousand words spoken in a place where thirst goes unquenched.

UN statistics conclude that a child dies every 15 seconds from water-related illnesses. Water-related illnesses prevent thousands of kids from regular school attendance. Bouts of painful diarrhea keep them out of school, underweight, and malnourished. If a community doesn't have clean water, its people will struggle with unstable health, miss out on educational opportunities, and ultimately remain in difficult economic circumstances. No one in those situations experiences the goodness of life. None of them can practice the advice of Ecclesiastes 3:12 and "eat and drink and enjoy the fruits of their labor, for these are gifts from God." They don't have those gifts from God because they don't have clean water.

WHO IS PROVIDING CLEAN WATER?

Numerous people have seen the effects of life without clean water and are doing something about it. I have actually counted 88 different U.S. charities focused on this issue. Three organizations that I have personally evaluated and seen a commitment to demonstrate the loving presence of God with clean water are: *Healing Waters*, *Water Missions*, and *Living Water*.

Each ministry takes a slightly different approach to providing clean water around the world. *Healing Waters* primarily builds water purification outlets in areas where the public water source is contaminated. *Water Missions* uses mobile purification tanks in rural areas for both disaster relief and community development projects. *Living Water* creates world-class teams of well drillers to dig and repair water wells in areas without an adequate water source. In each case the ministries deliver the water in the name of Jesus. The clean water is a sign of God's love provided by people compelled by that love.

Although the water-to-wine miracle seems worlds away and without clear significance at first glance, its purpose is little different than a cup of clean water given in Jesus' name. Both are signs of God's presence. All three organizations listed above have a vault of testimonies to that effect. Let me share just one story from *Living Water*.

BUILDING WATER WELLS TO REENACT JESUS' MIRACLE

Nigeria is one of 13 countries that lies along the "Tension Belt" of Africa. The "Tension Belt" is where the predominantly Muslim north Africa meets the predominantly Christian and Animist south. That clash of perspectives has fueled brutal violence in recent years.

The religious differences are exaggerated by ethnic tension. Nigeria alone has 250 unique ethnic groups. Often the ethnic groups that practice different religions fight each other for power all across the central region of the country.

In the central Nigerian town of Egbe, the tension is palpable. Half of the population is Muslim, and the other half practices Christianity or Animism. The Muslim half of the population comes from the Fulani tribe while the rest are from the Yoruba tribe. *Living Water* chose this divided community for one of its well projects.

Living Water started with one well at a hospital in Egbe run by the Evangelical Churches of West Africa. For a hospital that serves a local population of 600,000 people, clean water is a game changer. Before *Living Water* dug the well, patients with long hospital stays had to bring their own water! Can you believe that!? Just imagine if you had to bring your own water to relatives at hospitals in the U.S. It's easy to see how the sanitation and nutrition offered at the hospital has improved by leaps and bounds since *Living Water* showed up.

Living Water also went to a Muslim community outside the city called Okoloke and dug a well to replace the polluted ponds the people were using as a water source. In a country where some Christians have entered Muslim communities with machetes, bows, and arrows, *Living Water*'s local Christian staff came with commercial drilling equipment. Instead of a violent confrontation, the Muslims of Okoloke received access to God's good water.

The stories of Egbe and Okoloke are no exception. *Living Water* Nigeria has taken the same approach in Nigeria's capital Lagos. In one instance, *Living Water* dug a well on church property and that church ran water pipes to three taps that serve Christians and Muslims on Karimu Street. Even a mosque two blocks down the street now has access to clean water. That clean water source is a bold sign that Jesus brings the goodness of God's "good" creation to everyone.

In Lagos and in Okoloke, *Living Water* is re-creating the purpose of the water-to-wine miracle. They are demonstrating the loving presence of Jesus through the creation of clean water sources. As Muslims taste and benefit from the clean water, they are experiencing the loving presence of God. In fact, eight people in Okoloke decided right away to follow Jesus after tasting the water and understanding why *Living Water* had brought it to their village.

GET INVOLVED

We can all participate in the provision of clean water around the world. You could financially support any of the organizations above who are providing clean water in Jesus' name. For example, by supporting *Healing Waters* with $50 you give someone access to clean water for life. That seems impossible, but they have a self-sustaining business model that makes it work.

You could also visit the *Water Missions* manufacturing site in Charleston, SC and see how solar technology is being built into state-of-the-art mobile water purification systems. Then you could sign up to work a manufacturing shift and build one yourself.

If you want to get more involved, you can sign up for a volunteer trip with *Living Water* and learn how to drill and construct water wells. You will be able to learn the basics of drilling for water at their Texas training center and then fly down to help construct a well in Central America. It is an unforgettable experience for you and your friends and family. You will see first hand where the need is and meet the people whose lives you are changing.

I have been involved in providing clean water in a number of communities for the past few years. It is a ripe opportunity for demonstrating the presence of God's goodness. With the right explanation you can reenact the point of the water-to-wine miracle. You can actually give someone the ability to drink and experience this "gift from God."

GET CREATIVE

Don't let the water-to-wine miracle just be an intriguing story in the Gospels. Take action and make it your model for providing signs of God's loving presence in each new context you encounter. Whether you use water, trees, or another creative medium, you can follow Jesus now that you know what he was doing.

One of my son's friends decided to get creative this past summer. She committed to raising $50 so that another girl could have water for life. Since child labor laws prevented her from getting a job at 5 years of age, Ruthie decided to use her artistic talents.

Ruthie organized an art sale in her backyard (with a little help from her parents). To raise the $50, she slaved away for days making 50 unique paintings to sell for $1 each. Although she wanted to give up along the way, she kept her creative juices flowing so that another girl could drink clean water.

Ruthie's water-based artistic wonders did the trick. The art sale did turn into clean water for another child. Parents in our community brought their children to the backyard art sale to buy original artwork and to let their kids see Ruthie's example. Her labor of love raised $50 that night and who knows what her efforts will accomplish in the future. What I do know is that people will be drinking water given in the name of Jesus because she took action.

That's Ruthie's story. Now use the questions below to figure out how you will get started demonstrating the benevolent presence of God to people who are missing it.

Reenacting the way

1. Do you think the new sustenance that comes from the trees that *Plant with Purpose* plants and the wells that *Living Water* digs is a superfluous illustration of God's love—i.e., it just draws a crowd to hear about the Christian faith? Or do you think it actually presents God's loving presence?

2. If you don't want to participate in the Orthodox "Blessing of the Waters" at the beginning of each year, is there an activity or experience like a hike or a wine party or harvesting your house garden that would remind you of God's benevolence in the good things of life? Maybe a change to daily rhythms where you eat slower or savor things longer is your best embrace of God's goodness.

3. What actions do you take to create symbolic experiences of God's benevolent presence for people around you? Think about personal experiences you have had where the loving presence of God became palpable.

CHAPTER 7

MAKING A LAME GUY WALK: DON'T LET CULTURE TELL YOU HOW TO HELP YOURSELF

Focal Point: What directions does Jesus give to us by healing a lame guy putting his hope in culturally created powers behind water bubbles?

VOICES THAT LIE

Fabricated promises only disappoint. Problem is: who can tell the difference from a promise you can trust?

If I trusted the commercial advertising on TV last night, I could solve most of my problems with a few strategic purchases. My lack of style could be corrected by the latest Fall fashions. Problems with an undependable vehicle could be resolved by a $500 monthly lease payment. Purchasing the right light beer would stop people from mocking me. Even my old furniture could look new again with "stainz-B-gonzo." Only problem is then I'd be broke, in need of more closet space, disgusted with the urine flavor of light see-through beer and suffocating from an allergic reaction to an improperly tested fabric cleaner.

Promises of a better life and a better me fly around our world like pollen in a southern summer. We see them, hear them and read them everyday. Most of those promises don't offer the best solutions. They just pad the bottom line of commercial enterprises. So we better be discerning, or we will get sucked into the latest lie. We all know the world has a persuasive way of selling us a set of fabricated promises, but it's an arduous task to be one step ahead of the game.

I'll never forget the first time I dove into the world of prescriptopia. That's right. I just wrote "prescriptopia." I'm not talking about auditioning for a futuristic TV drama where telepathy has superseded the necessity of literacy. Yeah, think about that one for a while. I'm talking about the modern rage to manipulate every "abnormality" in our bodies with prescription drugs.

Rarely can you watch 1 hour of television anymore without an advertisement for new drugs. They promise to lower your body fat or control your bladder for the small price of nausea, dizziness, headaches, uncontrollable twitches, night blindness, and possible death. I don't have a clue how half these drugs get approved by the FDA after demonstrating the ability to do more harm than good, but that's life today.

That being said, I still decided to trust my doctor's advice about prescriptions. He said I could have a better quality of life with the simple addition of a couple prescription drugs each day. So I went to the pharmacy and waited for my prescripted utopia to take effect.

To give you the full story, you should know that I entered prescriptopia a few weeks before I got married. I wanted to be the best "me" that my wife could marry. Things did not work out as planned.

After taking the pills for a couple of weeks, I developed some side effects. Those side effects become "front and center" effects on my honeymoon. During the most romantic moments of my young adult life, my nose would suddenly begin streaming blood. Every other time we kissed, I'd immediately run for the nearest restroom to recover. And a nasty bout with dry mouth turned my tongue into a reptilian creature. These two effects would have been perfectly suited for a zombie in some second-rate horror film, but they scared my wife half to death. How would you feel if every time you kissed someone their nose started bleeding and lips felt like 60 grit sandpaper? It was not cool.

171

Prescriptopia was no utopia at all. The promise of a better life and a better me did not pan out. Needless to say, I stopped taking those pills right away. The soothing voice behind the commercial ads for those drugs was a liar.

When John wrote down his stories about Jesus, he was living in a world full of Greco-Roman voices. He'd moved into the region around Ephesus among thousands of Jews and new believers who believed the fabricated promises of the Greco-Roman world. He knew that it would take some serious work to expose the lies. So he decided to tell stories about Jesus that silenced the lying voices.

John wanted the actions of Jesus to dismantle the cultural voices that lie. So he chose episodes from the life of Jesus that didn't make the cut for most other Gospel writers. The cultural infrastructure of the Greco-Roman world weighed heavily on his mind when he picked out narratives for his scroll. That is why he chose a somewhat confusing story of a lame man looking for help in bubbling water.

In John 5, Jesus pulls off a classic miracle. He heals a crippled man. One minute the man is stuck on a mat, and the next minute he is walking around. Of course, John's message isn't that simple. He adds some details that you don't find in any other miracle story in the Gospels. Pay attention to the narrative detail in John 5:1-11, especially the bold highlights.

1 After these things there was a feast of the Jews, and Jesus went up to Jerusalem.
2 Now there is in Jerusalem by the sheep gate **a pool, which is called in Hebrew Bethesda, having five porticoes**.
3 **In these lay a multitude of those who were sick, blind, lame, and withered**, [waiting for the moving of the waters;
4 for an angel of the Lord went down at certain seasons into the pool and stirred up the water; whoever then first, after the stirring up of the water, stepped in was made well from whatever disease with which he was afflicted.]
5 A man was there who had been **ill for thirty-eight years**.

6 When Jesus saw him lying there, and knew that he had already been a long time in that condition, He said to him, "Do you wish to get well?"

7 The sick man answered Him, "Sir, **I have no man to put me into the pool when the water is stirred up,** but while I am coming, another steps down before me."

8 Jesus said to him, "Get up, pick up your pallet and walk."

9 Immediately the man became well, and picked up his pallet and began to walk.

Now it was the Sabbath on that day.

10 So the Jews were saying to the man who was cured, "It is the Sabbath, and it is not permissible for you to carry your pallet."

11 But he answered them, "He who made me well was the one who said to me, 'Pick up your pallet and walk.' "

This episode is Jesus' response to a mixture of first century voices. The obvious voice comes from Jewish regulators who didn't want to see any pallet-carrying on the Sabbath. Rabbis had developed strict rules about the appearance of work performed on the Sabbath. Picking up a mat and carrying it around broke those rules.

The religious regulators would rather see cripples stuck on the ground than a guy walking with his hands full. In a backwards manner, their regulations actually encouraged oppression over freedom. There was no space for people to break out of the molds that restricted them. This restrictive voice was a powerful force in Jesus' day.

Jesus' command to "pick up your pallet and walk" said that voice can't be trusted. The voice that touted restrictive regulation as the pathway to righteous living was a lie. Jesus wanted to expose it. Regulations that prevented people from prospering and celebrating the kindness of God had no place in Jesus' economy.

FREEDOM ISN'T FREEDOM TO DO ANYTHING

Regulations aren't always bad. Sometimes a little structure that keeps you away from self-destructive habits is a good solution. But waiting until the Sabbath ended to pick up a mat didn't protect this guy from harm. It kept him stuck on the floor hopeless. That is why

Jesus didn't give a rip about the established religious rule. That regulation didn't make any sense.

But Jesus did find the guy later in the day to give him a better restriction. He warned the former cripple, "Behold, you have become well; do not sin anymore, so that nothing worse happens to you." Yikes! That is a command that comes with a strong motivator. To be honest, that command is much bigger than just keeping your arms empty on the Sabbath. Jesus actually told the former cripple to stop sinning all together.

You may expect me as a Bible scholar to have a crafty way to lessen its impact. You might think I should say, "That was then and this is now." Or, you may think I should produce a better interpretation of the Greek that tones down the statement to an exaggerated statement for effect. But I have no grounds to dismiss Jesus' clear command to sin no more or face the consequences. He thought that this guy could mess himself up even worse than 38 years of disability if he kept sinning.

Jesus' confident belief that you could screw up your life by doing stupid stuff shouldn't be that surprising. If you decide to go against the grain of how life is best lived, you shouldn't expect the best. No one gets to escape the consequences of bad behavior even though we try to ignore them or excuse them. That's why Jesus puts a simple but serious challenge in front of this guy with a newly found freedom to walk.

FREEDOM TO SUCCEED

If you want to be in Jesus' business of freeing people to a restored life, it's going to take some concrete directions and restrictive guidelines. One of my favorite groups in the U.S. that sets boys free from the entrapments of poverty, broken families, and crime does this exact thing. H.O.P.E. Farm in Fort Worth, TX redirects urban boys headed toward detainment, death, or destitution (yes, that's my original alliteration) and puts them on a path to succeed. Started by a former street cop named Gary Randall, H.O.P.E. Farm frees these boys from the typical destiny of a broken, low-income home. And how do they do it? They create freedom while implementing restrictions.

If you are a single mom who wants her son to be mentored and tutored at H.O.P.E. Farm, you better be ready to sacrifice. Every mom must commit to having her son(s) at every required event on time. Every boy must commit to wearing his pants up at his waist and being well-groomed. If mom decides to have a boyfriend live in the home with her son, then her son gets kicked out of the program. If a boy decides he doesn't want to do his homework, then he has to find somewhere else to go. To free these kids from the statistically probable and personally painful outcomes of their peers, they must be punctual, dependable, academically committed, safe at home, and publicly presentable. If the restrictions were any less, it would be a disservice to the boys and their moms.

Some critics might call their regulations discriminatory. I call them necessary. H.O.P.E. Farm is protecting these boys and their mothers from living life in a way that leads downward. The restrictions prevent them from engaging in self-destructive habits. It is the same approach Jesus took when he found the former cripple and warned him not to sin anymore. You can't give freedom to people who keep putting themselves in situations that have negative consequences. True freedom isn't the ability to do anything you want. True freedom is the opportunity to do what is best.

H.O.P.E. Farm's ability to use restrictions to free boys from a life of self-destruction is a total game-changer. Boys have gone from angry victims of abuse to scholarship recipients at major universities. One participant used to be locked in the closet at home for such long periods that he began to eat carpet. Now he is a high-performing student at a local school with a growing number of extra-curricular successes. Boys on the street who used to insult you for walking through their neighborhood now greet you with respect, eye-to-eye contact, and a firm handshake. The revolution in how these boys look, perform, think, act, and even greet you sets them up for a whole new level of success in life.

Before coming to H.O.P.E. Farm, many of the boys had the freedom to do whatever they wanted in their neighborhood. But none of them had the freedom to succeed. That kind of freedom comes with life-giving guidelines.

A Greek Voice in the Room

Jesus had to quell the voice of Jewish regulators who put up the wrong restrictions. He had to tell the former cripple to disregard the pallet-carrying rule and now attend to his restriction on sin. Weeding through the religious noise of the time wasn't easy. Jesus' challenge made a lot of Jewish power brokers angry. However, the voice of Jewish regulators wasn't the only sound in the room.

The other voice bubbling up in the water where the lame man sat is a bit harder for us to hear. But every pilgrim to Jerusalem heard it crying out by the pool near the sheep gate. The message about magical healing waters resounded from an ancient Greek voice—a Greek voice that came to town a couple hundred years before Jesus. It's going to take an historical journey to tune your hearing into its fabricated promises. So hang on for the ride.

Most educated Americans have heard of Alexander the Great. You either remember it from world history class or saw the movie with Colin Farrell. If you can't recall much from either experience, he was the guy who conquered the known world of his time (Alexander not Colin Farrell). He conquered all the major cities and kingdoms from Greece to India between 334 BCE and 323 BCE. His conquest is impressive on its own and I could talk about fighting elephants and flanking armies for a while, but we have a more poignant question to ask about the healing of the lame man: How does Alexander's 11-year rampage across the world intersect with Jesus' miracle by a pool? Unfortunately, it has nothing to do with battle-ready elephants. It comes down to how the conquest changed the culture in Jerusalem.

After Alexander died his early death at age 33 in 323 BCE, the now conquered world was subjected to the language and customs of the Greeks. Jerusalem itself was ruled for a while by the Greek Ptolemaic Empire and later by the Greek Seleucid Empire until the Jews successfully revolted in 164 BCE. The period of Greek rule over 160 years left an impression on the Jewish homeland. The Jews had been forced to accept Greek customs (like running around nude in the gymnasium), the Greek language, and even Greek religion.

Turning the Jewish homeland into a Greek world was a process historians call Hellenization. One ancient Jewish historian captured the ins and outs of Hellenization in a history book called *1 Maccabees* (FYI, the book is named after the Maccabean family that led the successful revolt against the Greeks in 164 BCE).

Here is a brief summary of the orders that a king of the Greek Seleucid Empire decreed to fully Hellenize the Jewish homeland:

> The king sent messengers with letters to Jerusalem and to the cities of Judah, ordering them to follow customs foreign to their land: to prohibit burnt offerings, sacrifices, and libations in the sanctuary, to profane the sabbaths and feast days, to desecrate the sanctuary and the priests, to build pagan altars and temples and shrines, to sacrifice swine and unclean animals, to leave their sons uncircumcised, and to let themselves be defiled with every kind of impurity and abomination, so that they might forget the law and change all their observances (1 Maccabees 1:44-49).

This comprehensive program to replace the Jewish religion with Greek counterparts changed the face of Jerusalem. "Pagan altars and temples and shrines" appeared all over the city. One shrine to the god Zeus Olympios was even erected on the altar of burnt offerings in the temple itself. These acts of pure desecration ultimately led to a violent and successful Jewish rebellion. The Jews (led by the Maccabean family) freed themselves from Greek kings who had forced them "to follow customs foreign to their land." In the revolt of 164 BCE, the Jews took back the temple and purified it from every pagan desecration.

However, Greek influence didn't disappear. Remnants of Greek cultural and religious life remained long after the Jewish rebellion of 164 BCE. Customs and religious centers built outside of the temple survived the cleansing. One such pagan sanctuary lie just to the north of the Temple outside the city walls. That sanctuary was built around pools near the sheep gate. Sound familiar?

Now there is in Jerusalem by the sheep gate a pool, which is called in Hebrew Bethesda, having five porticoes. In these lay a multitude of those who were sick, blind, lame, and withered (John 5:2-3)

HEALING IN THE WATERS

The Greeks had long worshipped a god of healing called Asklepius. In his honor they built Asklepions (ancient healing centers) all across the Greek empire. The ill and disabled seeking god's help would flock to these regional healing centers. Patients would first drink and bathe in the waters at the Asklepion and then sleep within the temple precincts. They slept on mats laid out in a section of the inner sanctum of the Temple precincts called the *abaton*. During dreams, Asklepius or his serpents would reportedly appear to the sick and give them clues about their healing. Sometimes he would immediately heal them on the spot.

The recipes for recovery normally involved ritual bathing, abstinence from food, sacrifices, incubation, dreams, and then the healing. The dreams all took place in the *abaton*. The legends of what happened inside the *abaton* are quite entertaining.

One gentleman named Hagestratos suffered from an unflinching headache. So he went to sleep waiting for Asklepius to help him out. Surprisingly, his experience in the *abaton* took him beyond healing to a whole new level of insight. As the story goes,

> Hagestratos was oppressed by insomnia because of headaches. When he was in the *abaton*, he slept and saw a dream. The god seemed, after curing the pain in his head and standing him up naked, to teach him the attack used in the pancration. When day came he went out well and not much later won the pancration at Nemea.

The pancration was a Greek athletic contest that combined wrestling and boxing without any rules. It was the ancient Ultimate Fighting Championship (UFC) or Mixed Martial Arts (MMA). Hagestratos was probably suffering the effects of his last concussion from a fight when he first entered the *abaton*. And Asklepius gave him exactly what he needed. He got relief from his headache and learned the ultimate takedown move. Who knew the god of healing could be so versatile? Of course, Hagestratos's mat in the *abaton* was probably filled back up with the competitor he defeated at the pancration in Nemea. Looks like Asklepius had a racquet going for his recovery business!

I can't say I've ever had a doctor write a prescription and then show me how to knock someone unconscious, although that would have been more valuable than my prescriptopia experience. Then again, I'm not sure if I'd be impressed or just report the doctor for breaking the Hippocratic Oath to "do no harm."

I do know there are endless stories about strange healings at the Asklepions. One of my favorites is the case of Heraieus of Mytilene (Don't worry! No one but his mother could have pronounced that name and city of origin correctly the first time). Here is his story.

> Heraieus did not have hair on his head, but a great deal on his chin. Being ashamed because he was laughed at by others, he slept in the shrine. And the god, anointing his head with a drug, made him grow hair.

Yes, it is the first historical record we have of chemically-induced hair regrowth. Even the gods couldn't pull that miracle off without Rogaine! So my brother shouldn't feel that bad about having to use it either (sorry bro!).

Before I digress into too many Greek legends, let me explain the connection between pools of water and Asklepius. It's quite relevant to John's story of a lame man sitting by a pool waiting to be healed. Simply put, the Greeks attributed the healing powers of the Earth spirits to natural springs. This belief made its way into the cult of Asklepius. His temples were typically constructed near sacred springs with shallow pools and baths that offered healing and recuperative services. Mosaics of Asklepius representing this mythology picture him standing in a pool of water granting healing to patients.

The association between divine healing activity and water perpetuated itself at every Asklepion. It wasn't the only ingredient in the recipes for recovery, but it was dominant. It was a cultural mainstay throughout the Hellenized world. If the Greeks had taken over your country for a while, you'd probably get exposed to the same cultural phenomenon. And that is exactly what happened in Jerusalem.

THE ASKLEPION IN JERUSALEM

John 5:2-3 describes the place where the lame man was healed as a temple structure with 5 porticoes and a pool. Many commentators have mistakenly associated the structure with a pair of deep pools that stored water north of the old city gates (see archaeological remains of one of the deep pools in photo). Be careful that your study Bible or internet resource doesn't mislead you here.

The logic has been: 2 deep pools are separated and surrounded by walls. Therefore 4 porticoes would have surrounded the pools like a box with the 5th portico running through the middle. However, identifying 2 huge water storage pools with a depth of 15 meters as the location of the healing miracle doesn't' square with the facts.

The facts from the story imply a pool that a lame man could step into. That doesn't compute with 15-meter deep pools. Admittedly it would put a cripple out of his misery, but that wasn't the kind of ultimate healing the lame man sought. The stirring of the waters in the story implies that the shallow pools are connected to a spring that surged on occasion. Bubbling springs in shallow pools and baths are quite typical of sanctuaries for Asklepius.

Archaeological excavations have uncovered the base of a temple in the area just north of the Sheep gate mentioned in John 5:2. A number of small pools fed by bubbling springs have been identified next to the temple structure. Not surprisingly, the temple structure with 5 porticoes was a common design for Asklepions in the Hellenized world.

The 5 porticoes most likely formed an E-shape with pools tucked in between the walls. Temples to Asklepius have been excavated in other parts of the Hellenized world with similar E-shaped sanctuaries. The archaeological site is hard to make sense of today when you visit. The remains you see are a mixture of Herod's water system, Greek healing pools, Christian church ruins, and old Roman structures. In fact, the Romans appear to have built up a shrine to Asklepius and expanded the healing center around 200 CE. For our purposes, it is most important to know that healing shrines have been located at the site in rock hewn caves with three or four steps leading down to them. Those healing shrines built around spring-fed pools with steps leading down to them present the most relevant backdrop for the healing miracle of John 5 (see picture).

What does all this mean? It means Jesus was walking into another god's territory when he told the lame man to get up. He was confronting a cultural myth.

Why did Jesus heal a lame man next to a pool? What did his actions mean? That is the same basic question we have asked over and over again throughout this book. It is the question you should ask about every action you find in the Bible. Understanding the purpose of Jesus' actions in their original context is the key to reenacting it fittingly today. You have to understand the dynamics of the original situation or your imagination will run wild. In the case of John 5, you have to see that Jesus pulls off this miracle in another healer's territory.

When Jesus heals the lame man looking for divine aid in a religious fabrication, he is claiming to be the real deal. His actions are speaking a language that John's Hellenized Jewish audience understood. Asklepius is a fake. He is a pipe dream you can't depend on. If you are looking for restoration, you don't need to wait for the next bubble from the healing Earth spirits. Jesus can do what everyone is trying to find in spring-fed pools.

Here's the point. Jesus is your way out of every cultural myth that keeps you in an endless cycle of failed promises. He is the substance in a superficial world. Of course, our cultural myths don't look like Greco-Roman legends. We don't go to the local Asclepion for healing. We don't mistake natural phenomena for gods, but we do follow the latest trends promising a better life. And we find time and again that the new trends and the old lies don't turn into the life we seek. They often hardly work at all.

HELP THAT REALLY WORKS

Freedom from the cultural myths of our time is needed. We may not ask Asklepius for dreams that reveal magical medical treatments or wait by stirring spring waters for the cleansing powers of the earth (maybe you do but I don't). We may not go to divine healing centers instead of doctors, but we do buy into a hundred other cultural myths. We just don't always notice.

Cultural traditions that keep us wandering around in false hope don't stand out. They blend in. They are part of the common parlance and practice of our times. You've got to tease them out from the everyday scenery if you want to set yourself free. Typically, I find that you have to ask good questions to find what you're looking for.

The big question to ask is: Which recommended solutions in our culture keep us waiting for healing we will never find? The endless nuances of this question come up in every painful circumstance from which we wish to free ourselves.

One question I had early on in life had to do with programs offered to addicts. Why do we recommend that addicts go through a 28-day detox program if the success rate is rarely ever measured above 12%? It seemed like a classic case of fabricated promises that don't work. Why send someone through a hospital program that has little chance of success? That sounds dangerously close to telling a lame man to jump in a pool to heal himself.

Those low odds stood out to me because I had read about another program reportedly producing a 67% success rate. The organization Teen Challenge runs 12-18 month residential programs for people with "life-controlling problems." It is not an official drug rehabilitation program, but many beneficiaries of their residential programs are addicts in some sense of the word.

David Wilkerson started the first Teen Challenge program in 1958 when he moved to New York City to work with teenage gang members and socially marginalized people. He believed he had the solution to rampant problems among those populations. Simply put, he thought that a powerful and sustained introduction to Jesus could transform their lives.

As Teen Challenge grew and became known for freeing addicts from life-controlling problems, people wanted to evaluate the efficacy of the Christ-centered residential program. In 1975, Dr. Catherine Hess partnered with the University of Chicago and the National Medical Services to study a class of participants from 1968. The results were impressive. 67% of the graduates were drug-free as indicated by a urinalysis test. To be clear, the Teen Challenge definition of "drug-free" means abstaining from all use of narcotics, marijuana, alcohol, and cigarettes. Many other drug rehab programs consider consistent cigarette smoking and occasional use of marijuana acceptable.

Teen Challenge's success has been applauded by some and disputed by others. One doctoral student found that Teen Challenge's success rates were similar to other rehabilitation programs if the participants continued to attend Alcoholics Anonymous after graduating from the shorter rehab programs. The Texas Freedom Network Education Fund has also highlighted that 35-40% of program participants drop out of Teen Challenge programs before graduation. Therefore, the graduate long-term success rate is misleading. Another factor contributing to the success is Teen Challenge's ability to select its program participants rather than receive court-mandated participants.

Despite all these caveats and considerations, people that complete the program are more likely to stay drug-free than not. That is a whole lot better than giving someone a 1 in 8 chance of success. That is a promise of freedom that normally comes true. That is help that really works in a world of broken promises.

When the graduates from the 1968 class were asked about what makes the program successful, the most common answer was one word: Jesus. The camaraderie, the staff and the structure all played a role. But the number one reason for its impact on people's lives is the powerful and sustained introduction to Jesus. He is the one that helps them when nothing else can. He is the one who shows them a way to freedom. He is the one who provides the help that really worked. That's exactly what the lame man inside an Asklepion found when he met Jesus.

EVERY CULTURE LIES

Most of us have heard that you can't believe everything you hear on TV. But some of us just can't resist. We see the word "SALE," and it's over. We are sold. We find out that our food preparatory process has been hallow and hampered because we never had a Z1000 Vegetable steamer with auto-injection butter and olive oil side cars (hey, please don't steal my original idea here before I take it to the world on QVC). These messages are coming at us with mixed shades of truth and deception. It is remarkably difficult to differentiate between the false promises and substantive announcements.

I can remember one visit to an Express store where I let my guard down. I needed some Jeans, and the trend of the day was pre-ripped Denim. I consider myself a fairly hard-nosed analytical bloke so my mind quickly began to process the situation. My first thought: those Jeans look cool. My second thought: won't they rip farther in the washing machine? I faced a conundrum. Do I risk the ripping for the sake of the cool? Or do I trust my analytical mind and wait for the trend to go back to Jeans that aren't already ruined when you buy them?

Thankfully Express has clothing experts at every store. Those retail gurus are required to wear the store's products and run the cash register. So I approached the cash register and asked if the ripped Jeans somehow magically rip no farther in the wash. A well-intentioned young woman promised me: "I've got the same style and haven't had any problems." What a relief! And they were on "SALE."

Despite my better judgment, I trusted the brand name. Despite years of learning to research, analyze and read between the lines, I succumbed to the confirmation of a teenager working retail part-time. It's one of those moments that reminds me how you can't trust someone's judgment even if they have a doctorate. I may have earned the credentials to be a professor, but I am still sucked in by the simple antics of a good "SALE" and a false promise.

If you're wondering how it turned out, the Jeans ripped farther each time they were washed. I eventually had both knees exposed and an ever-increasing display of my upper right thigh. Try not to picture that.

Voices claiming to represent Jesus' way often don't give us much more dependable direction. The classic example is the message: trust God and he will make everything better. I'm not talking about prosperity preachers who say you will get rich. That's such a transparent lie I don't have to waste my words on it. The Christian cultural lie that presents itself more subtly has to do with the "easy life." What God wants to do for you is make everything easier to handle. The false promise is: Jesus creates an escape path from life's difficulties.

Of course, this false promise gets delivered in much more acceptable phrases and punch lines. "God wants to heal you." "God wants to protect you." "God wants to bless you." "God wants to take away your problems." "Jesus wants to calm the storms of your life." All these statements sound great and are true in some sense if placed in the proper context. But usually we interpret them as promises to resolve all the problems in our life. We hear them as one giant promise from God to make life easy whenever it feels hard.

The problem is: character is formed in the fire of difficult times. One of Jesus' first followers said, "Classify problems you face as pure joy" (James 1:3). That's something he learned from watching what Jesus did. Jesus exemplified a love that led to sacrifice and pain and all sorts of personal problems. He invites and even commands people to take the same approach. His suggestion to "take up your cross and follow" is not a pathway to relaxation and serenity. It's an invitation to suffer. You have to reconcile that reality with any understanding of God's promise to care for and bless you.

The inconsistency of Jesus' call to troublesome living and contemporary voices promising the easy life comes to a head for me in the Christian cruise phenomenon. The idea that one can develop his or her spirituality on the open sea next to the pool is hard for me to reconcile. Remember what Jesus said to one of his disciples that told him, "I will follow you wherever you go." Jesus warned him: "Foxes have holes and the birds of the air have nests, but the Son of Man has nowhere to lay his head." Jesus was making a point. This "following him" stuff is not easy. So how would sitting on a deck chair with a tropical drink in hand help me discover the way of Jesus? I'd certainly enjoy it, but I'd be deceiving myself if I mistook that piece of paradise as a path to know Jesus.

We've been hoodwinked if we think Jesus wants us living life with no problems. Now you might object. You might remind me that Jesus also said, "Come to me all who are tired and burdened, and I will give you rest. … For my yoke is easy, and my load is light." That sounds a lot like a Christian cruise, right? I'm glad you brought that up. Or at least I hope you're glad I brought that up.

When Jesus talks about giving you rest from a heavy yoke, he is adapting language that the Rabbis used to refer to "extra rules" they added to the Law. The "yoke" of a Rabbi consisted of all the extra instructions for life that were created from one's interpretation and application of the Hebrew Scriptures. Rabbis in Jesus' day were telling people how far to walk, when God would and would not accept them at the Temple, where it was acceptable to spit, whether to carry half a fig or whole figs on the Sabbath, when to cover your donkey on the weekend, etc. Jesus doesn't do that. He doesn't add thousands of microscopic rules to oppress you. He keeps it simple. He tells you to "love your neighbor." He also tells you to "deny yourself." But he doesn't tell you, "I'm here to solve your problems and give you an easy life."

I'm not saying Jesus doesn't want you to be blessed. But his idea of being blessed isn't a more comfortable, pain-free life. Jesus says, "Blessed are you when men hate you and ostracize you and insult you and scorn your name as evil for my sake" (Luke 6:22). That doesn't sound like a blessing I'd want. It doesn't sound like the protection and favor people falsely promise that God provides. That's because it's not. Jesus' way endures pain and problems. It doesn't avoid all of them.

Jesus' way only makes sense with the bigger picture in mind. Endurance through difficult circumstances builds character and leaves a counter-cultural witness. It serves a purpose. The idea that God wants to navigate you away from problems is a disappointing cultural myth. That myth hangs around too many discussions about the way Jesus walked. That myth excuses a growing industry of Christian comforts that promise spiritual renewal and growth in a vacation context that defies the path Jesus blazed. Don't buy it.

Just remember, the American culture and the Christian culture are equally culpable for creating new practices with fabricated promises that only disappoint.

NO MORE WANDERING

One of the most unusual details in the healing narrative of John 5 is the mention of how long the man has suffered. The man has been crippled for 38 years. Adding this detail about the duration of the man's condition makes the story stand out in the Gospel of John. How so? The fact is Jesus heals a bunch of people in the book. But no one else gets any mention of the length of their suffering. There is something about this man's 38-year battle that John wants his readers to think about.

What are John's readers supposed to be hearing in the reverberations of this man's 38-year battle? I'm going out on a limb to answer this question. I'm going to believe that the context and unusual detail reveal the author's intention to say something bigger—something symbolic.

Since Jesus performs this miracle during a feast that remembered the Jewish Exodus from Egypt, I believe the 38-year time frame is designed to recall the 38-year wilderness wandering. The 38 years Israel spent wandering in the wake of her sin encapsulates the lame man's experience and the plight of John's original audience. The lame man was stuck. He was stuck searching for freedom in a pool. Jesus pulled him out of that aimless venture. He put an end to his wandering in a world of false promises. He freed him from the consequences of a broken world built on sin.

In many ways, John's audience was stuck in the same set of cultural trappings. John's audience lived in a Roman province dominated by centuries of Greek influence. Legendary gods promised healing, entertainment, protection, opportunity, and just about everything else. John's message for them was one of liberation. Jesus could lead them out of their slavery to Greek cultural gods and practices. He could free them from a wilderness full of false promises.

John didn't think cultural norms were harmless. He saw too many people hoping in hopeless causes. He saw too many lies leading people to lives of wandering. And he knew that Jesus could lead them to a better place. So he told his audience that this man's 38 years of suffering is an image of their slavery to cultural myths. He told us all that Jesus can free us from whatever cultural myths had wrongly promised to help us. There is no more need for wandering.

EASIER STARTED THAN SUSTAINED

I must say the simplicity of miracle stories has the potential to mislead us. Jesus may have the way to freedom and promises that do come true, but there is no simple fix. Jesus can make a lame man walk again in an instant, but that's not the whole story. That man could put himself right back in the same position.

Don't forget that Jesus found the former cripple later in the temple and warned him: "Take note, you are better now. But don't sin anymore so that nothing worse happens to you" (John 5:14). This part of the story is unnerving. Apparently, the quick start to this man's redemption must be sustained. If he veers off the path that Jesus prescribes, the consequences could be worse than 38 years of immobility. There really is no quick fix. The rest of Jesus' wisdom for life must be implemented to sustain our new-found freedom.

The best rehabilitation programs and rescue missions understand this fact of life. You can't just throw a homeless guy in a pool and make him better. You can't just say, "Don't screw up your life" after a few nights in a shelter and some hot meals. You may be able to sober him up and get him a good shower, fresh clothes, and a job interview. But that quick turnaround doesn't mean a thing if his day-to-day decisions don't change. The quick start toward independence has to be sustained.

The Denver Rescue Mission knows what it takes. Their New Life program combines spiritual, emotional and addiction counseling with academics, Bible study and work therapy into a curriculum that lasts 12-27 months. The New Life program works people through five phases of ordered, staged growth:

- *Orientation*: Residents identify goals such as obtaining sobriety, overcoming personal problems and making educational progress.

- *Stabilization*: Residents accept and develop disciplines to reach established goals.

- *Application*: Residents attend church activities, complete educational tracks, may work part-time, and/or begin higher education classes.

- *Initiation*: Residents form new, healthy community relationships, continue higher education, mentor people in lower phases, and may work full-time.

- *Independence*: Residents develop an independent living plan and demonstrate self-sufficiency through career employment, savings and spiritual maturity.

Even when people graduate from the New Life program, many participate in post-graduate programs for further mentoring, accountability, counseling, and financial assistance. The quick start in an emergency shelter doesn't stop there. It goes on for years step by step.

Just go ask Dave, a graduate of DRM's New Life program, if he could have turned his life around without the methodical process of the Denver Rescue Mission. Ask him if he could have done it without Jesus. Ask him if he would be sober now and able to spend time with his son. He would say "no" to all of them. He now gets to go fishing with his son because the Denver Rescue Mission knew Jesus could turn him around and their ongoing counseling and mentoring keep him in that direction. Soon he'll have a full-time job welding with his new employable skills. Soon he will get to re-start his relationship with his daughter. The future is bright because his initial turnaround has been followed by wise day-to-day decisions.

As Jesus promised, nothing worse has happened to him down this path. Dave's quick start with sobriety has become a sustained life with friends, family, and a future.

GET UP AND START WALKING

It's time to get up. It's time to shout back. It's time to turn a deaf ear to the voices that lie. Every culture lies, and it's killing us. It's keeping us on a mat by a pool wishing we could jump into the next quick fix scheme.

We may not ask Asclepius for dreams or wait by stirring waters, but we have cultural traditions that promise us what we need in ways that never work. Don't believe them. We can't develop strong character in a problem-free life. We won't develop the resolve to live wisely on a comfortable Christian cruise. Blowing off Jesus' prescription for life won't free us from the oppression of religious requirements. It will set us up to punish ourselves.

Cultural invitations to antagonistically walk against Jesus' way are invitations to make something worse happen to ourselves. It is a one-way road to consequences that could have been avoided. Let us make sure we do not spend our lives wandering in search of what Jesus can provide. Jesus enacted a loud promise when he healed the lame man: Your wandering is over. Now that is hope you can believe in. Don't let the culture tell you how to help yourself when all it has are false promises.

Reenacting the Way

1. What cultural solutions exist for relieving our pain and problems? Use current examples regardless of whether you think they are effective or not.

2. Where has the Christian culture offered a quick fix to our problems and neglected to emphasize how further sin leads to worse consequences?

3. Where has Jesus set you free when other commonly accepted solutions didn't work?

CHAPTER 8

THE LOST MEANING OF THE LAST SUPPER: A CALL TO COMMITMENT NOT JUST COMMUNION

Focal Point: What are we missing when we only say thanks in our hearts while holding a cup and some bread in our hands that used to mean so much more?

STRANGE CEREMONIES WE PARTICIPATE IN

I still remember the first time I met my eventual roommate and lifelong friend from college. We weren't out on the soccer field or jumping off cliffs or flipping off snowboard jumps like we would eventually be. We were both in the college cafeteria—a place I'm still trying to forget. I was finishing up lunch like a normal human being. He was sitting across from 3 other guys drinking tea.

Why does that matter? According to the way I was raised, guys didn't drink tea. Girls drank tea and guys drank coffee. To be clear, old ladies drank tea and men drank strong black coffee. That's how my family did it. That's how I thought everyone should do it.

When I saw 4 guys drinking tea after dinner, I was worried. I wondered if they all grew up without dads or were raised by their grandmothers. I started to get concerned that they had never played competitive sports or got their hands greasy changing leaky water pumps. I know. I've got strong opinions about the way a man should be. Thanks dad.

As these empathetic emotions welled up in me, my mind noticed another odd element in the scenario. None of the guys were talking. Each guy was holding a tea cup in one hand and carefully eyeing the rest of the group. This was getting stranger by the minute.

The unusual character of the scene captured my attention. I was hooked. I didn't know if they were about to start a food fight or a flash mob or a rebellion against the cafeteria ladies at some predetermined time. I wondered if someone might have slipped sleeping pills into their drinks, and I was about to witness a simultaneous 4-man faint. I was wrong. It was much less exciting. All of the sudden the 4 guys lifted their tea in unison, swallowed the remaining backwash, and slammed their cups on the table. Then they laughed at themselves and parted ways. That was it.

I must admit it was a bit anti-climactic. I expected a bigger finale at the end of the "old lady" tea cup liturgy.

A few weeks later I eventually found myself at the same all-male tea cup ceremony. I had penetrated their ranks with some leaf-flavored tea in hand to find out what it meant. I wanted to know the real significance behind the after dinner ceremony. The sad thing is: there was no point. My eventual college roommate just loved playing arbitrary games.

Knowing when to take the final synchronized sip did give each participant a certain acceptability in the group but nothing else. All I ended up learning is the difference between green tea and peppermint tea—not a meaningful life lesson.

Why do I tell you the story of my meaningless tea cup ceremony? It's because I find the Christian practice of the Lord's Supper to mean about the same thing for most people. If you go to a church for a while, you know when you are supposed to take the bread and drink the cup. Eating and drinking on cue confirms that you are part of the group. However, it doesn't mean much more than that. At best, people think it's a time to remember the value of Jesus' crucifixion. At worst, they think it's an adult snack to hold you over until lunch. The real meaning of the ceremony has been lost.

Have you ever wondered where Jesus got the idea of eating bread and sipping wine as a ceremonial enactment of our relationship with him? Most folks who ask that question quickly turn to the Passover. That's not a bad place to start. If you haven't participated in a Passover meal to learn more about the dynamics of the Last Supper, I'd encourage you to try it out.

Exodus 12:14 labels the Passover meal a "memorial." It is a time to remember God's great act of redemption. Passover is the climactic moment in history when God freed Israel of her slavery in Egypt. As Moses says about Passover in Exodus 13:3, "Remember this day on which you came out from Egypt from the place where you were enslaved because the Lord brought you out of there with a mighty hand."

The Passover was a memorial. The Lord's Supper is also a memorial. As Jesus said, "Do this in remembrance of me" (Luke 22:19). The Lord's Supper is a time to remember the sacrifice of Jesus just like the Jews remembered the sacrifice of the Passover lamb.

If we fail to reflect on the great sacrifice that Jesus made to free us from slavery to sin, then we do fail to fully participate in communion. If we turn it into a ceremonial snack that has been separated from Jesus' bold act of redemption, we miss something. Eating the bread and drinking the wine should be a flavored memory of painful sacrifice. It should alert our sensations to the reality of Jesus' excruciating death on our behalf. It should cause us to remember and be thankful.

However, reducing the Lord's Supper to a "memorial" just like the Passover still misses half of what Jesus was doing through the bread and the wine. When Jesus described the significance of his symbolic actions with the bread and the wine, he used the word "covenant." "This is my blood of the covenant, which is poured out for many" (Matthew 26:28; Mark 14:24). Jesus never used the word "covenant" anywhere else in the Gospels.

When Jesus announced that his body would be broken and his blood poured out to inaugurate a new "covenant," he was moving beyond a memorial meal. He was turning his Last Supper with the disciples into a "covenant" meal. And the books of the Law never call Passover a covenant meal. So we have to look elsewhere to understand the dynamics of a "covenant" meal that Jesus' Jewish disciples would have understood more naturally than we do.

Since Jesus is introducing a "new covenant" at the meal, it only makes sense to explore the meal that inaugurated the "old" or first covenant between Israel and God (Hebrews 9 calls the Mosaic covenant the "first covenant"). That meal took place in the Sinai wilderness a few weeks after the first Passover. Unfortunately, the Passover often overshadows the first covenant meal when people explore the meaning of the Last Supper. That neglect has led to a hallowed out Last Supper considered only to be a memorial—or a time of remembering rather than also a time of committing.

THE FIRST COVENANT MEAL

The first covenant meal is captured in Exodus 24:3-11. It begins with Moses presenting God's requirement for his people and ends with a big meal.

> 3 Moses came and told the people all the words of the Lord and all the rules. And all the people answered with one voice and said, "All the words that the Lord has spoken we will do." 4 And Moses wrote down all the words of the Lord. He rose early in the morning and built an altar at the foot of the mountain, and twelve pillars, according to the twelve tribes of Israel. 5 And he sent young men of the people of Israel, who offered burnt offerings and sacrificed peace offerings of oxen to the Lord. 6 And Moses took half of the blood and put it in basins, and half of the blood he threw against the altar. 7 Then he took the Book of the Covenant and read it in the hearing of the people. And they said, "All that the Lord has spoken we will do, and we will be obedient." 8 And Moses took the blood and threw it on the people and said, "Behold the **blood of the covenant** that the Lord has made with you in accordance with all these words." 9 Then Moses and Aaron, Nadab, and Abihu, and seventy of the elders of Israel went up, 10 and they saw the God of Israel. There was under his feet as it were a pavement of sapphire stone, like the very heaven for clearness. 11 And

he did not lay his hand on the chief men of the people of Israel; they beheld God, and ate and drank.

The Bible never calls the blood of the Passover lambs in Egypt the "blood of the covenant." The "blood of the covenant" first comes from the oxen sacrificed in Sinai mentioned here in Exodus 24. The only other reference to "blood of the covenant" in the Bible refers to the sacrificed body of Jesus. That connection must not be missed.

What's the big deal? The big deal appears twice in the passage above. Read it again. Before Moses takes the "blood of the covenant" and sprinkles it on the people, what do they commit to doing twice? Exodus 24:3 and 24:7 record a very specific corporate commitment. "All that the Lord has spoken we will do, and we will be obedient." That is what God required of the people entering into a covenant relationship with him. It's no small commitment.

The "blood of the covenant" doesn't just signify God's willingness to accept a sacrifice as payment for human sin. It signifies a two-way commitment. God will reach out and over the sins of many, but those whom he reaches have a major responsibility. The responsibility is obedience. God's ways become your way of life if you want God's sacrifice to become your forgiveness.

Every word God gave Moses to share with the Israelites became their guidelines for life. It's no different when Jesus raises his glass of wine and calls it the "blood of the covenant." That covenant comes with expected obedience to all the words he delivered to his disciples. The disciples weren't expected to just say "thanks" for Jesus' sacrifice. They were expected to commit to do "all that the Lord has spoken."

Now some of you might be getting nervous that I have made an in interpretive leap. But don't worry. I'm not creating this connection out of thin air. I'm not trying to read more into the Last Supper than Jesus really meant. I'm just highlighting what someone wrote back in the first century.

Hebrews 9 spells out the parallel between Jesus' blood and the blood of the first covenant in plain terms. Specifically, Hebrews 9:11-22 is an extended argument for the superiority of Christ's blood and the new covenant compared to animal blood and the first covenant. I'm not the first to see the connection or communicate its significance. Hebrews 9:14 clearly states that Christ's "blood of the covenant" frees people "to serve the living God."

The end goal of the new covenant isn't for you to just say "thanks" for a clean conscience. God steps toward you so that you might fall in step with him. The "blood of the covenant" comes with a commitment from both parties. God commits to cover your sin with the blood of his son. You commit "to serve the living God."

THE DANGER OF ONE-SIDED COVENANTS

At first glance, I wish I had a few more one-sided covenantal relationships. If my job was to say "thanks" each time people serve me and everyone else's job was to serve me, I'd have it made. My boss could send me a paycheck in exchange for a "thank you" card. My wife could serve me at every meal, and I'd remember to be appreciative with each sip of wine and bite of bread. The government could provide me with good roads, public schools, and police protection, and I could schedule "memorial" meals instead of paying taxes. That'd be a pretty attractive lifestyle (apart from the fact that I'm horrible at remembering to send "thank you" cards).

The only problem is it wouldn't work. My company would flounder, my marriage would fail, and government workers would go on strike. Covenantal and contractual relationships have to go both ways. Both sides must play their role to maintain a healthy relationship.

The reason one-sided covenantal relationships don't work goes even further than lop-sided and unsustainable service in one direction. A more subtle danger lies in what happens to a person who simply takes without any service in return. The basic result: character dissolves.

I will admit that being thankful and giving recognition is a positive in itself. A person who learns to do nothing more than say "thanks" to those who serve him is definitely better than a "thankless" beneficiary. But a person who escapes the inherent responsibility in his relationships will lose out on the development of the courage and character that make human beings great.

I see the loss of character from one-sided covenants all the time. The person who games the unemployment system for free paychecks without work has lost character. The son who lives off his parents' inheritance may remember his parents fondly but loses the need to cultivate the wisdom and will power to succeed. The spouse who recklessly spends every dollar the other partner makes without taking on equitable responsibility forfeits temperance and self-control. As a result, that relationship struggles rather than strengthens. The Christian who thanks God for a clean conscience and a hell-free future but doesn't embody the way of Jesus bankrupts his very existence.

One-sided covenantal relationships turn you into a shell of a human being. It looks attractive until you lose the soulful substance that we were created to incarnate.

I can still remember watching a young man I was mentoring game the unemployment system and then get caught. Suddenly he found himself owing the government $8,000. He came to me bummed about it. I not only told him "I told you so," but I told him it was a good thing. He now had the opportunity (and a legal necessity) to put together the kind of character that endures to do the right thing. He's a better man for it today (even though he didn't really appreciate my comments in that moment).

THE TWO-SIDED SUPPER

When we approach the reenactment of the Lord's Supper as a time to say "thanks" for Christ's sacrifice, we are missing half the picture. We should definitely remember and be thankful for the sacrifice. It is in part a memorial meal. But we can't drink the cup that symbolizes the "blood of the covenant" and pretend we are passive recipients. Drinking that cup is a commitment.

Exodus 24:11 recalls how the people "ate and drank" at the first covenant meal. That consumption didn't just celebrate God's acceptance of burnt offerings and peace offerings for their sin. The meat did come from such offerings, but the meal meant much more. That meal was the culmination of a response to do "all that the Lord has spoken."

Now thankfully we don't have to repeat the part of the first covenant meal where Moses threw bowls of ox blood on the participants. I honestly don't think I could handle that covenant responsibility. And I'm not sure people could afford to remove blood stains from their Sunday best after every communion service, especially those traditions that celebrate it weekly.

Although the blood-smattering does not carry through to the Last Supper, the commitment to do "all that the Lord has spoken" does. The bread and the cup should only be enjoyed and appreciated by those who are committed to embodying the way of Jesus. Jesus should be thanked for forgiveness of sins but also praised for providing a path to follow back to authentic human existence. Communion is not only a time to remember the cross but also every word that Jesus spoke leading up to the cross. Those words are the ones we are committing to do when we drink the cup.

AVOIDING COMMITMENTS

I have found it's a lot easier to tell my wife "I love you" than to say, "I'll clean the bathrooms and windows on Saturday instead of flyfishing in the mountains." Saying "I love you" is a general affirmation that means so many things it hardly means anything. I can proclaim my love each time I walk by the soap scum in the sink. I can shower my wife with compliments while I stare out our filmy windows. Then I can take my endless love to the Colorado River on Saturday and leave the chores behind. It's quite easy to verbalize my appreciation without making any specific commitments that require action.

If you're anything like me, avoiding specific commitments has become an art form for many of life's daily activities. For example, my wife may ask, "Are you going to be home at 5:30pm for dinner tonight?" My preferred response is, "I will be home for dinner when I can." It almost sounds like a commitment at first until you think about it. And my wife does.

My wife usually gives me the benefit of the doubt that I can't promise 5:30pm and follows up with another question. "Do you think you can make it by 5:45pm?" My response, "That's a great time for dinner. Thanks for getting it all together." Somewhat impressively, I have been both positive and thankful without yet committing to a specific arrival time. I'm practically a genius (or so it makes me feel). By thanking her for planning dinner, I am kind and thoughtful in my response and completely vague about what I will actually do. I can arrive late and feel no twinge in my conscience.

Of course, now that I'm writing my secrets in this book I may run into problems with this approach. She has already dismantled one of my best strategies. When asked to pay a bill or swap out some dirty sheets on a sick kid's bed, I love to say, "That'd be a good thing to do." It affirms her idea. It lets her know I support the action. Who could disagree with her anyway? It would be a good thing to avoid late charges and give my children a sanitary sleeping environment. But I'm certainly not going to commit to it. What if I don't feel like doing it later? What if I forget? What if I fall asleep? I'd rather leave myself an out so that I don't feel bad when I say "thanks" to her for doing tomorrow what I avoided today.

COMMITMENTS TO THE ORPHANED

I think we are quite accustomed to avoiding commitments. That is why I love people and organizations that communicate their commitments clearly. They are the noble exceptions. One exemplary ministry is Lifesong for Orphans.

Lifesong for Orphans cares for orphans in 6 countries around the world and facilitates adoptions in the U.S. Lifesong has set up adoption loan funds and grants with over 100 American churches to make sure orphans at home and abroad get into loving families. In each country around the world Lifesong tests business models that can create profit to fund ministry to orphans. In fact, their entire administrative costs are covered by an endowment from its founder so that 100% of your donations can directly help orphans. Lifesong has made a string of smart choices to help the most children in a lasting way.

Why has Lifesong for Orphans made these decisions and worked tirelessly to maximize their service to children? It's because of a commitment. Lifesong does not settle for vague statements about loving orphans around the world. They do not stop at general affirmations of God's concern for orphaned children. Lifesong has made a concrete and definitive commitment to orphans. That commitment has been boiled down to four standards.

Lifesong's children will have:

- No want for food, clothing, medical care, or shelter.
- Fundamental Christian training and discipleship.
- A quality education to provide a foundation for the future.
- Continued love and support as they transition into adult living.

These four standards make it clear. You know and Lifesong knows what they are going to do. Lifesong is going to care for mind, soul, and body both now and in the future. This commitment guides program decisions and pushes leaders toward higher quality care and long-term planning. To fulfill this commitment to as many children as possible Lifesong has to maximize its resources. That is why they have started profitable Strawberry farms that fund schools.

Although I find myself avoiding commitments, I don't trust any organization that can't clarify their commitment. I want to know what the commitment is and how central it is to the way the leaders operate. I want it to be simple enough so that leaders and staff members remember it. I want it to be engrained in the life of that organization. I want to read a clear plan of action to which everyone has committed: "All that has been written we will surely do." Lifesong for Orphans does just that.

The correspondences between the Last Supper and the first covenant ceremony don't tell the whole story. The pattern and significance of the Last Supper looks a lot like another covenant ceremony from Jesus' day. What other "covenant ceremony" possesses striking similarities? It's called *Kiddushin*.

Kiddushin means "betrothal"—or "getting engaged to marry" in modern American culture. *Kiddushin* became a fairly standardized process during (or shortly thereafter) the time of Jesus, as best as we can tell. As most cultures do, the Jewish people established a socially approved pattern for bringing two young people together for marriage.

The Rabbis debated, refined, and ultimately codified the "betrothal" process. We can still read their conclusions in an old document dating back to about 500 CE—which elaborates on the betrothal practices first recorded in the *Nashim* section of the Mishnah dating to 200 CE. You may have no desire to know the names and dates of Rabbinic writings, but they do help us understand what Jesus was doing in the Upper Room.

The ancient *Kiddushin* tractate from the Babylonian Talmud (i.e., oral Rabbinic teachings written down around 500 CE) provides a series of recommendations for how the betrothal process should work. Of course, the betrothal process would have varied from region to region and family to family, but four stages were generally observed. The young man who was taking a wife would:

1. Establish terms for betrothal with the bride's family (i.e., her father)
2. Make a down payment for his future bride
3. Have his proposal accepted by the bride
4. Go back to his father's house and return for his bride in a year or so when their new home was ready

The betrothal process could involve written contracts or verbal agreements ratified in the presence of witnesses. Down payments generally consisted of money, food, temple offerings, oil, or any other valuable object. The most relevant down payment for our purposes is *wine*. In the *Kiddushin Tractate* the requirements for using wine in a betrothal ceremony are spelled out with some detail.

Kiddushin Tractate 7:2 instructs young couples about what to do and to say during the betrothal ceremony. The young man is instructed to say, "Be betrothed to me with this cup of wine." Then the young woman must drink the wine to accept his offer if the wine is valuable enough. The *Kiddushin Tractate* reads,

> If a man gives a woman a cup in kiddushin, then: if the contents are wine, she is betrothed only if the wine is worth a perutah; otherwise she is not betrothed even if the cup is worth a perutah standing alone. Of course, she is expected to return the cup after drinking the wine.

The betrothal process may not seem relevant at first, but note the parallels to the Last Supper:

Kiddushin 7:2	Mark 14:23-24
"Be betrothed to me with **this cup** of wine."	"This is My blood of the covenant, which is poured out for many." When He had taken **a cup** and given thanks,
…If **a man gives a woman a cup** in kiddushin, then: if the contents are wine, she is betrothed if the wine is worth a *perutah*.	**He gave it to them**,
Of course, she is expected to return the cup **after drinking the wine**.	and **they all drank from it**.

The parallels don't suggest a mysterious heavenly betrothal ceremony that no one ever imagined before at the Last Supper. They simply point to common features in covenant ceremonies. The disciples drank wine to accept Jesus' covenant proposal in the same way that women drank wine to accept a marriage proposal.

When a young woman drank a cup of wine that a young man offered to her in an explicit covenant ceremony, it carried with it enormous significance. It was no different for the disciples. Drinking the wine that Jesus gave to them as a sign of a new covenant was an act of commitment. They were signing up for a life-long relationship that obliged them to a wealth of duties.

The significance of the parallels between the Last Supper and *Kiddushin* should be no surprise. The parallels can be found throughout biblical sayings from Jesus. In John 14:2-3 Jesus refers to step 4 in the betrothal process where a man leaves to prepare a home for his new family. "In My Father's house are many dwelling places; if it were not so, I would have told you; for I go to prepare a place for you. If I go and prepare a place for you, I will come again and receive you to Myself, that where I am, there you may be also." The new home was consistently prepared on the land owned by the young man's father, some times as another room of the father's house. Jesus is alluding to the climax of the betrothal process when he issued the words in John 14.

You may also be familiar with how Jesus employed the analogy of betrothed girls to his disciples. It wouldn't be the most flattering comparison in my male opinion, but he did do it. In the "Parable of the 10 Unmarried Girls" in Matthew 25:1-13, Jesus talks about being prepared for step 4 of the betrothal process. As the parable goes, on the night when the bridegroom has announced his coming, five brides are wise enough to bring oil for their lamps. Five fail to prepare for the unknown hours of waiting for the bridegroom to arrive. Jesus wants his disciples to be ladies in waiting who are prepared for his return. It's an awkward analogy, but the betrothal stages are being used to paint the picture of Jesus' relationship to his disciples.

In addition to these analogies to the betrothal process, the apostle Paul does make a direct link between the Last Supper and the betrothal process. In Paul's estimation the Last Supper is a re-enactment of *Kiddushin* steps 2 and 3. The down payment was Jesus' death (step 2) and eating the bread and drinking the wine are his disciples' acceptance of the new covenant (step 3). That is why Paul says to eat and drink the Lord's Supper while you wait for step

4: "For as often as you eat this bread and drink the cup, you proclaim the Lord's death until He comes" (1 Corinthians 11:26). What Jesus started at the Last Supper isn't finished until he comes. That meal had multiple commitments from both sides.

RENEWING YOUR VOWS

I still remember how dumb it seemed the first time I heard about couples renewing their vows. Of course, I was 12 and had no clue about the difficulty of managing healthy relationships over a lifetime. As an adolescent who grew up in a stable family, I just assumed married people stayed married. So why would they put on some repeat ceremony that just rehearsed worn out lines from a wedding book?

Now that my parents are divorced, I have a different perspective. Committing and re-committing to do all that my wife and I promised each other makes sense. The very act of rereading the vows calls upon the residual nobility in me to rise to the occasion. The greater distance that grows between our wedding day and now results in a vague memory of the commitment. The specific details of what we promised get blurry and forgotten. Rereading or reenacting them provides a timely reminder of all that I said I'd do.

Re-committing to the extensive demands of our marriage vows also causes me to ask: why would I work so hard to do all these things? That may sound like a heartless question to ask. However, it actually drives you to the heart of the matter. You begin to bring all the reasons for loving your spouse back into focus.

MEMORIAL + COMMITMENT = LORD'S SUPPER

Our reenactment of the Last Supper is a renewal of our vows. It is not just a memorial service. At a modern memorial service, we remember all the great things that an absent friend or family member has done. We appreciate and treasure their finest moments and greatest accomplishments. That does not capture all the dynamics of the Last Supper. The Last Supper is an unexpected combination of both the memorial service and a renewal of vows. It is unlike the common cultural practices of Americans and many other nations.

Too often our reenactment of the Last Supper is only a shallow remembrance of Jesus' love demonstrated for us in his death. What do I mean by a "shallow remembrance?" I mean we feel loved by his sacrificial act and remember how good we have it because of that love. But we don't dive into the depths of what his love makes us do. We would be wise to remember Jesus' words about basking in God's love: "Just as the Father has loved Me, I have also loved you. So live in My love. If you keep My commandments, you will live in My love." Doing what Jesus told us to do is central to basking in his love.

I won't lie. I'm concerned. Do we remember his sacrificial love but ignore our commitment to his commands? I've been through hundreds of Communion ceremonies and Eucharists that have failed to acknowledge our side of the covenantal relationship. It's time to remember Jesus' finest moments of selfless love symbolized in the Last Supper but also stir our noblest desires to do everything that he commanded.

COMPASSION FOR INDIA REDEFINES CHURCH

If the last supper was a ceremony of commitment, how does that redefine your definition of church? In India, one church planting organization knows exactly what changes.

Compassion for India does not believe a church has been established when 30 baptized adults meet together for weekly prayer, worship, sacraments and teaching. A church only exists when that group is actively and compassionately reaching outside of its community. Compassion for India (or Empart as they are known in the US) knows that Jesus wanted more than a group of believers who are profoundly thankful for his sacrifice and forgiveness. Jesus wants us to embody all that he said and did in the way we love others.

Compassion for India is so focused on doing all that Jesus commanded that they can register in India as a social benefit charity rather than a church denomination. Their reception of God's sacrificial love turns into service to others. At the risk of their own lives (and some have been killed), Indian leaders reenact the way of Jesus by ministering to the poor and excluded and sick. Sewing programs empower women. Mercy Homes for the mentally ill demonstrate the amazing love of God in tangible form. Education centers for children are giving illiterate kids the chance to develop literacy skills necessary for schools. Churches are planted that go beyond the spiritual narcissism of what God's love does for us to what God's love does through us for our neighbors.

When Compassion for India churches gather across north India to celebrate the Lord's Supper, they know it is a ceremony of commitment not just remembrance. They are not only filled with inward gratitude but also motivated to look outward in obedience to all that Jesus commanded. They have a clear understanding of Jesus' final commission. He didn't just want people to hear what Jesus did for them and become baptized believers. He wanted his disciples to teach everyone to do all of his commands. When a congregation is not considered a church until it embodies the way of Jesus, then the full significance of communion can be experienced. Remember, we drink and eat as a sign of our promise to "do all that Jesus commanded us." Empart's churches embody that reality.

A PLEDGE OF GRATEFUL ALLEGIANCE

In the private school I attended as a boy, we would recite our pledge of allegiance to the American flag every morning. I can't say I understood everything I was saying or why it mattered, but I did it. Some times I even led the whole class in the pledge.

My main memory from those early morning recitations is a deep fear of mixing up the words and saying "indivisible" at the wrong time. As I can remember, I had no trouble with the beginning of the pledge. We would all be staring at a flag so it made sense to say, "I pledge allegiance to the flag…" My problem came after we said the next line, "and to the Republic for which it stands." The pause that followed that phrase sent chills up my spine. What in the world do I say next?

Half the time I would get it right and the rest of the time it was like a "choose your own adventure" book. I'd say the wrong word and get lost in a maze of futile attempts to recover. It would go something like this: "and to the Republic for which it stands, indivisible, with liberty, and God, one nation, under justice, for all... amen." I'm not sure why I would add the "amen." But it just seemed right to give people some indication that I would no longer be spitting out random phrases in front of the class. I like "closure." It also may have been because I closed my eyes half way through the botched pledge and had a habit of saying "amen" whenever I opened my eyes and saw a group of people.

Even when I could remember to say "one nation under God, indivisible, with liberty and justice for all" (I think that's how it goes), I'd screw up pronunciations. Who in the world thought it was a good idea for 5 year olds to say "indivisible"? That word has just as many syllables in it as kindergarteners have years on the earth. That syllabic nightmare would cause something different to come out of my mouth each time.

One day I'd pledge my allegiance to a "nation under God with *invisible* liberty and justice for all." The next day I'd commit myself to "a nation, and *individuals*, not just God, but liberty for all." I'm not even sure what that means, but that's where I'd end up. One time I pledged my loyalty to "one God, in the visible nation of justice for all." I didn't even know where to insert "liberty" that day. Eventually, the 5-syllable word did help me learn the difference between other complicated terms I would need in high school: residual, interorbital, and intravisual. Just so you know the last two aren't actual words.

The years of learning by screwing up were painful. Thankfully I have recovered from the trauma of those Kindergarten years. However, it has been a long time since I've recited the pledge of allegiance in a public setting. I may still be averse to the risk of losing face from mispronouncing big words.

A DEEPER COMMUNION

I think we could learn something from that 15-second pledge in our communion ceremonies. It may cause fear and flashbacks for people like me, but I'd recommend adding the pledge from the first covenant ceremony to our reenactment of the new covenant ceremony. We could read the biblical account of the Last Supper and then respond in unison: "All the words which Jesus has spoken we will do." This simple yet profound pledge from the first covenant ceremony could resurrect the covenantal character of communion. Verbalizing our commitment could help us overcome the common default into a one-sided relationship.

As a practical suggestion I recommend reading and contemplating a portion of Jesus' teaching each time communion is taken. Take a section of the Sermon on the Mount in Matthew 5-7 and read it out loud. Or take a section of Jesus' teaching on the topic being discussed or taught that day. This way participants can specifically consider the commands in the covenant to which they are committing—to which they are declaring in action, "All the words which you have spoken we will do."

Reading an excerpt full of Jesus' commands and asking people to rededicate themselves to those words can restore the lost meaning of the Last Supper. It can bring back the response to God's love that leads to obedience. Reenacting the Last Supper should be a frequent practice that both orients our lives around the grace of God in Christ and inspires us to embody that graciousness and love in a faithful life. It should be a pledge of grateful allegiance to Jesus.

COMMITMENT IS ESSENTIAL FOR REDEMPTION

All this talk about committing to do commands can rub people the wrong way. Isn't it by grace that we are saved? Shouldn't we focus on Jesus' loving sacrifice for us rather than what we will do in obedience to his words? Unfortunately, we have separated the two elements over time into independent activities.

We think grace simply leads to a sense of freedom from guilt. We forget what Paul knew early on. Grace leads to obedience. And obedience ushers in freedom from the consequences of destructive habits—what the Bible calls "sin." Both the freedom from guilt and the freedom from sin's destructive consequences are wrapped up in the redemption Jesus seeks in the world.

Paul taught the Romans about the relationship between grace and obedient decisions in Romans 5:21. Here's my translation from the Greek: "Grace unleashes its power by directing us to live God's way." That unexpected connection between grace and righteous living must not be broken. They go together.

In Romans 5:21 Paul is tapping into an old paradigm from the Ten Commandments. He isn't rehearsing the ten "dos" and "don'ts," but he is rephrasing the motivation to obey them. It is often misunderstood that the Ten Commandments are all about obeying God's law and Jesus is all about accepting God's grace. That misconception needs to be expelled by taking a closer look at the immediate context before the Ten Commandments are given.

In Deuteronomy 5:2, Moses reminds Israel that "The Lord our God made a covenant with us." Understanding covenants is quite relevant to the discussion of this whole chapter. So how did God describe the first covenant? He began with a reminder of his grace. "I am the Lord your God, he who brought you from the land of Egypt, from the place of slavery" (Deuteronomy 5:6). Obedience to God is a response to and motivated by an experience of his grace. For the first covenant, God's grace meant freedom from slavery in Egypt.

The instructions that follow are designed to keep people out of every other form of slavery. The Ten Commandments protect people from falling victim to fake gods, jealousy, murderous hate, and all sorts of other activities that would bring harm. The reason to keep those commands is God's grace. His grace has freed you and his words can keep you free.

When you take full stock of the order to how God presents his ten commands, you see he first provides grace and then the path to experience the fullness of grace and freedom. There should be gratitude for what God did to free Israel from Egyptian slavery that then translates into obedience. And that obedience keeps us free from every other form of slavery that sin can contrive. That is how God's covenants with people work. His gift of freedom requires ongoing commitment in order to experience the fullness of that freedom.

NEW LIFE REQUIRES COMMITMENT

Ministries like the Denver Rescue Mission understand how to let God's grace flourish in people's lives. First they provide access to the gospel and encourage a fresh experience of God's love and forgiveness. Then they lay out a path with 5 phases for people to follow toward holistic restoration. It's grace and obedience together to overcome addictions and destructive habits from the past. The Denver Rescue Mission has aptly named the program New Life.

As highlighted earlier in the book, the New Life program at Denver Rescue Mission requires participants to complete specific assigned duties at each phase. If they refuse to comply, they cannot remain in the program. The New Life program cannot promise new life for those who do not respond to their gracious assistance with compliance and good decision-making. As Paul said, the grace of God unleashes its power through right living. You can't experience the power of God's grace if you just say thanks and then make up your own path forward.

The commitment that the rescue mission requires and that I've discussed in this chapter is both motivated by grace and required to experience grace's power. It is a disservice to Jesus and to ourselves to separate the reception of grace from the commitment to obey. Grace leads to obedience. And that obedience preserves the freedom grace provides.

If grace doesn't drive you to do all the words that Jesus spoke, then it cannot set you free. The destructive habits that are wrecking you, your relationships, and your world will continue to crush you while you stop at internal "thank yous" for Jesus' loving sacrifice. Don't discredit the power of God's grace by stopping it before it can get started in you. Commit yourself to the freeing words of Jesus.

LAST SUPPER AS COVENANT CEREMONY

The next time you take the cup and a piece of bread, I hope it's different. I hope you realize that Jesus didn't just want a memorial service for his sacrifice. I hope the parallels to the first covenant ceremony at Sinai and the Jewish betrothal ceremonies have shown you it's so much more.

It's both a ceremony of remembrance and of covenantal recommitment. It is a time to remember the love of God in sacrificial action just like when He led Israel out of Egyptian slavery. It is also a time of whole-hearted commitment to a two-sided covenant. It's a time to resurrect Israel's pledge to God's first commands, "All the words which you have spoken we will do."

If we leave out the re-commitment to Jesus' way, we run the risk of covering up our covenant responsibilities with lavish appreciation. It starts to look more like a big "I love you" that avoids committing ourselves to the life he prescribed. Our ceremonies then become slick and emotive while our character collapses from a one-sided relationship.

Saying "thanks" is a good first step. Following through with a commitment to embody his commands must be the second. Don't go through another reenactment of the Last Supper without hearing the words of Jesus and committing to reenact them. You will never experience the freedom and life made possible by Jesus' sacrifice if you don't embrace both sides of the covenant.

Reenacting the Way

1. What meaning, if any, has Communion (or the Lord's Supper or the Eucharist, as you may call it) had for you personally?

2. What effects would it have on you and other followers of Jesus if you added time during Communion to read Jesus' words and commit to doing everything he said?

3. Where has Jesus set you free by commanding you to live in a way that redirected you from destructive habits and self-inflicted consequences?

CHAPTER 9

REENACTING THE WAY:
DOING TODAY WHAT JESUS DID BACK THEN

Focal Point: Why should we reenact the purposes behind biblical actions rather than just extract biblical ideas to believe and propagate?

FOLLOWING IDEAS DOESN'T MAKE SENSE

It is hard to follow an idea. Ideas don't go anywhere. It is much easier to follow directions.

If we only define Jesus by who he is rather than what he does, we lose the ability to imitate him. You cannot follow a person who is just standing there being himself. If you daily imagine Jesus as a heavenly being standing in the clouds in all of his eternal perfection rather than a man on mission, you'll be left taking clues for how to make your next move from everything but Jesus himself.

That's why this entire book has focused on Jesus' movement. We have deciphered the meaning of mysterious actions. We have seen that his actions are not superfluous connecting material between teachings. His actions were making profound statements in and of themselves. He was challenging and changing the world by what he did. And he was setting an example for all who would follow him.

If we are going to honor Jesus, we must begin to reenact his way of doing things. We must find creative ways to be faithful to his example. Jesus understood the symbolism of wine and water in his culture. He knew what pigs and storms meant to pagan regions around the Galilee. He didn't take deformities and debilitating diseases at face value. He used their cultural significance to his advantage and took action. We must do the same today.

ACTION GROUPS VS. IDEA GROUPS

If you think of Jesus as a great teacher who walked around giving all the right answers, following him will mean doing the same thing. You'll look for opportunities to learn the right answers to tough theological questions and pass them along. You'll be attracted to small groups and churches that pull out new principles and truths from the Bible each week. Refining your ideas about God and life will be everything you want to find in a community of faith.

But to be brutally honest, your faith will be more like the appendix to a math book than a way of life. In that paradigm, your faith becomes the summation of all the right answers to all of life's tough questions. It becomes a way to be right about everything. That pursuit of all the right ideas and answers distracts you from following Jesus because you have to spend so much time learning how to prove others wrong and defending why you are right.

That's why I have pushed you to change your vision of Jesus. If you look at Jesus as a man on a mission who is calling people to fitting action, then static group settings characterized by "discussions" and "sermons" won't be enough. You'll want to find a group on the move. You will quit a Friday morning "study" group for a Friday night "action" group. You'll cancel your next Christian conference so you can volunteer for the weekend to pack nutritious food for starving children. You won't stop discussions, but you'll want them to grow out of what you are doing rather than what you are debating. You will be more concerned about embodying the love and justice of God than figuring out how those two divine characteristics could work together throughout eternity.

If you are wondering where you might find a community of like-minded Jesus followers who are charting new and culturally relevant paths for Jesus' purposes today, I'd encourage you to attend a Q conference or a Catalyst conference. You can find upcoming Q events at www.qideas.org and Catalyst conferences at catalystconference.com. At Q and Catalyst, you get a rapid-fire introduction to cutting edge cultural engagement from a Christian perspective. Q and Catalyst are built on the idea that Jesus has called us to restore God's original intent for creation within our cultural context. Presenters and participants are all driving toward that goal. They are creating action groups testing out new ideas for cultural engagement. The people you will meet at Q or Catalyst may just be the friends you need at your side to reenact Jesus' way faithfully and fittingly in our time and place.

HOW CAN YOU RESEARCH THE ORIGINAL CULTURE?

To discern fitting ways to reenact Jesus' ancient purposes today, you will need to figure out the purposes behind his actions locked away in ancient dynamics from the first century. The same is true for finding culturally appropriate ways to follow all the trajectories from God's mission spread throughout the Bible.

Discerning the original meaning of biblical actions is easier said than done. Even if you have recognized the value of discerning the purposes behind biblical activity, that is still a far cry from knowing how to figure out what the words and actions meant in their original context. Although I cannot provide a full explanation for how to research the historical context of each biblical passage here (because that takes a few years of guided practice), I can tell you what to avoid and where to start.

First, don't search the internet and assume that blogs or Bible sites you find provide any type of dependable information. Amateurs in this space routinely find the first thing that seems relevant to a passage and make up as much as they can from it. It takes more time and discipline than that to get it right.

I spent years learning and practicing the best of modern biblical scholarship to discover what I did. Although I purposefully left out hundreds of research footnotes to shorten this book for a broader audience, every conclusion is built on a careful cumulative case with ample evidence. That same approach is necessary when interpreting ancient documents in light of their historical context. Don't fall victim to the convenience of internet ideas when dealing with the importance of interpreting the Bible correctly.

Even if you find a real "commentary" online that was a published book at some point in history, be cautious. Most commentaries that you can access for free online were written 100 or more years ago by authors who did not have the benefit of the game-changing archeological discoveries of the twentieth century. There is a reason these commentaries are free to access. No one would pay for their outdated and sometimes misleading conclusions.

So where should you start when looking for the historical context of a passage? The easiest place to start is a Bible Background Commentary. Two great background commentaries are (1) the IVP Old Testament and New Testament Bible Background Commentaries and (2) Zondervan's Illustrated Bible Background Commentaries. Both background commentary sets are great, but here is how to get your hands on one set and a whole lot more for the best price.

I have had all my college and seminary Biblical Interpretation students buy the IVP Essential Reference Collection software (compatible with Logos Bible Software—the best Bible study software I've used for the last 15 years). The IVP Essential Reference Collection can be purchased for about $100 and includes not only the IVP Old Testament and New Testament Bible Background Commentaries but about $400 more of Bible reference books that you can electronically search on your computer, tablet and smartphone.

If you buy the IVP electronic reference collection (which they will hopefully keep updating and expanding over time), you can start all your historical background studies by reading the comments organized by chapter and verse in the background commentaries. Then you can dig deeper into ideas, historical figures, geography and customs by searching the rest of the reference books by relevant terms mentioned in the background commentaries. The search function allows you to pull from over a dozen reference books in an instant.

It is a bit of an investment of both money and time, but it can help you move from misinterpretation to a true understanding of the purpose behind biblical actions. If you use these reference tools to answer each question in the 2-step Reenactment Model for biblical interpretation (introduced in Chapter One), you will move a long way toward understanding the original meaning of biblical actions and getting the right directions to follow for today.

FAITHFUL NAVIGATION NOT PUZZLE-MAKING

Taking action takes work. You've probably felt that tension as you read my advice for how to research the original culture. The same was probably true when you read each chapter and discussed imitating Jesus' actions with your group. I wish it wasn't so hard. If the same set of directions would work for everyone in all places and times, it would be simple. We could create an exhaustive list of "dos" and "don'ts" and be done with it. But Jesus showed us just how much work has to be done. We have to understand culture and take appropriate action.

The good news is our faith gives us the tools to navigate. Our vision of Jesus challenging cultural myths, welcoming outsiders, and acting out new covenant ceremonies gives us direction to follow. But that direction comes from the purposes he had in an ancient culture and not specific actions we were meant to repeat thoughtlessly. We are tasked with reenacting his way in a whole new environment.

Too many times we think of the Bible like a puzzle box with no picture on top. We spend our time pulling out pieces that we call "truths" and "principles" and "commands." We then try to logically put all those puzzle pieces together to create one clear, universal plan for what everyone should do and believe. We end up having to throw out many pieces to simplify and organize the final picture.

The puzzle-making approach can be an arduous process of extracting all the clear ideas and simple commands from so much outdated material and seemingly irrelevant place names and metaphors. But many of us were told to study the Bible this way, looking for golden nuggets to pull out. We have been told to believe that the salient ideas are lost in irrelevant activity.

This Bible study model can bring up tough questions. Maybe you have wondered deep down why the simple truths got so muddled in ancient history books, Hebrew poetry and prophetic tirades. Maybe you have even asked: why didn't God just give us a basic rulebook or at least organize the ideas by theme? It's hard to make a puzzle without the picture on top.

Here's the problem with puzzle-making. When we extract parts of the Bible like puzzle pieces and put them together in a way that seems logical to us, we destroy the Bible's design and power. We cast off the stories and poems and relationships and diversity of opinion and plot. We turn the Bible's contents into what we are looking for: a list of answers to our ultimate questions and a fence of rules to bind our behavior. At the moment we tame the Bible to spit out golden nuggets of truth and universal guidelines for living, we denude its ability to direct us in an ever-changing world. The Bible is not a puzzle with one static picture that has been jumbled up in the diversity of genres in Scripture. The Bible is not Humpty Dumpty. You're job isn't to put it back together again.

It would be better for us to imagine that the Bible is a compass. It is not a GPS-enabled mapping system that spits out step-by-step directions for anyone trying to get from point A to point B. It is a compass. It gives you a trustworthy trajectory in ever-changing terrain. The trajectories of Scripture do not change, but our place and time constantly change. The purposes of Jesus' actions do give us direction to follow, but blind reenactment of exactly what he did may have you walk off a cliff in Judea or drown in the Mediterranean Sea. You must faithfully follow biblical directions but creatively adapt it to new terrain.

The terrain that Jesus navigated is not our terrain. He does still want us to celebrate the true source of life and introduce an alternative path to peace and justice in the world. However, turning water into wine and invoking a heavenly host to sing praises won't work. Our cultures don't wait for Dionysius to appear at wine-making ceremonies. No emperors pay male choruses in Asia Minor to sing of the good news and great joy that Roman emperors have brought to the known world. We must create new symbolic actions to communicate the same old purposes. That is what the trajectories of Scripture give us: directions good for any culture that must be combined with our creative navigation of new territory.

In my experience, cultivating this wisdom and nuanced living wears you out. It is much like using a compass when you are lost in the mountains during a snowstorm. It takes work to navigate. It is difficult to discern the personal and cultural patterns that keep us fearful or make us thankful for all the wrong things. It is hard to go beyond a simplified faith that just thinks things or a basic set of rules that everyone must obey. It takes resilience and energy.

Where do you get that energy? That energy bubbles up from the gratitude for a meaningful life that Jesus offers. It's an energy produced from experiencing the love of God and support of friends on the same journey. It's an energy rooted in our recognition that we have a chance to find the way to live in a world full of meaningless ways to spend your life. When you tap into that motivation, you will put in the work to find directions from Jesus and every other approved actor in Scripture to faithfully navigate the terrain in front of you.

FINDING THE WAY TOGETHER

Figuring out how to act meaningfully and creatively does take energy. That's why we need community. You cannot succeed on your own. You need friends to point out your blind spots, and multiple eyes on your subculture to know how to reform it. You also need inspiration along the way.

I had the privilege of developing the right kind of community for a few years in my life (before my last move). During my doctoral studies, my wife and I connected with three other couples who committed to weekly gatherings. We didn't sing songs or light candles. We didn't follow curriculum or appoint a leader. We didn't even go to the same church or come from common backgrounds. We just lived life together and discussed what came up.

We tested our theories and refined our decision-making process in community. We got feedback on family matters and professional plans and community activity. We served each other, embarrassed each other, and challenged each other. We helped each other figure out how to act.

I'll tell you that kind of community is an absolute "must" if you are going to reenact the actions of Jesus today. If you haven't figured it out yet, following Jesus is tough. You need friends at every step. I hope you have had a community of this sort to discuss all the questions in this book.

FINDING YOUR ROLE TO PLAY

You do have a role to play in the most meaningful story you will ever know. The Bible isn't a dead end of "dos" and "don'ts" or a static batch of concepts to consider. It provides a wealth of actors who have gone before you in the greatest drama ever performed on the world's stage. Those actors can all inform what role you play.

In Paul's epistle to the Romans, he commends a role for first century Christians to play that he first saw in King David. Romans 15:1-4 reads:

> But we who are strong ought to bear with the failings of the weak, and not just please ourselves. Let each of us please his neighbor for his good to build him up. For even Christ did not please himself, but just as it is written, "The insults of those who insult you have fallen on me." For everything that was written in former times was written for our instruction so that through endurance and through the encouragement of the scriptures we may have hope.

In these four verses, Paul is calling the Romans to forego their personal preferences and do what is beneficial for others. He is asking his brothers to considerately care for their neighbors rather than pleasing themselves.

Why did people in Rome need this reminder from Paul? In first-century Rome, new believers in Jesus had trouble getting along. Jews wanted to celebrate holy days from their Jewish calendar and thought every believer should fast on those days, even non-Jews. Gentile believers thought they were crazy. Jesus had brought the Old Covenant to a close and launched the New Covenant era. Why keep fasting on old holy days to show one's devotion to God when Jesus has taken us beyond all that? Gentiles didn't want to eat only vegetables for Sunday lunches just because their Jewish comrades told them it pleased God.

When Paul heard about Gentile and Jewish believers arguing, offending each other, and splitting up, he wrote Romans 15:1-4. He wanted Gentiles to put down their personal preferences and do instead what pleases the Jews for the sake of unity.

Although the context may lead us to downplay Paul's command since it focuses on eating vegetables at shared meals and celebrating holidays Gentiles didn't like, there is something more important going on here. There is a paradigm for how we move from stories in the Bible to directions for how to live today. Paul doesn't just see a group of Gentiles who need to respect the culture, habits, and holidays of messianic Jews. He doesn't just think they need to suck it up a little so that Jews and Gentiles can get along at worship gatherings. Paul thinks the Gentile Christians in Rome have the opportunity to play the time-honored role of the righteous sufferer in God's drama of redemption.

How does he do it? Paul first points to the example of Christ. Christ did not please himself so neither should you. Paul is calling the Romans to reenact the role that Jesus played when he sacrificed his life for others. Of course, that sacrifice looks completely different for the Romans, but the purpose behind limiting their pleasure out of respect for the Jews is the same. The Romans should imitate Christ's sacrificial attitude.

But Paul doesn't just point the Romans to Jesus. Paul connects Jesus' sacrifice to a Psalm of David. That's where the quote from Scripture originates in Romans 15:3. In Psalm 69, David is praying to God as he suffers for doing what is right. In context David is suffering, humiliated, and being treated horribly by those around him. So he is crying out to God for help. In Psalm 69:9 he laments, "I endure the insults of those who insult you." He is taking it on the chin because he is doing the right thing. He is being faithful to God.

The words of Psalm 69 are the words of a righteous sufferer. David played that role. Jesus played that role. And Paul calls the Romans to play that role once again in God's great drama. Every time the role looks different in the details, but it is a role that God's faithful must play in every generation. The righteous will suffer.

Biblical stories and poetry and epistles are full of these roles. In Paul's epistle to the Romans he finds direction for his readers in the lives of Abraham and Adam and Isaiah and Pharaoh and David and Esau. They have all taken action with words and choices that Paul wants his readers to emulate some times and avoid other times. For example, David's Psalms are full of activity, from praising and thanking to cursing and condemning. They give a blueprint for all the ways we should be expressing ourselves to God. The Gospels as we have also seen are full of Jesus' cultural subversions and symbolic actions. Jesus embodies his message as an example for us and fights to reform a religious system that is misrepresenting God and cutting people off from forgiveness. The wealth of history books and prophets in the Bible all portray a string of people to imitate and an even bigger batch to avoid.

All these characters' recorded deeds and the activity of authors' written words give us options. We find a hundred different roles to play that must be adapted for our time and place. It is often a shame that Christian education moves from biblical stories for children to abstract discussions for adults. I can't embody an abstract idea, but I can imitate a righteous sufferer. I can witness how Elijah spoke out in his generation and see how John the baptizer reenacted that same role. Then I can leave the fixtures of Elijah's floating axes (2 Kings 6:1-7) and John's locust diet (Mark 1:6) behind as I discern what it looks like for me to speak out in my culture. We can all find roles to play from the patterns of biblical characters.

JUST LIKE MY DAD

I'm a father of three children under five. That means I am loved lavishly. It also means the kitchen floor has to be cleaned after every meal. And it means that someone is always on my back when we're hiking. I'm sure it means more, but that's all I can recall after another night spent not sleeping. You understand if you've ever had three kids four and under.

When my oldest son was one year old, I could still hike with a certain sense of freedom. I would just stick him in the backpack and act like nothing had changed. Sometimes that worked in my favor and other times it caused family discord. My wife wasn't always sure I was taking adequate precautions to protect her male family members. On one hike along a cliff's edge overlooking Devil's Lake in Wisconsin, it nearly ended my marriage.

Along the trail I found a clearing at the edge of the cliff created by an exceptionally high rock formation. Of course I had to get a good look. So I walked out to the edge of the rock and gaped down the cliff.

I quickly realized that no one else had followed me to the edge. When I turned around to see where my wife was, I received that "get away from the edge of that cliff" look. Having the maturity of a 12-year old, I pretended to slip and then catch myself just to egg her on. She didn't find it funny and demanded I get back on the trail. I somehow interpreted her comment as a request to find something more daring to do on the rock ledge. The opportunity came up right away.

As I took a step back toward the trail, a gust of wind swept up and blew my hat off my head. My immediate reaction was to lunge after the hat and save it from falling off the other side of the rock formation. Due to the sudden wind speed, the hat did roll off the rock platform where I stood. But it stopped on a rock outcropping below. So I jumped down to it in an act of valor and rescued by favorite Wisconsin Badgers lid. I couldn't resist the thrill. I knew I could do it, and I knew it would alarm my wife on a whole new level.

I stood up proud of my save and waited for some applause. Not surprisingly all I got was an earful of "what the heck were you thinking putting the lives of my 2 favorite guys at stake for a $10 cap?" I tried to play it off, but it was futile. My wife, my wife's friend, and my wife's friend's husband all had the same look on their face: "What were you thinking you immature 12-year old with a kid on your back?"

As I thought about it later, I had an epiphany. Scaring my wife on the edges of cliffs is normal to me. That's right. It's normal because I've seen my dad do it a hundred times. My dad did the same thing to my mom on every family vacation. In fact, I had rocks buried into my scalp after one incident, but it didn't stop him in the future from fooling around at the edge of the Grand Canyon, the bluffs in Wisconsin, or the Chimneys in the Smoky Mountains. My dad's antics are engrained in my mind next to the best family memories I have. When I get a chance to reenact "the husband who scares his wife on the edge of a cliff" role, I'll take it every time. I know exactly what to do and every consequence it creates. It may look different at each rocky ledge with wind gusts or fake jumps or false trips, but it's a familiar role. I can't resist.

I BECOME WHO I'VE SEEN BE

Playing familiar roles is how we create our identity. The people we have observed, known, and heard about give us options to become. We pick our roles from a pool of possible selves that we've collected throughout our lives. We do mix and match them in fresh ways, but we don't create ourselves from scratch. Picking our roles from a pool of possible selves is how we form our identity. That is why deep familiarity with biblical characters in action is critical.

We can't become a collection of disembodied ideas. We reenact the roles that we have seen other people play. We yell at people like our father did. We talk about people like our mother did. We create games like our brother did. We find solace in caffeinated beverages like our sister did. We become who we have seen people be.

That is why we must become intimately familiar with the ins and outs of what Jesus did. We must know what made him tick and how he would act in each situation in which he found himself. We must know why he did what he did.

Too many of us set out to follow Jesus without knowing him very well. Most of us know he was born miraculously, taught profound truths, died, and came back to life. So we say thanks for the death and resurrection part, particularly around Easter. We celebrate Christmas to remember the miraculous birth part. And then we are left with a vision of Jesus teaching profound truths. So we tend to set out to do the same. We read. We study. We debate. And we look to tell other people what we know. That isn't all bad, but it isn't all there is. If your knowledge of Jesus doesn't extend into the purposes of everything else he did between the birth and death parts of the Gospels, you are in trouble. You can't follow Jesus if you don't know what he was doing.

That is why we worked through the cultural dynamics of each mysterious action in this book. We must see Jesus in action. We must be familiar with what he does. We must see the roles that he plays so we can reenact them in our world today. If you have had trouble following Jesus in the past, maybe it's because you didn't know where he was going.

WAYS TO BEGIN

In this book, I have provided contemporary examples from dozens of nonprofit organizations that are following Jesus' way. They are creatively and faithfully doing today what Jesus did back then. I'd encourage you to get involved with any one of them if you haven't identified other avenues to begin reenacting the way of Jesus. The website for each organization is listed at the back of this book (see Appendix A).

If you want to learn more about their operations and impact, go to IntelligentPhilanthropy.com and get everything you need to analyze nonprofits (*Note*: I created IntelligentPhilanthropy.com so that the performance of ministries could be evaluated by anyone with an interest to do so). I make these recommendations so that every one of you can know how to make one clear next step like Jesus. I want you to know that these groups are taking action, not just propagating ideas. They are reenacting the way of Jesus.

THE ADVENTURE HAS JUST BEGUN

Hopefully the emphasis on Jesus' actions pushes you in a new direction. You should be able to see that inviting people into the way of Jesus doesn't just involve words. Jesus made huge statements with his actions, and we can too. We should be reading headlines and driving through our hometowns with that in mind. We should be meeting with friends and fellow Jesus followers to discern our cultural misnomers and take action.

If I have succeeded, then you have just begun a brand new adventure. A flattened and bewildering Bible has become a 3D action film. The silent actions of Jesus tucked between supposedly more important teaching sections now have a voice. Jesus isn't just standing there anymore.

He is finding ways to announce an alternative path to peace (chapter 2). He is welcoming outsiders and breaking down cultural barriers (chapter 3). He is acting out the message before explaining it (chapter 4). He is correcting your false imaginations about the powers that be (chapter 5). He is surprising people with reminders of where the true source of life lies (chapter 6). He is demolishing cultural promises about the latest self-help solutions (chapter 7). And he is ceremonializing habits of recommitment to all his ways (chapter 8). That's just the few actions we covered in this book.

Jesus has begun an adventure and called us to follow. He has given us a litany of memories in the Gospels like my father did for me growing up. Now it is time to play our redemptive roles. It is time to find in the ways of Jesus the possible self that we can become. It is time to do today what he did back then.

Remember, we can act in remarkably powerful ways in our time and place, but we have to move beyond the quickly conceived "applications" of biblical ideas. We have to be both faithful and creative when we reenact biblical intentions. There is no one-size-fits-all set of rules, and that's why I didn't give you such an imaginary, stripped-down summary of what you must do in this final chapter.

Your future lies in a group of friends finding the way together. It lies in the trial and error of navigating our terrain in ways faithful to Jesus' actions. Most students of the Bible have spent too much time debating ideas and not enough time testing incarnational and enculturated action plans. We can be different.

It will force us to meddle with cultural norms, to question accepted spiritual practices, and to unseat things that have been "settled." We will step on toes. We will be branded a radical or a nuisance. However, we may just push beyond religiosity to the discerning creation of a new kind of culture that Jesus showed us how to make. We may just reenact the way of Jesus.

Appendix A

Nonprofit organizations highlighted in the book

Organization	Website	Chapter
1. ALARM	www.alarm-inc.org	2
2. CARE	www.care-international.org	5
3. CURE International	www.cure.org	3
4. Denver Rescue Mission	www.denverrescuemission.org	7, 8
5. Dalit Freedom Network	www.dalitnetwork.org	3
6. Empart	www.empart.org	8
7. Healing Waters	www.healingwaters.org	6
8. He Intends Victory	www.heintendsvictory.com	3
9. Hope Farm	www.hopefarminc.org	7
10. Kindernothilfe	en.kindernothilfe.org	5
11. Lifesong for Orphans	www.lifesongfororphans.org	8
12. Living Water	www.water.cc	6
13. Luis Palau Association	www.palau.org	4
14. Plant With Purpose	www.plantwithpurpose.org	6
15. Q	www.qideas.org	9
16. Questscope	www.questscope.org	2
17. Save Our Youth	www.saveouryouth.org	4
18. T4 Global	www.t4global.org	2, 5
19. Thornston Educational Fund (No website)		3
20. Teen Challenge	www.teenchallengeusa.com	7
21. Torchbearers International	www.torchbearers.org	6
22. Vapor Sports	www.vaporsports.org	5
23. Water Missions	www.watermissions.org	6